GET TUSKED

GET TUSKED

The Inside Story of Fleetwood Mac's Most Anticpated Album

Ken Caillat
and
Hernan Rojas

GUILFORD, CONNECTICUT

Published by Backbeat Books
An imprint of The Rowman & Littlefield Publishing Group, Inc.
4501 Forbes Blvd., Ste. 200, Lanham, MD 20706
www.rowman.com

Distributed by NATIONAL BOOK NETWORK

Copyright © 2019 by Ken Caillat & Hernan Rojas & Daniel Hoffheins

Book design and composition by Michael Kellner

All rights reserved. No part of this book may be reproduced in any form or by any electronic or mechanical means, including information storage and retrieval systems, without written permission from the publisher, except by a reviewer who may quote passages in a review.

Library of Congress Cataloging-in-Publication Data available

ISBN 978-1-4930-4771-0 (hardcover)

∞™ The paper used in this publication meets the minimum requirements of American National Standard for Information Sciences—Permanence of Paper for Printed Library Materials, ANSI/NISO Z39.48-1992

Ken Caillat
To my wife, Diane, my two lovely daughters, Morgan and Colbie,
and my faithful dog, Scooter.

Hernan Rojas

*To my beloved wife, Pascuala, my dearest sons, Diego and Santiago,
and to my late mother, Maria Teresa, the "Belladonna."*

Contents

Preface		I
1.	**NEEDLES AND PINS**	1
2.	**LINDSEY'S HEAD**	17
3.	**THE STARS MUST BE MY FRIENDS**	37
4.	**INTENSE SILENCE**	61
5.	**DO YOU HAVE TO HAVE ME?**	73
6.	**TRANSCENSION**	87
7.	**SLEEPLESS CHILD**	97
8.	**THE HILLS ARE FILLED WITH FIRE**	113
9.	**HERE COMES THE NIGHTTIME**	125
10.	**LIFE ON THE LEDGE**	141
11.	**DROWNING IN THE SEA OF LOVE**	159
12.	**REAL SAVAGE LIKE**	175
13.	**DON'T WORRY BABY**	195
14.	**EVERYTHING YOU DO HAS BEEN DONE**	209
15.	**MISTRESS OF MY FATE**	223

CONTENTS

16.	**A YEAR GONE BAD**	243
17.	**A CHARMED HOUR**	259
18.	**UNDOING THE LACES**	277
19.	**NAIROBI TO LOS ANGELES**	297
20.	**LAST CALL FOR EVERYONE**	311
21.	**TUSK IS HERE**	333
Acknowledgments		351
In Memoriam		353
Selected Bibliography		355
About the Authors		359
Index		361

Preface

The term *get tusked* basically means "Go fuck yourself." This was the attitude Fleetwood Mac had adopted under the onslaught of its newfound fame and fortune. Successful beyond all measure, the band members found themselves at loose ends, looking for a way forward in the face of insurmountable expectation. They reacted in the most outrageous way possible: *Tusk*.

Every album has a secret life, a story untold that lives only in the men and women who gave birth to it. This is the story of an ambitious band and the making of its most ambitious record in that frozen moment. This is a book about a band in the midst of unexpected stardom, wealth, and independence. A band that took a stand, challenged its confused audience with a style made up of many styles, and made a noble failure. It's also a story about a misunderstood double album that resiliently endures and continues to resonate with younger generations.

Seven years ago, I decided to write my memoirs of what is was like to work with Fleetwood Mac and to describe, truthfully and expertly, what the process of making a "big time record" was like. For this book, I invited my engineer on *Tusk*, Hernan Rojas, to help me tell this story by sharing his. Hernan's voice will be in *italics* for easy distinction. Every

PREFACE

working day, from the summer of 1978 to the fall of 1979, Hernan, Richard Dashut, and I were the men responsible for putting every second of *Tusk* on tape and seeing that we reached the end of our journey.

It's popular to write off *Tusk* as a flop or one of the "great albums that never were," despite having two Top 10 hits, reaching number four in the album charts in the United States and number one in the United Kingdom, and earning double platinum sales. Too often, the story of *Tusk* is told too simply as one of Kleenex boxes and narcotics. This book does not attempt to correct these misconceptions so much as explain what our lives were actually like at that time and the creative decisions we made in the recording studio. As of this writing, this is the only authoritative book that relates the story of the *Tusk* album.

At no point, do we intend to make any of the characters in the *Tusk* saga look bad. We acknowledge that these stories took place nearly forty years ago and none of us is who he was then, nor is our culture the same that it was. All of the stories in this book are as accurate as our primary materials, secondary sources, and personal memories, as well as those that we have interviewed, can determine. We hope that you find them both insightful and pleasurable.

Ken Caillat
Los Angeles
August 2018

1

NEEDLES AND PINS

> It's not like *Rumours* was "the best album ever made" because it sold the most copies. It did well for a lot of different reasons, many, I'm sure, that had little or nothing to do with the music. If I'm going to believe it sold so well because it was so great, how am I supposed to interpret *Tusk* selling so many fewer copies? I like *Tusk* better. I just can't take it too seriously. Sales are not necessarily indicative of quality.
>
> —Lindsey Buckingham

Since finishing *Rumours* a year and a half ago, things changed a lot for us. *Rumours* went platinum a month after it was released with 1 million in sales and hit no. 1 in April 1977, and stayed no. 1 all the way until November, breaking and setting records established by some of the biggest names in the music business. A year later, my coproducer, Richard Dashut, and I won a Grammy as the producers of the Album of the Year for our work on *Rumours*, and were also nominated for Best Engineers at the twentieth annual Grammy Awards.

I traveled with the band on its victory lap around the world—all across the United States, Europe, Australia, New Zealand, and Japan, recording its live shows to millions of rapturous fans. Everywhere Fleetwood Mac played, it was more than just a rock band; it was a phenomenon, one that required hours of hard work behind the scenes to maintain. After a much-needed rainy winter break, the band rented Joe Walsh's house on Mulholland and began rehearsing and writing again. The band's popularity hadn't waned one bit. If anything, it was growing. Fleetwood Mac had the magic touch, with more hits than Rod Carew. Even its side projects, such as Warren Zevon's "Werewolves of London" and Walter Egan's "Magnet and Steel," were burning up the Top 40.

On September 16, 1978, construction began on our new custom-built studio on the edge of Santa Monica, a new addition to the renowned Village Recorder Studios, and by June, Studio D was complete. The owner was an eccentric midwestern tycoon, Geordie Hormel of Hormel Foods, and the studio that Spam built was his favorite toy. If he was low on money, he'd sell an island. If someone didn't let him play piano, he'd buy the place. Geordie was a very nice guy and mild mannered with long hair well down past his shoulders, a former socialite once married to Leslie Caron now turned California hippie. Geordie's clients were some of the biggest stars in the music business, and he was constantly paranoid about the rampant drug use and parties going on only half a block from the local precinct. Therefore, the entrance to the Village was a maze of mirrors intended to confuse and delay a police raid. Inside his office he even built a fake wall that he could open and disappear behind. It truly was a different time.

After getting loose on the road, the band was itching to record. Now that its studio was complete, it was time to get down to business. I was confident that this time around would be easier. I was no longer the new kid, and I now knew the band intimately and how to better fulfill its needs. Its storied relationship issues had apparently all but healed. John McVie was engaged to his secretary, Julie Rubens, and Christine McVie was head over heels for LA's most eligible bachelor, Dennis Wilson of the Beach Boys. Christine and Dennis spent most nights either sleeping on his 52-foot yawl, *Harmony*, docked in Marina Del Rey or at her mansion in Beverly Hills. They were now rock royalty. Lindsey Buckingham, for his part, had won the heart of a stunning blond model named Carol Ann Harris, and the two soon moved in together and were nearly inseparable.

In less than a year, Stevie Nicks became one of the most famous, distinctive, and lusted-after singers in the world with an amoeba-like entourage around her at all times. The band's little sister dated celebrities and musicians at such a rate that we stopped keeping track. Mick Fleetwood may have been a lunatic on the road, but he was still the married family man who doted on his children and his parents. What we didn't know at the time was that Stevie and Mick had already embarked on an affair during the *Rumours* tour. Over the next year, the Fleetwood Mac saga would only become more epic. But for now, the business at hand was to record the most anticipated follow-up album of the '70s.

I drove my new metallic blue 1973 Ferrari Dino down the hillside from my ocean-view home in Malibu. Foreigner's "Hot Blooded" was on the radio and my beagle, Scooter, had his head out the window, ears flapping as I zigzagged in and out of busy beach traffic on the Pacific Coast Highway. Other drivers did a double take at Scooter, who appeared to be driving because I'd bought the car in London. It was a beautiful day. I felt good. I was in the mix.

Foreigner, another collection of crazy Brits and Americans, had asked me to produce the album that would become *Double Vision* right after I finished *Rumours*, but I was too tired and probably too scared to jump back into another album after spending over a year locked up in a studio. Instead, the job went to Keith Olsen at Sound City, who had produced Fleetwood Mac's self-titled breakthrough three years before. He was a straight-ahead rock-and-roll producer who got amazing sounds, and I was admiring his work on the drive in, hoping I would be able to replicate that same magic that day. The best part of working in the recording industry is you never know what day you're going to be a part of something historical. Despite the egos and the money, the doubt and insecurity, the potential is always there for something special.

I looked over at Scooter, "Here we go again. Are you ready for another Year of Crazy, buddy?"

He looked at me like, "Sure, what the fuck, how bad can it be?"

If I had only known, I might have turned around and gone back to bed.

Scooter and I pulled into the Village parking lot before noon. I was excited to get this album going. I felt bold. I wanted to surpass *Rumours* with more great songs and more great sounds. Fleetwood Mac was the perfect package and now I had home-field advantage with my bespoke studio and team, built to my own precise specifications. This was my house; what could go wrong?

On the way in the door through the hall of mirrors, I passed a very attractive new receptionist—she looked to be about twenty-three, with flawless skin—and thought, *Why not sit down in the waiting area until Richard gets here?* When Richard entered a few minutes later, he took one look at the beauty and immediately did one of his fake stumbles, right into her desk. "Well, excuse me, but I think I may be falling for you," he said in his Rodney Dangerfield voice. He started laughing and when he finally stopped, he introduced himself to the new girl, who was engrossed in a copy of *The Thorn Birds*. "Hello, I'm Richard Dashut," he said, reaching out with his hand to hers and giving a gentlemanly half bow.

She put down her book as I instinctively jumped up to her rescue and apologized, "Yeah, yeah, don't mind him; he's always this way."

"Why, thank you, but I have a boyfriend, and besides, he looks pretty harmless to me, though," she said with a smile, looking straight into my eyes.

"Boyfriend, huh? If he ever screws up with you, please let me know, and I'll be there for you." Scooter barked reproachfully at us. I put my arm around Dashut as he continued to snicker and took him down the long hallway that led to our studio.

"Hey, when did she start working here? She's hot!" Richard wondered, turning his head for one last look.

"Here we go again, Casanova. I guess Geordie hired her last week to go with the new room," I joked.

We opened the double doors of our studio and into the lounge that was directly behind the control room. "Want a beer?" I asked. We made sure to install a tap of Heineken, Mick's favorite beer, to prevent any more bottle pyramids next to his drum set like last time. (Fleetwood Mac was getting classy; even Christine had switched from Blue Nun to Pouilly-Fuissé.) I grabbed two chilled glass mugs from the fridge and handed one to Richard.

"Hey, get away from that beer! That's Mick's!" Ray Lindsey, the band's roadie, chauffeur, and occasional second guitar player walked in the room.

"Just try to stop us," Richard countered.

"Hey, buddy," I said, putting my arm around Ray, giving him a hug. "How do you like our new home for the next year?" I asked. "Did you see the room we built for you and Rhino? It's on the other side of the studio. It has a bench where you can work on the equipment with special lights and tall chairs."

"Yeah; they showed me when I got here—pretty cool!" said Ray.

"How was the tour?"

"Bitchin'!" said Rhino, who had been sitting in the corner unnoticed.

Rhino was Mick's drum roadie. I have to admit Rhino came off as rough around the edges. Born Ron Penny, he got his road name for, well, being a bit obnoxious. He had a chipped front tooth, which I think he got in a bar fight. Rhino grew up on the road and that was the life he loved. They're a special breed.

"I got a lot of hot punters to use those Mac knee pads to get backstage access," he boasted. "'No head, no backstage pass'—that's my rule!"

Sometime during the *Rumours* tour, somebody in the merch department okayed the making of official Fleetwood Mac knee pads. You see, those in the Mac's road crew prided themselves on treating their women properly.

"Nice, Rhino," said Ray, sarcastically.

Ray was a sweet guy at heart. He had a baby face and a keen sense of humor, but could be pretty biting when he wanted to be. Nobody in the Fleetwood Mac family, I noticed early on, was thin-skinned.

"When will the band's equipment be here?" Richard asked.

"It's out in the truck. We were just waitin' for you two losers to tell us where to set it up," Rhino said flatly.

"Follow me, gentlemen," I said, "and I use that term *very* loosely."

Richard and I led the two roadies into the small kitchen, past the two private bathrooms and into the control room of Studio D. The control room was about 1,000 square feet, shaped in a hexagon with big double glass windows that surveyed the spacious sound room, giving us a commanding view of the action. The control room was paneled with dark, ornate, recessed walnut panels. In the back of the control room, there was a long couch and a credenza in front, which served as a coffee table. Additionally, it was a handy coke chopping surface, a prerequisite for any recording studio of that era.

In the opposite corner, on the far side of the couch, was the tape machine station. We had designed it to hold everything we needed. We had two brand-new Studer A-80, 24-track tape machines, two Ampex ATR-100 2-track machines, and a full complement of forty-eight channels of Dolby SR noise-reduction units. Attending to all these fabulous machines was our pal, assistant engineer Hernan Rojas.

"Good morning, Hernan!" I said.

"May I call you Ernesto or Ernie, my good man?" Dashut said, while lighting a cigarette.

Hernan half-groaned, half-chuckled.

"Hello, it's nice to see you guys again. It's pronounced 'Air-nan,' by the way."

Hernan was a proud, ruggedly handsome Latino with a cleft chin like movie stars have. He had emigrated from Chile because of his love of music and desire to work in a top studio in the States. He had been an assistant engineer here at the Village for the past four years, where we met him during the remix of singles for *Rumours* and other FM side projects. He had married a California girl for mutual convenience, so he could get his green card and she, a male companion for her and her young four-year-old daughter. This album would be Herman's big break, and he knew it.

"Well, Hair-non, you've got your work cut out for you with Dashut and Caillat, that's for sure!" replied Ray and Rhino, nearly talking in unison like Heckle and Jeckle, their laughter trailing them out into the studio.

"Very funny coming from you two guys," Richard yelled after them, laying down the law. "Remember you're in our world now, not on the road!"

Richard and I followed after the two roadies and showed them where the drums, bass amp, guitar amp, electric keyboards, and Leslie organ should be placed around our new studio. Each musician would have his or her personal station, surrounded by portable isolation walls, and with its own individual headphone controls. Now that we were all set up, all we needed was a band.

"When will the band be here?" I asked.

"I talked to Mick a while ago," said Richard, "and everyone will be down later this afternoon to check out our new digs."

"Great. I want to be all set up when they arrive. Hernan, let's get some help in here to get the mics on stands, connected to the board, listed, and tested. I want this album to start off perfectly."

"Aye, captain," Hernan acknowledged in what may have been a Chilean's attempt at a Scottish accent. *Everyone's a comedian*, I thought to myself.

Back inside the control room, I saw Hernan was busy making final adjustments, labeling each microphone's identity on the channels of our new sixty-channel Neve 8078 console, an amazing and very expensive piece of equipment. Hernan set up mics like a bullfighter, always with pizzazz and always fun to watch. This was the Big Day and you couldn't help feeling a certain nervous energy in the air, among other things. Richard was already smoking a joint with Ray. I gave him a look and he headed over to help me finish setting the mics.

"Hey, buddy! Are you going to share that with me?" I asked, pointing to the glowing joint.

"Cutlass," Dashut said, calling me by his nickname for my tape-editing abilities, passing me the joint. Richard added, "I talked to Lindsey this morning and he didn't sound so good. Had a rough night with Carol, apparently; he said he'd be a little late coming in today."

"No problem; we'll get everyone else's sounds perfected while we wait for Lindsey to arrive."

It was uncharacteristic of Lindsey for him to be the last to arrive. Fleetwood Mac was unique among big rock bands in that it had Mick as its manager and Lindsey as the band's de facto producer and arranger. It was all in-house, which streamlined the process, of course, and made every decision more personal, but also made the burden that much heavier. Lindsey especially liked to be a part of the day's planning, and to have the first pick at the prime time of the day.

Mick and John arrived next and soon hoisted frosty mugs of Heineken, cheering their own luck and success, like two village blokes who won at the races. They were best friends and great battery mates, who always reminded me of Peter Cook and Dudley Moore. They just had that chemistry. Almost immediately after entering the live space, Mick started tuning his drums with Rhino and Dashut at his side. Mick carefully tuned each drum to his unique liking, which is one of the secrets to his sound. Also, because Christine had perfect pitch, tuning up and staying in tune were a Fleetwood Mac obsession, which as an engineer, only endeared them to me. Over in John's bass area, all of his basses were lined up neatly on stands so John could immediately have the right instrument for each song. John is one of the most tasteful and instinctive bass players I've ever met. When he was sober, he worked quickly and he worked well.

Half an hour later, Stevie arrived with her gorgeous friend, Sara Recor. Sara was a natural beauty with long brown hair and a killer body. In a room full of famous people, she was the one you couldn't ignore. She was Stevie's best friend and was the inspiration for the one of *Tusk*'s standout tracks, "Sara." Both Stevie and Sara went directly out to talk to Mick. He always had a way with the ladies. It seemed to me that they were both flirting with him. I didn't know about Stevie and Mick's affair at the time, nor did I know that things were starting to fall apart between the two of them.

Stevie came back into the control room and handed Hernan a cassette for him to play.

"I want you guys to hear two new songs of mine," Stevie said.

Hernan put it into the cassette player and pushed Play. One of Stevie's new songs, "Storms," came on. It was a somewhat depressing song with only a few chords. I know now that it was written about Mick, but at the time it was assumed that it was written about her and Lindsey. She told Hernan to pause the tape. "What do you think of that one?" she asked us.

"Nice," we all said, even though it was a bit of a downer for the first day.

"I really love it, Stevie," Sara was sure to add, and she meant it.

Stevie was, and still is, a prolific songwriter and lyricist. She knew that she was competing with Lindsey and Christine for song space and for some reason always had to fight harder than the other two to get her due consideration. This would come back to bite the band in a couple of years.

Just then, Christine and Dennis Wilson came into the control room. Chris and Dennis had been dating for a while now. Christine often wrote songs on his boat where he had a keyboard for her to play which led to a slew of new love songs from her. I had known Dennis for a while now. He'd always come down and check on our studio's progress, always smart and inquisitive and generous with advice, having been in the business since he was a teenager. I liked him.

"I heard a bit of that last song through the door," the always outspoken Christine remarked. "It's a bit dodgy, don't you think, Stevie?" Christine drawled like a duchess, so you were never sure whether she was being bitchy or not. The English were hard to read that way.

"Don't listen to her, Stevie," Dennis said. "Chris really likes it."

Dennis, no stranger to family quarrels, always had a kind thing to say if the air got tense.

"No, it's just a demo. It will be great after we work on it," Stevie said, undeterred. She was far more self-confident now than she had been, especially in Lindsey's absence. Stevie learned she could no longer be the front woman onstage and a shrinking violet in the studio. "Storms" did sound like another breakup song, and I had secretly hoped that we were past this breakup stuff. Stevie had written it on the couch of Studio D, looking up from her journal occasionally and somehow ignoring Mick during the insanely long hours we spent in the control room.

The next song on the tape was "Sisters of the Moon," which I recalled from a few years back, written about her failing health on tour. The new voice-and-piano demo was depressing and not very exciting, but it would evolve into a rocker more like "Gold Dust Woman," becoming one of the few driving hard rock songs on *Tusk* and another mystical milestone for her wandering gypsy persona with a chorus that foresaw '80s heavy metal.

"That one's gonna be fucking great, Stevie!" exclaimed Christine, an old rocker at heart, holding her cigarette in the same hand as her glass of Burgundy. "We should play it live this summer. I'll play the Rhodes on that one."

A Fender Rhodes is the most mysterious sounding keyboard of all time, and a perfect fit to the aura this song was giving off. We all agreed this song had some real potential.

"Do you want to hear my two new ones?" Christine asked.

"Absolutely!" said Stevie, slightly relieved.

Hernan cued up two of Christine's new ballads, the alluring "Brown Eyes" and the lilting "Over & Over." By this time, Mick and John had come into the control room to join us. They had been listening to the demos through their headphones out in the studio, thanks to Hernan's efficient thinking, and were already coming up with parts, such was their innate gift and craft as superb sidemen. We were all very excited with the new songs and couldn't wait to get started. There's a certain euphoria that comes with hearing a new song for the first time and all the creative possibilities it invites.

All of a sudden, Lindsey and Carol walked into the control room, looking as if they had been fighting. Most startling, though, was Lindsey's extreme haircut. He shaved his Dutch beard and his long curly locks of hair had been hacked off, leaving only his handsome, square-jawed face. He looked less like the California hippie arena rocker, and more like a New Wave punk. I also noticed he had slashed up his pants pretty badly.

NEEDLES AND PINS

"Lindsey, what the hell did you do to your beautiful hair?" Christine asked, clearly dumbfounded and anxious for his explanation.

"I don't know. I was in the shower after Carol and I had a fight and I just lost it. I grabbed a pair of scissors and just started chopping my hair off," Lindsey said, "and once I started, I pretty much had to finish the job." This story, although strange, was not atypical of Fleetwood Mac in general. Lindsey explained he was in a rut and needed to shake things up in his life. Dennis chose this moment to excuse himself and left us to get on with the album, kissing Chris on the way out.

"We just listened to two new songs of Chris and Stevie's," Mick told Lindsey, "and I'm very pleased."

Lindsey brushed the topic of his new look aside and strode confidently to a seat at the mixing board next to me and Richard. Not surprisingly, he said he'd prefer to get started with one of his new songs first and handed Hernan a cassette.

It was the first time we'd heard "The Ledge," although at the time, Lindsey referred to it as "Can't Walk Out of Here." The cassette was distorted and I thought, *Yikes—that sounds horrible and very unlike his previous demos*, which were always clean and meticulous. I wondered what was going on in Lindsey's mind and life. His look may have been clean-cut, but his music definitely wasn't.

We all liked the song fine, but Lindsey had also tuned his guitar down, so it sounded as if he was playing an inner tube, and a distorted one at that. He listened patiently to our comments but nevertheless was anxious to get started. Lindsey asked for me to get his guitar sound first because it would determine what we'd do next. Lindsey went out to his station to adjust his guitar tone on his amp. He plugged in his Les Paul to his Marshall amp and through my direct box, the Fat Box, just as he had on the last album. He started to play the main riff of "The Ledge" and Richard and I started playing with the EQ, reshaping and improving Lindsey's guitar tone to sound perfect through our equipment and out of our speakers. This was high-end technology at its finest.

"I think it sounds great!" Richard said to Lindsey through our talkback mic into Lindsey's headphones.

Lindsey smiled oddly and then said to me, "Ken, are you happy with the sound you guys got on this?"

"You bet!" I said truthfully.

Then, he said something he had never said before to me during *Rumours*.

"Okay, now I want you to turn all your knobs one hundred eighty degrees in the opposite direction!"

"What?!" I asked, totally astounded and confused at his request and his intention behind it. "Lindsey, if I do that, it will ruin the sound that we have in here," I pleaded, even though he knew that just as well as I did.

"*Just do it now!*" he said in an agitated tone of voice. Then, he paused for declamatory effect, "I don't want this to be another *Rumours*. I don't want to make the same record twice like the Eagles did!"

"Okay," I capitulated, "but how am I to do my job? I can't just turn all the knobs a hundred eighty degrees the wrong way the whole album." This wasn't my first time dealing with a frustrated guitarist, especially this one. "Do you want to change your guitar sound? Are you saying you'd like this album to emphasize the bottom end more, to have a darker tone with less sparkle?" I reasoned.

Lindsey thought for a moment and then said, "Umm, yeah, I guess that's what I'm saying."

"All right, then; let's try that, a darker album," I relented.

It was an auspicious beginning to what was supposed to be the follow-up album by California's sunniest band. Somehow his new look made everyone feel even more ill at ease. For the rest of the night, Lindsey built his song brick by brick without the contributions of the rest of the band. After everyone was spent, He announced his vision: that he saw a different direction for this album, and if the rest of them didn't do what he said, he'd quit the band. He looked around at the band nervously, almost to see whether he had gotten away with his demand. Everyone was aghast.

'What is *wrong* with this band?' I thought.

It was a depressing and dramatic end to a day that had begun so hopefully, but then again, this was Fleetwood Mac we were talking about.

"Come on, Scooter, let's go home."

2

LINDSEY'S HEAD

> That's the magic of this band. If we made it like a military operation, we probably wouldn't be together.
>
> —Mick Fleetwood

The making of Tusk *started for me as I was boarding a merchant ship bound for the United States. It was a foggy morning in January 1974, and I was departing from Valparaiso, Chile's most important port. I wasn't leaving my home on a luxury liner, but on a merchant ship departing on its last voyage before being sold for scrap metal. My personal odyssey had finally begun after years of dreaming about it. I wanted to be part of the music revolution that was taking place in California, where people lived the hippie lifestyle, a counterculture where I could find a new life away from the forces that were beginning to limit my own life and those of my fellow countrymen. Augusto Pinochet's coup d'état, assisted by Nixon and Kissinger, of the first socialist democratically elected government under the unsuccessful presidency of Salvador Allende the previous fall, had thrown my homeland into disarray, resulting in blatant human rights violations that included torture and forced disappearances. I was determined to leave at all costs.*

The seeds that grew into this dream were planted the first time the

GET TUSKED

Beatles came roaring out of my grandfather's old RCA tube radio in 1963. I didn't know what to make of it. My only thought was, Who the hell are these guys that are playing this music?! *The groove was intense and the melody was attractive and pleasing, with an edge. The epiphanies kept coming with the Rolling Stones, the Animals, the Beach Boys, Bob Dylan, the Yardbirds, the Kinks, and many more over the next couple of years. The joy ride had started, and I realized viscerally that the energy contained in rock music was unique. The gospel of Dylan so prophetically worded in his "The Times They Are A-Changin'" inspired me through its truth. The song was an indictment, a news flash, and a call to arms. It was happening, and it was happening now. Something special and powerful had been brewing for our generation during the '50s. It was hidden and misunderstood by headline news, an explosive cocktail of blues and country music, shaken with a hard, danceable beat. I wanted nothing more than to drink it and be a part of it.*

Arriving at the port in Valparaiso, I found that the ship had not docked due to weather conditions, so I had to board it on the open sea from a small craft with part of my family accompanying me to the boarding stairs along the side, making our good-byes all the more dramatic. Those last minutes gave me the chance for one final look into the eyes of my grandmother, aunt, father, and brother. Their silent expressions spoke the sorrow of separation that would last years. The night before, holding the tears back as much as I could, I said good-bye to my mother and sister, since they didn't have the strength to see me leave the next day.

As the ship sailed away, the fog that surrounded the port turned to sadness, and thoughts of leaving my family and home consumed me. But I was resolute, and with a month's long journey ahead, I knew this wouldn't be a pleasure cruise. My thoughts turned to survival mode. How was I to keep my mind active and my spirits up and prepare for my landing in California? My only spiritual sustenance came from three cassettes, which consisted of Revolver *by the Beatles; a mixtape of Neil Young, Crosby, Stills & Nash, America, and Jethro Tull; and a compilation of early Fleetwood Mac that included "Black Magic Woman." In that music was my salvation, whole worlds of imagination and emotion to lose oneself in. That was one of the first signs planted by destiny about the journey ahead of me.*

Time and time again, I would be presented with events that would change and define my life forever. I knew very little about what I was getting myself into, but like most adventurers, that mattered very little. In those days, I had no knowledge of the music production process, or the types of professionals that were required in the recording industry, those trusted to build an artist's career through engineering and producing. Los Angeles was weeks away, the home of the music industry, and I was going to submit myself to it one way or the other, because in my case, there was no turning back.

Four years later, Fleetwood Mac and its crew are going to enter the studio I work for, the Village Recorder, to embark on a new album. A new album is always a big project, but in this particular case, it was going to be a very special one. The world had crowned Rumours *as the most popular album of all time, which is a mind-blowing achievement. In addition to its sales, all of the necessary awards and recognition created a cultural phenomenon. The band's success had become bigger than life, and the expectations for the follow-up were impossible to overstate.*

Fleetwood Mac's style and demeanor were not entirely new to me since I had worked with the band as an assistant engineer remixing some of the Rumours *singles for radio in Studio B at the Village Recorder. I connected well with its engineers, Ken Caillat and Richard Dashut. They made a* great team, with technical know-how and the attitude to back it up, and they were fun people to be around, which is vital for long-term projects like this one.

This new recording journey with Ken, Richard, and the Mac at the newly built Studio D happened thanks to the intricate designs of fate and a series of crossroads. The sessions we did for Rumours were a key milestone It began when I got a call from Gary Starr, the manager at the Village, urging me to quit my vacation in Marin County early and return to LA. Fleetwood Mac had booked time, and my previous experience with the hottest band of the moment was required for such an important client. I did a fast rewind of all the fabulous musicians and bands that has passed through Village Recorders, which included Prince, Van Halen, Milton Nascimento, Wayne Shorter, Neil Diamond, the Band, Steely Dan, Santana, and Joe Cocker. "There must be a logic to all these series of sessions to prepare me for this moment," I said to myself. This had to be something very special to cut short my vacation. Then I remembered the Fleetwood Mac cassette that had accompanied me through the ocean voyage, with Peter Green's raunchy voice and those chilling riffs and solos, layered on top of that great rhythm section. Fate was intervening.

"Gary, I'll be on the next flight."

I arrived to the brand-new Studio D early that morning to attend to my technical duties that, in those analog days, and given the amount of amazing equipment we had, required at least an hour or more of careful setups, alignments of our console, multitrack and stereo tape machines, microphones, reverb, effects, and outboard gear. During the proceedings, I felt a rush of adrenaline, a potent mix of emotions that included anxiety along with and a strange sense of tension and calm, almost like a Fleetwood Mac song. I did feel reassured somewhat by a slight advantage I had in being accepted by the band. I had suffered through a British school education in Chile with rugby, prefects, and caning administered by rigid, British teachers, all of whom answered to a despot of a headmaster. It always seemed as though the meanest and strictest teachers were sent from the United Kingdom to find employment in Chile. Little did I know how my mind-set, so grounded and proud, was going to be quickly beaten into submission, starting that very first Monday morning by Mick and Richard's remarks and jokes. Ritual humiliation was the way of life in the Fleetwood Mac family.

From the start, my instincts told me that recording with the world's most successful band was going to be a larger undertaking than I had previously imagined. A powerful set of circumstances and twisting energy was brewing to unleash something very special to all involved, and hopefully to the fans and the rest of the outside world. It was clear to me that this endeavor was going to require much mental and physical endurance, something I was familiar with from school. Indeed, during our sessions, Mick would often repeat the typical British call for the resilient "stiff upper lip," and he was fond of quoting Winston Churchill's "We shall never surrender. We shall fight till the end."

During the remixes of the singles for Rumours, I remembered the comical slings and arrows that were directed at the newcomers, as if there was a need to haze all new members of the Penguin brotherhood. This was confirmed repeatedly by the band's battle-hardened roadies, Ray Lindsey and Rhino, but also Mick, who renamed me Fernando, as sung to that line in an ABBA song "Do you hear the drums, Fernando?" When I wasn't Fernando, I was Hernandez or Hernesto. It didn't matter. I was Chilean, so I instantly became all Latinos. This didn't really bother me as I realized that with this band, humor was not just cruelty, but acceptance. This was my job. They were our guests and our clients, and we were going to be spending a long, long time together, so I had to become one of them.

As the clock hit the arranged start time of eleven a.m., neither the crew nor the band had shown up. I glanced through the window of the control room out onto the unchristened Studio D, admiring the first luxury, multiroom studio at Village Recorders. It was palatial, and customized for the biggest band on the planet. It featured a bespoke Neve 8078 console, which was the Rolls-Royce of consoles. It had twin, synchronized Studer A880, 24-track tape machines; forty-eight Dolby noise reduction channels; top-notch condenser, ribbon, and dynamic microphones; and the latest in outboard gear, such as Lexicon digital reverb.

I walked through the different rooms in the studio, which could go from dry to wet with different woods and lava rocks from Hawaii. There was a large echo chamber and a variable acoustic ceiling with motorized blinds. The studio came furnished with expensive instruments, such as a Yamaha concert piano and a Hammond B-3 organ with a Leslie rotating speaker. Fleetwood Mac's own gear was set up around the live room, including three full drum kits, acoustic and electric and bass guitars, a bank of electric keyboards, a pump organ, various percussion instruments, and amplifiers. All that was left were the musicians to bring it all to life.

There was also a fully equipped tech room for the roadies, also handy for any discreet needs like sex and drugs, also known as "rest and relaxation." The interior design of Studio D leaned toward antiques and home decor, with a kitchen tiled with a medieval village scene out of Brueghel and a lounge designed for plush leather comfort for the band and any hangers-on that visited on a regular basis. It was designed to look like a wood-paneled English manor library with paintings of fox hunting and other country scenes along with a dining space and a full bar with changing lights that could make it feel like day or night for any studio vampires.

Finally, Ken showed up excited to do the honors of beginning the new and long-awaited Fleetwood Mac album. He was inseparable from his dog, Scooter, who I really got to like from our previous sessions and outings. Richard tagged along with the roadies firing off lighthearted threats like, "Hey, guys, these are our stomping grounds, so you'd better submit and behave," as if they were a pack of hounds. The band arrived eventually with no sense of urgency that the clock was already ticking because money was no longer an object. Rock superstars often have an aura, either from their look or their onstage persona, which presumes an attitude of bad behavior. But, in my role as an engineer for these flesh-and-blood human beings, the connection had to be as normal as possible, observing I couldn't cater to them as a fan and I had to observe the highest professional standards as the session required, no matter what their attitude was that day.

The British members of the band had their own trademark personalities, which in the early days, conveyed the sense that there was a distance to keep. Mick would purposefully linger over the Neve console, overshadowing all of us, which I found a bit intimidating. John McVie would wander unnoticed into the control room with his vodka tonic, take a seat, and quietly pore over Mad Magazine *to take his mind off the tribulations that he knew was to come. Christine was a pro lounger, always smiling with her ever-present cigarette and glass of Champagne, but always menacing with her sharp, sarcastic tongue.*

The Americans couldn't have been more different. The common bond between Lindsey and Stevie, from my perspective, was a more authentic closeness that offered the chance to have normal conversations and an openness to listening. Lindsey and I talked about music from the beginning, and Stevie opened up to me as if we had known each other forever. As the sessions *progressed, the depths of her pain from those days became clear. The unique white witch hippie look that she cultivated, along with her cute face framed by a curly shag haircut, reminded me of Carrie Fisher, and made an impression on me instantly. The dynamics of this group of people and the time we spent together would intertwine all of us, shaping not just the music on the album, but all of our lives to come.*

Scooter and I cruised down the Pacific Coast Highway toward Santa Monica through the seasonal puffs of the late morning fog, what the locals call "June Gloom." The 12-mile drive along the coast from my home to the studio took about twenty minutes, unless I chose Ferrari power, and then it was a blurry shot to our new home at the Village Recorder. This was going to be an interesting week, I thought, still waiting for my coffee to fully kick in. It was Saturday morning, June 24, 1978, and the construction of our new custom-built Studio D was only finished days ago. The band was about to start rehearsals for its "Penguin Country Summer Safari" tour, and the feeling among the band and its team was, "Let's get in there and see what our sweet new studio could do."

Even better, I was now officially promoted to coproducer of this new album along with my buddy Richard Dashut and the band. Ordinarily, this would come with great prestige, since the producer is responsible for most of the logistics and scheduling along with the musical direction for the album and its songs. But since Lindsey played the "You will all do as I say or I'll quit" card, we were all caught reexamining our options and pondering life under the rule of Buckingham. This situation wasn't entirely new to me, but every day presented its own set of challenges. It was clear he didn't want to compete with "Shadow Dancing."

LINDSEY'S HEAD

At this point in Lindsey's life, he was very serious and tense. I guess when you're trying to reinvent yourself or keep up with the new kids, it's got to be tough without some yardstick to guide you. Looking back on the situation now, the new album must have been an unfolding contradiction in his mind: wanting so much distortion on his songs, but still knowing he had to conjure the same ear-pleasing sounds for all the girls' songs. On Chris and Stevie's songs, he literally created some of the most beautiful and sophisticated guitar sounds ever recorded, while on his songs, he goaded us to distort his guitar to the point where I thought we were going to damage our speakers. I couldn't suppress my disappointment that this album wasn't going to sound like *Rumours*, an album that I was very proud of and whose sound that I didn't think the band was done exploring, even if Lindsey had. Since he was insisting we create a new Fleetwood Mac sound for this next album, and I was its producer and engineer, it fell on me to help the band achieve it.

Step one was getting to the studio first to come up with some sort of cohesive game plan that we could operate under for the next year. It also happened to be Mick's birthday, so I was fairly sure the day wouldn't be entirely productive.

I pulled into the small parking lot and took some pride that I was guaranteed a prime spot. My mid-engine V8 rumbled with a deep-throated growl and instantly stopped. I stepped out and looked up at the enormous painted mural on the side of the Village. Titled *Isle of California*, it depicted the aftermath of a great earthquake that dropped California into the sea, with ocean waves crashing on the cliffs of Arizona below a severed freeway overpass with a green sign showing the border town of Blythe in white lettering. Every day I parked under it, it made me think about how unique this part of the country was and how many bridges we were burning ourselves, and yet the view was from an island, a new land created from the old.

The trusty Heineken truck arrived at the same time to drop off a half-barrel keg for our lounge tap, the only such one at any of the studios that we knew of, and we were very proud of that fact. I was thankful we wouldn't have empty bottles rolling around studio floor like last time. The English members of the band loved their beer and drank it more regularly than their afternoon tea. I walked in the door of the mirrored lobby, nodded to the receptionist, and hung a sharp left down the long hallway lined with gold records, past Studio A where the members of Steely Dan was working on the follow-up to their masterpiece, *Aja*, what would eventually become *Gaucho*. They would be our neighbors, of and on, for the next year. They, too, would be plagued with personal and artistic setbacks that would push them past their release date, resulting in the end of their marvelous streak of albums.

Passing the double-wide, stained-glass doors and marble staircase of the building's original entrance, I ducked right up the corridor that led directly into Studio D's control room and nerve center, where Hernan was already in full swing setting up, making notes, and labeling the console. Being methodical, efficient, and early are invaluable traits in an assistant engineer, and we were lucky to have him. Hernan lived walking distance away—a rare thing in LA—which probably added to his chronic cheerfulness.

"Morning, my friend," I said to Hernan.

"Mr. Caillat, good morning to you and your fine dog, too," he jested with me. It was somewhat of an eccentricity that I took my dog to work. Scooter trotted around the corner behind the massive console where he had his dog bed.

"Quite a day yesterday, huh? Lindsey wanting to go all mysterious on us?" I confided, trying to gauge Hernan's opinion before offering a positive spin. "I've given it some thought, and it could work out okay. I usually go bright and jangly, so maybe we go low and dark. That way, we can balance it out with some sizzling cymbals."

"You know," Hernan said after a pause, "I think that could work. That would make a fucking amazing-sounding album." I was glad he concurred. Sometimes, Hernan sounded like a scientist with his better-than-average Chilean English, I thought.

"Ken, I know you recorded *Rumours* slower at 15 ips for a tighter bottom and controlled top, but how about we record this album at 30 ips for a bigger bottom and higher top end?" Hernan suggested.

"I love it, Hernan; let's do that. The top end transients will be better, but I still want to use Dolby noise reduction. I hate *hisssss*," I exaggerated. "We'll have to be alert when it comes to Lindsey and make sure he trusts us enough with his sound. A darker album it is . . ."

Hernan nodded knowingly, and I walked to the lounge to get my first beer and found Richard already at the tapper and kibitzing with the crew and John McVie.

"Hey, Dash, Hernan and I came up with a plan for this album, regarding tape speed," I said, taking a sip of beer.

Richard was already in high gear, "I love it already. Don't tell me any more. Finish your drink and get on with it, man! Oh, and Cutlass, I talked to Adams this morning and he told me there's a baseball team of bean counters called the Messiahs of Money, and they're challenging us to form a team and play them. He told them we're musicians, all soft and high and no match for greedy accountants!"

"Oh, really? Those guys are all fat and out of shape—we'll kill 'em! Plus, I can pitch."

GET TUSKED

"Hey, we're going to need uniforms for the Fleetwood Mac Groin Pulls!" he joked, and we all laughed.

For the next half hour, we got down to work discussing the pros and cons of Lindsey's "The Ledge" that he had played us the day before. Politely speaking, the song could best be described as raucous. It was more vicious than a *Rumours* song, which were also lyrically edgy yet so musically pleasing that they didn't come off as spiteful. Those songs inhabited both worlds, which was the secret recipe of that album. This song, though, started with a very non-McVie bassline on the 1 and 3 and simplistic kick-snare track on the 2 and 4. Lindsey layered on electric rhythm guitars so distorted that it sounded more like a tuba than a guitar. There were no lyrics to speak of as yet, because Lindsey preferred to write those last. Instead of lyrics, he grunted and mouthed words fast and furious, which added to his demo's nervous energy.

After listening to the playback, I turned to the others and said, half-jokingly, "When we get back into it today, we're going to make the tuba sound amazing!"

"I'm going to tune that snare up so high it's going to break," Richard threatened.

"Maybe try to tune it with the song?" Hernan mentioned helpfully.

"Let's see where it goes when the band arrives," I said.

"Where what goes when we arrive? Good morning, lads!" Mick said, suddenly towering over all of us. He looked suave as always in his dress shirt, embroidered silk vest, and watch fob.

"Hey, Mick! Happy birthday! I have your present for you, my lord," Dashut sneered with a strange tone, bowing and scraping like a jester toward Mick.

LINDSEY'S HEAD

"Knave, I'll have your *head*, if I'm not pleased with your gift," Mick said, playing along.

"I'm sure you'll find this jeweled dagger to your liking. This is from me and all the peasants in the kingdom who *hate* you, my lord!" Dash then thrust the imaginary dagger into Mick's chest. Mick collapsed into my engineer's chair as the two broke into hysterical laughter, proud of their on-the-spot improvisation. We all joined in on the laughter.

Mick's corpse rose and spoke in a foreboding voice, "Lindsey's just outside saying good-bye to Carol. He should be right in . . ."

"Great," I said. "Since we've got the birthday boy here, why don't we get started on that snare sound, then?" Mick and Dash agreed and headed off into the live room to pick out a snare and start tuning it.

Our practice of tuning Mick's drums started at the beginning of the *Rumours* while Richard and I were trying to save our asses from being fired. We discovered that Mick's drums never sounded the same from day to day. His drum roadie would just pack and unpack his drums, and that was it. Drums have a top and bottom head made out of either skin or plastic and can be stretched tighter or looser to eliminate overtones and buzz, deliver clarity, and match them to a particular song or room sound. Fortunately for me, Dashut took it upon himself to learn how to tune and dampen drums to perfection. So, every day before recording, Dashut would tune each and every one of Mick's toms, plus the snare and the kick drum. The result of all that painstaking work were the bold tom sounds in the verse of "Go Your Own Way." That's just one famous example of the many times when a savvy engineer can make all the difference in the finished sound of a recording. No matter how good the song was, Mick never tired of reminding us, "The song can't survive if the drums aren't right!"

GET TUSKED

As Mick and Richard got down to work, Lindsey and his beautiful girlfriend, Carol, walked into the control room, nodded, and said hello to everybody. Carol was a model with long blond hair that did little to conceal her breasts bouncing inside her half-unbuttoned blue silk blouse. She was adorable. *She should have chosen me*, I couldn't help thinking. Apparently, Carol had cleaned up Lindsey's spontaneous haircut from the other day and added a slight bit of eyeliner, making him look like a mix of punk rocker and Venice Beach cult member in his designer jacket, jeans, and flip-flops.

A few minutes later, Judy Wong walked in the door with Christine McVie. Christine was wearing one of her favorite outfits, a denim shirt ironically decorated with Boy Scout merit patches to match her high-waisted bell-bottom jeans. Judy was short and of Asian descent with long black hair and a British accent. She had been friends with the band for nearly ten years now, sharing in its members' early blues heyday and bohemian lives in England. Judy was completely dedicated to FM; I believe she would have done anything for it. When I first met Judy, she was living with Christine while also running the band's business affairs, that's how tight its circle used to be. I always credited Judy for coming up with the running order for *Rumours*. She had an impeccable feel for music, which was why she remained so close to Fleetwood Mac for all these years.

"Good morning, Kenneth," Judy said to me. I think she had a slight crush on me.

"Good morning, Judy. You look great as always," I responded, cheerfully.

"Chris, would you like a beer, to celebrate Mick's birthday?" Hernan chimed in, trying to be accommodating.

LINDSEY'S HEAD

"Fuck no, I hate beer. Can someone bring me a glass of chilled Champagne?" Christine was from Birmingham, and her accent had a thick, Brummie lilt. She lit a cigarette in the new control room, as we all did then. By the end of *Tusk*, the control room smelled permanently of Merit cigarettes. Christine turned to us. "What are we working on today? And where's Stevie?"

I wasted no time. "She's not here yet, so I thought we'd start with Lindsey's new song. We've been talking about it and have some fun ideas for it."

"Great," Lindsey said, obviously satisfied, "let's get started," acting as though nothing had happened the day before. He began rubbing his hands together rapidly, one of his quirks that indicated he was ready to get down to work, which always boded well.

Ray came in from his work area and asked Lindsey which guitar and amp combination he wanted to start with. Ray had the uncanny ability to anticipate situations. Even though he just entered the room, he was already thinking about our next setup.

"Let's use my Strat and the Fender Twin. I might just go direct and not use the amp, but let's set them both up anyway," Lindsey answered. Like all big league guitar players, he was obsessed with his sound. Being able to play guitar extremely well is a given at this stage in the game, but achieving a perfect tone in the recording studio is what differentiates the pros from the punters.

"Hernan, let's put the amp in the iso room with two close mics on it," I instructed.

"Okay, boss." Hernan nodded and made his way to the isolation room to our left. We had designed the studio with the control room looking out 270 degrees into the studio, and then on either side, we had smaller sealed rooms that could isolate the sound from the rest of the live room. In addition, the iso rooms were tiled to sound like a bathroom, but they also had carpets and drapes that could be closed, giving you the option between an "echoey" and a "dead" sound. We designed our studio in such a fashion to make it extremely flexible, to be able to achieve any sound an artist required.

Studio D gave us the ability to see and control everything that happened from our own vantage point, like being in a ship's bridge, surveying the musical seascape changing before us and communicating with all parts of the ship. In a big-time studio situation, working with multiple renowned musicians, who may at any given time be creating musical history, our job is to anticipate and accurately capture the recording at hand. There is no room for error, because sometimes you only get one shot when something truly special happens. It's sound photography. You can snap as many photos as you want, but you can't replicate that perfect moment.

For instance, at a very basic level, Stevie might come into the control room one day and say, "I want to record a new piano song." Hernan, Richard, and I would have to consult with Stevie on which piano or keyboard she would prefer and what area of the studio it would sound best for the recording. Subsequently, Christine, Lindsey, and Stevie might want to record background vocals on this new track that Stevie just laid down. Again, we would have to decide which microphones would be appropriate and how many we should use. We might use one microphone for all three of the vocalists, or we might decide to have more control and use three separate microphones for each of the singers. Then, we'd need to choose which room they should sing in: an ambient room, such as the main live area of the studio, or a dry room, such as the right iso booth. These decisions would have to be made for nearly every day of the life of the recording, so it's imperative that the band have the utmost confidence and trust in its control room team.

The first step of recording, though, is listening. We blasted Lindsey's enigmatic cassette demo of "The Ledge" over the studio's JBL speakers before the musicians went to their stations to make personal adjustments. We determined the tempo that he wanted and we set our digital metronome to play a click into everyone's headphones so everybody could play in time with one another. Mick's drums were set up in their designated area to our right, and John's bass amp was set up in the small iso booth next to Mick. That way, John would be able to stand in front of Mick's drum kit while his amp was isolated to prevent bleeding into the other microphones. Continuing counterclockwise, Christine's Yamaha keyboard was plugged directly into the console with no amplifier. Past Chris and moving farther left was Lindsey's guitar station. Like John, he was able to stand in the middle of the room and walk around, as if onstage, while his amp was stationed in the left isolation room. The musicians each had their own headphones so they could hear one another perfectly yet also possess the option to have more or less of any of the instruments in their "cans." Adjusting each member's headphone mix was an incessant, but necessary, chore that we had to monitor, for better or worse.

After piping the song through their headphones a couple more times, the band felt it was ready to make some music. Hernan loaded up a blank reel of 2-inch tape. Richard and I went out into the studio to make sure we were pleased with all the microphone placements on the instruments, then he and I returned, lit a joint for luck, and then Richard addressed the party on the talkback, "All right, ladies and gentlemen, please take your positions, and let's get this fucking record started!"

"Grammys, here we come!" I said, continuing the tradition.

Hernan, a bit confused, asked, "Aren't we gonna wait for Stevie to arrive?"

Lindsey shot back, "No need. I don't hear her on this. Let's just get started."

Hernan shrugged as the musicians fussed with their headphones, put down their drinks, and rested cigarettes on their ashtrays. Richard asked whether they could hear us in their headphones, and they all nodded yes. I followed suit and said, "I'm going to play the click in your headphones. Go ahead and play the song down and we'll get levels on you in here." Hernan pressed Record on the Studer 24-track tape recorder, and the reels of tape spun into motion and the VU meters started to dance into the red as the band played.

I hit the talkback and announced, "'The Ledge,' take one," and Richard pressed go on the metronome. As soon as Mick heard the click in his headphones, he counted off the song, "And one, and two, and three, and four," and all the musicians kicked into gear. Mick was playing straight 2 and 4. His snare was tuned so high it sounded as though he was hitting a trash can lid; his 26-inch kick drum was muted by a large pillow and held in place by a heavy microphone stand so it wouldn't tumble out from the relentless pounding of Mick's kick pedal. Lindsey had tuned down his Fender Stratocaster, and again it was emitting these unprecedented muddy tuba sounds. John, remembering his confrontations with Lindsey for playing too eloquently, kept his part simple, while Christine stuck with a straightforward blues part.

Lindsey again sang gibberish in place of the unwritten words he didn't have yet, and a short two minutes later, Richard held up his hands to indicate "Silence, please," as Hernan stopped the recording.

LINDSEY'S HEAD

"Not bad for a first take," Richard chirped reassuringly into the talkback. Lindsey had already put down his guitar down and was striding back into the control room. He walked over to his stash box of Hawaiian pot, which he'd bring into the studio in a garbage bag right in front of the police station, and he immediately rolled a joint, lit it, and barked at us, "This is going to be a hell of a long album!" I thought I heard him mutter under his breath, "*This is all wrong.*" With his eye makeup, I remember thinking he looked more serious than ever before.

He then walked back out to the studio and started sharing his thoughts on how everyone could get closer to the sound in his head. He didn't want Mick to use any cymbals or tom fills; and to John, he reminded him, "No fancy turnarounds"; and to us, "Take a little low end off his bass." He suggested Christine switch over to the Hammond organ and just play some pads. We spent the next two hours running through seven takes of "The Ledge," until Lindsey gave up and said he needed to go home for a while and think. He grabbed Carol and they left wishing Mick a happy birthday on their way out. We spent the rest of the session drinking and drugging and trying to figure out what tomorrow was going to bring.

Several days ago, it all had seemed to be going to so well. We were following up a fantastic album. We all had money and nice cars. We had built our own state-of-the-art studio with every trick in the book built in. The band had just conquered the world with a hugely successful tour. We were all thinking that we were more experienced now and on our home turf of Los Angeles. All we had to do is do what we do best: make great music.

Suddenly, there was a dark cloud above us all. Mick said that he didn't feel that he could follow his instincts anymore when it came to playing drums on Lindsey's songs, and John said, "Well, I sure as hell know I play what I want, thanks to Fuckingham!" For a moment we all laughed at John's black humor. Truth be told, it was a heavy moment, and the entire control room felt the foreboding that the next sixteen months would have in store, the insecurity of taking the leap and making an album with the whole world watching. Fleetwood Mac, though, was a band that thrived on tension, and on the lighter side, there was the new desk girl who was drop-dead gorgeous, and I seemed to have the inside track with her. Maybe, being here every day wouldn't be so bad after all? Besides, I hadn't struck out yet.

3

THE STARS MUST BE MY FRIENDS

Tusk is years more mature. If you're complacent, you stagnate.
—Christine McVie

In the middle of making *Rumours*, I had fallen in love with a stunning nineteen-year-old girl named Cheryl, and we continued an on-and-off relationship; however, the past six months while I was busy building the new studio and working with the band at its rehearsal house on Mulholland had been very hard on us, and I suspected she had begun to see someone else. I had to ask myself whether our relationship could stand up to another long album. Being in the Fleetwood Mac family takes over your life. The album is everything.

So, before leaving the studio that night after Lindsey's many takes of "The Ledge," I called Cheryl and invited her to meet me at my hillside home in Malibu. Her birthday was coming up in a few days and I was hoping to convince her to spend a long weekend with me before the madness resumed in the studio.

I had been depressed with the realization that after we had meticulously planned this next album to be *Rumours 2*, invested $1 million into the perfect studio, and rented a celebrity's home to rehearse and work the kinks out of the new album's candidates, Lindsey Buckingham wanted to become some other type of musician, dashing all our hopes. Lindsey went from folk rocker to punk rocker overnight in an attempt to exorcise his demons. All of our dreams unraveled. That change would end up gouging a deep rift in the band's psyche for the next year. The absolute confidence that we had coming off the world tour quickly turned to tense insecurity. For better or worse, this was the way Fleetwood Mac worked—nothing came easy.

When I got home, Cheryl's little white BMW 2002 was there in the driveway. My house clung on the edge of a steep slope directly above the Pacific Ocean and the LA basin. Every room of this long, single-story home looked out at the ocean. The city lights glittered romantically in each window from Santa Monica Bay all the way to the Palos Verdes Peninsula. There was a constant stream of airplanes coming and going over the dark bay into LAX and the City of Angels.

I pulled my Ferrari into the garage. Scooter and I walked into the living room expectantly, glanced out at the amazing view, and called out to Cheryl. There was no answer. On the table was a full glass of wine already poured for me with Cheryl's leotard and pants lying across the chair. There was also a dry towel, presumably for me. I could hear music coming from the pool house. Scooter had already gone outside through the sliding glass door that was left ajar.

The colored dimmer lights above the pool were turned down to take in the city lights. The glass sliders on the pool were pulled open so the steam wafted off the water. And there in the dim light was Cheryl in the pool, sipping a glass of wine, completely naked. "You better get in here quick, mister, before I start without you," she taunted. I pulled my shirt over my head, unzipped my pants, and let them drop to the damp tile floor. I slid into the pool next to Cheryl. For a moment all we did was look at each other. I pulled her in closer and she arched her head back into the water while she wrapped her legs around my waist. She was so beautiful with her long black hair and perfect body. She lay back in the water, letting her hair fan out over her breasts. Her silhouette was breathtaking in the dim moonlight, and quite stimulating. All worries soon disappeared.

The next afternoon, we took Scooter down the steep, windy roads to Topanga Beach to play. Big Rock Mesa, where my dream house sat, was a mountain that was in process of settling and shifting. Many of the water pipes and sewer lines had been rerouted above ground. The road was undulating and marked with fresh pavement where breaks in the soil had occurred. *No wonder I got such a great deal renting this house. It'll probably fall down any day now*, I thought. *Maybe I could buy it for a steal.* Closer to the bottom of the hill, where it got dramatically steeper, several homes were already red tagged as dangerous and uninhabitable. But I had to admit the house was paradise, and also a babe magnet. When we got back, we showered all the sand and salt off us, and then I broke out the blender and made some of my famous margaritas, with only the finest ingredients and whipped to frothy perfection with a thin layer of ice floating along the top.

While my concoction purred in the blender, I turned on the stereo. Strangely enough, I couldn't receive local radio here, but I could get a great FM station, KCBQ, from 140 miles south near San Diego. I made sure the house had speakers installed in nearly every room plus the outdoor patio and pool house. "Baker Street" by Gerry Rafferty came blasting through the house. It was the perfect summer song and the echoed sax parts just lit up my beach home. I poured two margaritas and took them out onto the patio where Cheryl and Scooter were already watching the view.

"Cheers!" I said to Cheryl.

"You're spoiling me, mister," she said, turning around. "Would you like to some lotion on my boobs or should I?" she teased.

"Well, I hate to get my hands all greasy. I might drop my margarita," I teased back, but I wasn't fooling anyone. It was a good thing we had a large covering of trees obscuring the view of us for the next few hours while Cheryl protected me from the sun's harmful rays.

Sunday morning came to a groggy couple of heads as the warm summer sun broke our needed rest and announced Cheryl's birthday. "Good morning! Quite a night last night," I said to her and raced naked down the long hall. "Don't go anywhere. I'll be right back!" I ran to my kitchen where I had placed a bottle of Perrier-Jouët. I returned minutes later with two glasses of bubbling Champagne, "*Happy birthday, babe*! Welcome to Twenty-One! Please move in with me." Cheryl's face lit up and she thanked me for the gift, but she demurred.

I didn't know it then, but that was going to be one of the last times I would be with Cheryl. The band had its Penguin Country Summer Safari Tour looming and more band rehearsals to get road tight. Starting in July, Fleetwood Mac would rent out the large Hollywood soundstage, Studio Instrument Rentals (SIR), familiar to fans as the location where the Mac recorded the videos for *Rumours*. These rehearsals were indicative of the band's new decadent lifestyle and rock-and-roll working habits, surrounded by its growing entourage and crew, a Japanese masseur, and massive buffets of neglected food. With friends, relatives, partners, and pets sitting in on each day's rehearsal, the musicians' focus would wander. Thankfully, this didn't include me, as I would have gone crazy. I was strictly "the studio guy," and never volunteered to just show up and stand around.

The 1978 Penguin Country Summer Safari tour consisted of fifteen shows across the United States from July 17, 1978, to August 30, 1978, hitting cities and areas that the band missed the previous year:

7/17/78	Alpine Valley Music Theatre	East Troy, WI
7/18/78	Alpine Valley Music Theatre	East Troy, WI
7/19/78	Alpine Valley Music Theatre	East Troy, WI
7/21/78	University of Texas	Austin, TX
7/23/78	Cotton Bowl	Dallas, TX
7/26/78	Saratoga Performing Arts Center	Saratoga, NY
7/28/78	Rich Stadium	Orchard Park, NY
7/29/78	JFK Stadium	Philadelphia, PA
7/30/78	JFK Stadium	Philadelphia, PA
8/6/78	Capital Centre	Landover, MD
8/7/78	Capital Centre	Landover, MD
8/24/78	Rupp Arena	Lexington, KY
8/26/78	Cleveland Stadium	Cleveland, OH
8/28/78	Jefferson Civic Auditorium	Birmingham, AL
8/29/78	The Omni	Atlanta, GA
8/30/78	LSU Tiger Stadium	Baton Rouge, LA

The summer tour gave the band a chance to get back to what it did best: being a kick-ass live band. At that time, its members were untouchable, as both performers and entertainers. Onstage, they were all equal. The initial *Tusk* studio experience had left a slightly sour taste in everyone's mouth, and I think getting back on the road was going to be therapeutic for everybody. The band would also play its first *Tusk* song on that tour, Stevie's rocker, "Sisters of the Moon," that it worked up during rehearsals.

Throughout the summer as the band toured, I became close friends with the gang at the Village. Geordie Hormel had hired twenty-four of the nicest bunch of young engineers and musicians to work there. He believed in equal opportunity, hiring both women and men engineers, techs, and assistants. During that summer, we all gathered at my Malibu home around the indoor pool, laughing and partying, loud music intermingling with the whir of the blender. What was nice about this group was they were my kind of people, folks who loved music, but also understood everything that went into making it. We'd always talk about how to get certain sounds or wondering how other engineers did this or that.

Earlier in the year, I had taken my new windfall and purchased a lakefront home in Lake Tahoe, a mile from my parents' place, with a serene view of the majestic, crystal-clear water. Lake Tahoe is a very special place on the California-Nevada border near Reno and is the largest alpine lake in North America. Since my new home was only a 7-hour drive away, many of my new friends and I would go take the party there to gamble, drink, and lose our studio tans boating on the lake.

During that summer of 1978, Ken and I partied all the time with a cast of characters that included my Chilean ex-pat friends, my co-workers from the Village, Ken's old colleagues from Wally Heider's, such actors as David Cassidy and Bill Mumy, and such musicians as Gerry Beckley from America and the guys from Supertramp who were recording Breakfast in America *at the time down the hall in Studio B. The mix of people was fantastic. I loved throwing parties, a trait inherited from my father who was a registered party animal. I learned from him the basic elements that were key to any successful event: a list of diverse guests with personalities that will add spice and humor to any conversation, the best music mixes timed to increase in intensity as the party rolls along, hearty cocktails from the start (not just beer and wine), and a good environment to mix them all up. We'd have pool parties at Ken's Big Rock house in Malibu and late night parties at my place because it was stumbling distance from the Village.*

We were all young, restless, immature, and looking to emulate the likes of Keith Moon and John Belushi. Of course, no one knew they weren't long for this earth, but it was summer and we felt invincible. We made Ken's waterfront place in Tahoe our own personal Animal House in those days. One time, we met two gorgeous girls at a local bar, and the plan was to invite them for a ride in Ken's speedboat to cruise the lake and spend the day on a deserted beach somewhere. We prepared a good stash of Quaaludes, pot, cocaine, and white wine that we all started taking as soon as we left the shore.

Ken and I were like two wild and crazy guys, navigating and feeling no pain, landing upon a sandy, white pebble beach far away from the roaring crowds. Safely "docked," the girls smiled as they asked us if it was okay for them to remove their tops. We looked at each other like kids and answered in unison: "Of course, not!" This was all going swimmingly.

Then, the perfect moment was suddenly broken.

Ken turned to me and screamed, "Oh no, Ernie! We're finished! The boat is full of water and we are miles away from help!"

"No way, captain; we are not surrendering to this one!" I said, showing off my daring to score points with the girls.

But all joking aside, the boat was indeed filling with water fast as the waves were crashing in, which obviously had gone unnoticed by us because we were happily distracted by more important things. Ken's inventor brain somehow cleared enough through the foggy, overrelaxed state we were in to devise a plan in seconds. He instructed me to push the boat out, jump on the bow, and hold on tight to the anchor chain while he manned the wheel.

"The plan is simple, Ernie. We turn the boat around, take the plug out of the back of the boat, and drive it fast to make the water rush back out of the boat. You hold on tight to the bow to keep the weight up front. We will not run out of crystals!" Ken added, imitating Scottie from Star Trek.

It all sounded perfect. Ken revved the motor to the max with me holding tight to the bow's cleat so not to be expelled along with the water. Off we went, full speed ahead, bouncing off the choppy waters of Lake Tahoe. The plan was working, but our Quaalude-impaired capacities played against us. In an instant, yet in slow-motion, I saw Ken turn around in desperation and, letting go of the steering wheel, unthinkingly throw his arms in the air, trying to catch his wallet as it flew out of his pocket and into the lake. The boat swung violently to the right, jettisoning Ken into the cold water as though he weighed nothing.

Realizing the danger of the boat's propeller injuring him as the boat made circles at full speed, I leaped like a cat toward the wheel. Trying to maintain my balance by holding onto whatever I could find, I finally got hold of the wheel, lowered the throttle, and steered the boat away from Ken.

As I pulled around to him, to my surprise, I saw the wallet floating in the boat. Ken was treading water, happy to be rescued, and finally, after what seemed like the longest minute of my life, he was onboard, and we managed to laugh at our stupidity. The adrenaline surge had erased all the effects of our drug cocktail and we felt lucky to be alive. We emptied the boat of the floodwater, replaced the stern drain plug, and returned to our beach paradise to take care of our ladies.

When we got back, our fine companions were standing, clothed, looking very worried, as they must have seen the whole bizarre Three Stooges scene play out from the shore. The mood of the romantic getaway that we had left just a half hour before was no more. Ken and I were all wet and it was now late afternoon with a cold alpine wind making us feel that we were close to hypothermia. The Casanova Stooges were now out of the game, but our friendship had grown through the misadventure.

Soon after, Ken and I left our playground and headed back to LA to continue recording Tusk *in earnest*, revitalized to endure the long campaign that was approaching fast. Fleetwood Mac had crisscrossed the heart of USA with a caravan of rock stars, blowing the doors off every auditorium and charming the rising multitude of fans wherever it stopped to deliver its hit-loaded setlist.

Working with sophisticated machines and solving problems had run in my family and came naturally to me. My father had been a craftsman and model maker for NASA, and my grandfather invented the "Ridger," a series of horizontally mounted disks pulled behind a tractor to cut the troughs in orchards for seeds to be planted. My mom's parents had been ranchers and owned acreage in what would become Silicon Valley. They sold their 40-acre ranch and moved to Lake Tahoe, settling there soon after highways were built in the late '50s. My family often made the drive from San Jose to stay with Gramps. Eventually, my parents retired early and moved to Tahoe after investing wisely in real estate.

Gramps was a tough old bird when it came to money. When he

moved to Tahoe, he went into real estate. After I graduated from Santa Clara University, I had turned to music and pot and turned into a relatively conservative hippie. Gramps hated my shaggy hair and beard, offering me a job with his friend, the governor of Nevada, if I cut my hair and went to law school. At one point, he even stopped talking to me, until one day he read about *Rumours* smashing all music business sales records in the *Wall Street Journal*, which was his bible. Later, when I pulled up to his real estate office in Carson City in my new car, beard and all, he welcomed me with open arms and said, "Kenny boy, I'm so proud of you!"

My mom and dad were proud, too; however, they weren't quite sure what to make of a son with a hit record who was making money; to be honest, it was new to me, too. *Rumours* immediately started selling as no album had done before. I started receiving gold and platinum record awards faster than I could hang them on my walls, so naturally, all my family received these hangings for their walls and participated in the bragging rights ritual that goes along with these accolades. To my family, it was like having a decorated war hero in the family. To this day, I'm embarrassed to meet their neighbors, "Here he is, the Grammy winner!" Massive success is in many ways, harder to deal with than total failure. People soon forget about failure, but success raises expectations so high that they become impossible to meet. After my friends and I spent Labor Day on the lake, I said good-bye to my parents and grandfather and headed back to LA to get back to work.

Fleetwood Mac spent its Labor Day finishing up its tour at Tiger Stadium in Baton Rouge, before heading home in a hurry—Chris, home to Dennis Wilson, who didn't like going on the road; John, to his new wife, Julie Rubens; Mick, home to uncertainty, and Lindsey and Carol, who were inseparable on the road, returned to their new home in Hancock Park. Stevie, on the other hand, wasn't too excited to go home because, as fate had it, she and Mick ended their affair after the short summer tour.

During that summer, we found out that Judy Wong had been dating one of the Los Angeles Dodgers. Judy, besides being one of Christine's best friends, also worked at the band's office, Penguin Promotions. She introduced me and Richard Dashut, who were longtime fans, to Dodger teammates Bob Welch, Steve Garvey, and Ron Cey. Dashut and I were soon being asked to attend some of the Dodgers' final games that season, sitting in the field-level seats next to the Dodgers' dugout. This was an especially exciting season because the Dodgers were contenders to be in the World Series, eventually facing off against the New York Yankees in a rematch from the previous year. After some coaxing from Judy and Dashut, third baseman Ron Cey and rookie pitcher Bob Welch agreed to coach the Fleetwood Mac All-Stars when the band's tour was over. I couldn't wait to see the look on the other teams' faces when we brought our ringers out!

I pulled into the parking lot the weekend after the band got off the road for our first practice. Dashut was already there, holding court and getting everyone in a good mood. The team practice was located out in the San Fernando Valley, where it was September hot, which means about 105 degrees. Our uniforms weren't ready yet, so we played in Levi's and tennis shoes. Dashut chose a ball park in Woodland Hills so that in case the Brits and hippies proved not to be baseball players, our friends from Wally Heider Studios in Hollywood could join in.

The Fleetwood Mac All-Stars consisted of me and Richard, Mick and John, their attorneys, and the roadies. Mick and John make a good-faith attempt to learn the game and hit and catch, completely different from having played soccer as a team sport in England growing up. John and Mick both played outfield, where they would presumably see less action. Lindsey bowed out, but Christine and Stevie came for moral support. Richard was team manager and I volunteered to be the pitcher for the team—I always imagined that I could have pitched professionally.

The usual suspects arrived either drunk, stoned, or amped up and not taking it seriously that we were actually going to be playing other softball teams like the Eagles, the Doobie Brothers, and Studio Instrument Rentals, to name a few. The entire practice lasted about two hours, but it was hard to play baseball with a beer in your hand. We realized quickly that we were not prepared to really play baseball hungover and in the heat. We threw the balls around to at least make an effort, but as the minutes passed, more and more of us disappeared under the shade or into an air-conditioned car. At one point, we found ourselves standing under a large sycamore tree, drinking beers and sharing a joint, and I looked around and said, "Why the hell are we trying to play baseball in the Valley?! Why don't we find a nice, cool place on the west side or near Malibu to hold these practices?" It was instantly and unanimously decided that baseball practices would move from the torrid San Pornando Valley to the cool saintly confines of Pepperdine University next to the Pacific Ocean.

Richard continued to be our back channel, talking to Lindsey regularly while he was in self-imposed exile, getting updates on his progress or lack thereof. Lindsey said it was slow going trying to reinvent himself right at the most crucial time in his career. And since he didn't think he was very good at writing lyrics—it wasn't his strong suit—he spent most of his time looking for interesting sounds and melodies to sing against the chord progressions he had. While I loved Richard to death, he was more often part of the problem rather than the solution when it came to Lindsey, because the two of them were close friends first and business associates second. Richard would often side, out of the blue, with Lindsey on a position that made no sense, reversing direction on decisions that the rest of us had already agreed upon. Lindsey was fond of saying that rock bands were a democratic dictatorship, but this was more easily said than done, and Richard was between a rock and a hard place, the loyal friend and the voice of compromise, always trying to keep everybody happy. It was tough on him. We were starting to make progress on the album, but it was a grind, and Richard had to keep the machine greased so it didn't come to a halt and make Fleetwood Mac just another cliché of massive success.

In the weeks to come, Lindsey continued to play Hamlet in his castle, living in his head and quite content to experiment in complete isolation and privacy as a one-man band. The rest of us were starting to get bored. I discovered the road crew had a cute little saying that applied to our current state: "Let's get high and wait for something to happen!" The band's most trusted roadie, Ray Lindsey, put it thusly:

> That era was when it started to unravel and everyone was doing too much of everything because you could. They were so successful at doing it their way, that the argument was, "What do you mean this is the wrong way?" That's also when it brought out all of these personality traits that just playing the music wasn't powerful enough to overcome.

GET TUSKED

▼

As one of the album's producers, I knew this was not good. Stevie was already a will-o'-the-wisp, but to make matters worse, the always practical Christine followed Lindsey's lead and decided to go away, too. Chris spent nearly two weeks on Dennis's boat, writing songs and trying to be a normal couple, but probably just got hammered. One of the songs she did return with was "Never Forget," which was a complete version of a song called "Come On, Baby" that we had tinkered with in June

We enticed Christine back into the studio to work on her lead vocals because we knew with Lindsey out of the picture, Christine and Stevie were probably itching to get their songs tracked. Stevie had also begun drafting her new epic poem, "Sara," but had no music to set it to as yet. Christine wanted to revisit "Never Forget" and record "Brown Eyes." Mick and John, as always, were dying to play some music, especially on a record where the songwriter appreciated their talents. They lived to play music, and we had the luxury of taking our time in our own million-dollar studio, which is was not, and still isn't, the standard way of doing things in the music business.

The liberties that Fleetwood Mac took with studio time was earning it a notorious reputation for excess and gave birth to the legend that *Tusk* was one of the most self-indulgent albums ever recorded. The truth was somewhere between hard work and enjoying the spoils of that hard work. Fleetwood Mac wasn't a normal band under the best of conditions, and this was a group that was in the midst of artistic crisis, so there weren't many "normal" days. Every day was a cycle of tension and release. The Mac didn't "fix it in the mix." They made damn sure the mix justified what was already perfect.

THE STARS MUST BE MY FRIENDS

We were setting up when Lindsey arrived at the studio to get some advice and cables for his home studio and he surprised us by his excitement to stay and play on the session. Lindsey grabbed his acoustic and the band got down to work as we listened to them bickering and joking their way through the song. Thanks to Mick's obsession with having everything that transpired in the live room documented onto a 1/4-inch reel-to-reel tape machine, here's a partial transcript of the session for "Never Forget:"

CHRIS: Whatever sounds best, John, just a little passing thing that goes with what I'm singing.

JOHN: Let's just play.

CHRIS: Don't be difficult, John; remember our conversation? Big Sis is watching you.

JOHN: Go on, Chris, strike it.

LINDSEY: Do you wanna hear more of your bass, John? Because it's not that loud.

CHRIS: The bass is louder than anything else in my cans.

JOHN: I can hear it, Lindsey.

LINDSEY: Also, just a touch more snare.

CHRIS: You were getting a bit deafening there, Mick, geez. Are we rolling?

The band starts another take.

CHRIS: Why'd you stop, Mick? That was probably the tightest one we've done.

LINDSEY: Maybe he thought he got a little too cute?

The band warms up and then stops. Chris counts them off and Mick fumbles the beat.

MICK: Sorry 'bout that.

CHRIS: Mick had a bottle of schnapps in one hand and a joint in the other!

MICK: Shuuuutup! Let's get on with it, Chris!

LINDSEY: The click is fucking it up.

MICK: John, give us a quick schnapps.

CHRIS: Should I count what we're playing then?

LINDSEY: Don't count at all. Just start singing whenever you feel like it.

They try another take, but it breaks down.

CHRIS: It's speeding up. Can someone turn up the click in my cans? Mick, drink a half a pint of schnapps or something.

LINDSEY: I just want to have a hit off a joint real quick and then try a few more. It's nice for the singing, anyway.

CHRIS: Yeah, it seems right to me.

RICHARD: It feels better. Mick, how's your rimshot?

MICK: I get mesmerized by it. Like trying to shake to a track.

LINDSEY: Think about something else while you're doing it.

MICK: I know. I'm trying desperately. It's fuckin' driving me crazy.

LINDSEY: That was rock steady. Y'know, what was neat is you went off the cymbal after about halfway through.

MICK: Yeah, I liked that.

LINDSEY: And maybe start to do that kind of feel for the second half. It was great.

MICK: Yeah, I enjoyed coming off the cymbal.

LINDSEY: That take is definitely overdub-able.

CHRIS: Overdub-able?!

LINDSEY: Yes. I think the one before that was better. I know, but there were some loose-ities to it, but still that doesn't matter. All right, it's sounding *de-luxe*.

CHRIS: Lindsey, I like what you're playing, whether you want to play it tighter, but what you're playing is great.

LINDSEY: Oh, thanks.

CHRIS: John, you're just real tired.

Mick starts playing loudly.

CHRIS: Mick's trying to wake you up, John. It's the roll call.

LINDSEY: Let's go for it!

CHRIS: Here we go.

Another take.

CHRIS: Gonna be some really pretty harmonies there, too.

LINDSEY: I know. Boy, this is great to sing along to.

CHRIS: Mick, are you wired or something? Why don't you turn the lights down on Mick a bit. When he was sitting there in darkness, he was doin' real good.

LINDSEY: The first one we did was great, I thought. That could have been The Take.

CHRIS: Well, yeah. Let's do a couple more and go and listen to that one.

LINDSEY: John, aren't you gonna play?

JOHN: Sounds terrible. Stereoflack.

LINDSEY: The first one sounded good. I mean, I can't play what I'm doing unless you're playing and I have you to play off of.

CHRIS: John?

RICHARD: We can always overdub the bass.

CHRIS: We just want to get the feel of the song to start with, y'know.

MICK: John, c'mon, ya putz.

KEN: John, that bass really helps the feel.

CHRIS: It's true. It does. If John doesn't do that, then I have to play the bass in my left hand. C'mon, Johnny.

JOHN: It's embarrassing.

CHRIS: (*Sings the song's melody.*) C'mon, Johnny, don't be a putz!

Mick and Lindsey join in behind.

LINDSEY: Oh, young Juan!

JOHN: Sounds awful. It just sounds so terrible.

LINDSEY: Oh wow, John.

CHRIS: Oh god, John. Listen, I mean, you think you're exposed, it's my bloody song!

MICK, *in fake Italian voice*: Heeeeey, I wanta wanta do the toota!

LINDSEY, *in a growly voice*: C'mon baby! Mau mau gau gaaaau!

Band kicks into another take.

John plays too hard on purpose to ruin the take.

CHRIS: Johnnn, please.

KEN: John, with that bass, you don't have to hit it as loud.

CHRIS: Ken was very diplomatic about it.

LINDSEY: John, just play like you played on the other take. (*Sings.*) Ohh-hhhhh Johhhhhhhhn . . .

Mick starts playing along.

CHRIS: *Big baaaad Jooooohn.*

JOHN: Just play!

LINDSEY: Do you want to go listen to any of these? The first one felt real good to me. This is the kind of song that you can't seem to play too many times before you start losing the spark, y'know? Even if we do some more, we have to go listen to it and then go out.

CHRIS: That last one did feel real good.

THE STARS MUST BE MY FRIENDS

Mick starts bashing around.

CHRIS: Oh, Fleetwood, fuckin' 'ell.

In under a couple of hours, we eventually had everything we needed. Lindsey had an ear for parts and the technique to play them in a variety of different ways. If he wasn't in Fleetwood Mac, Lindsey could have made a handsome living as an LA session man, I thought. He suggested we also try doubling the rimshot snare throughout the song for an insistent metronomic beat that never let the tempo lag, but also had the hallmark of Lindsey's avant-garde percussion ideas, simultaneously interesting and challenging the ear. We chose one of Mick's smaller Ludwig snares and an AKG 451 mic plus a 414 for overhead ambience.

I'm always amazed at Mick's versatility. He can play a twelve-piece drum kit or only one drum and make it sound engaging. Playing straight rimshot for hour upon hour must have been agony, but Mick was a pro, and tenaciously kept at it, experimenting a bit with fills as he went. John eventually warmed to the song when he plugged in his Fender Mustang bass which offered a low hollow bass sound that fit right below Chris's right hand electric piano figure. John's supple bass playing never stopped moving and sounded like something out of Muscle Shoals or Stax/Motown. Combined with Mick's rimshot and Lindsey's gorgeous fingerpicked arpeggio fills, John's bassline made "Never Forget" more stripped-down folk rock than ballad. Lastly, we added Chris's Hammond B-3 organ part, playing in the upper register of the song, giving the band a waterfall of sound falling behind them.

Of course, we knew there would be background vocals, and later we would overdub Christine, Lindsey, and Stevie doing what they did best. It just came so naturally to them, the wordless ghosts in the night who later repeat the song's chorus: "We'll be alright / We'll never forget tonight." The background vocals added the necessary energy and richness, the human element to match the instruments. It was moments like these that convinced me I was working with the best pop band on the planet. Christine and Stevie's writing and performance could match, if not better, anything by Heart, Carly Simon, Rickie Lee Jones, Kate Bush, or Patti Smith.

When we sequenced *Tusk*, "Never Forget" was given the honor of being the album's closer. It wasn't quite the grand statement that most rock listeners had come to expect at the end of big albums. The song "Tusk" would have made far more sense in that regard, but we liked the idea of using "Never Forget" to stifle expectations. In our minds, *Tusk* had become a concept album about a relationship with its ups and downs, its lovemaking and fighting. Thus, ending the album back in mother's arms with "Never Forget" right after "Tusk," from the pain of D minor to the joy of D major, was akin to the Beatles' closing the *White Album* with "Goodnight" after "Revolution 9." We chose to end it on an optimistic high note, the highlight reel we usually remember. The message now wasn't about thinking about tomorrow, but rather never forgetting tonight, the anticipation of nostalgia and giving a farewell kiss to the '70s.

We spent another three and a half days on "Never Forget" and getting the other lead vocals on Christine's songs to date. Recording lead vocals can always be a challenge. The artists know they have to bring their A game. This could be the vocal that they have to hear and sing forever. As an engineer and producer, I usually have two choices in microphones, expensive or inexpensive—elegant or intimate. Sometimes an expensive tube mic captures an exquisite vocal, but can sometimes makes it sound less intimate or less sexy. Do you want to feel an artist's breath on your neck or not? Sadly, some engineers listen with their wallet and not their heart.

To complicate things further, artists always sing wearing headphones to hear their pitching better. What they hear in their "cans" will determine how long of a day you will have ahead of you. One trick that really worked when I recorded Stevie's vocal for "Dreams" was I lined up about eight mics from elegant to intimate and turned them all on in Stevie's headphones. I then invited her to walk down the line and try each one without me doing or saying anything. When she got to one particular mic and sang into it, she said, "Oh my god, I love this mic! It sounds great!" and my job was done. She fell in love with a relatively inexpensive Sennheiser 441 dynamic mic all on her own, so she sang better because she felt better about her vocal. If you can make singers forget about their voice and place their trust in the mic, they will be less insecure, more relaxed, and have more fun. Music studios can be intimidating, so any edge you can get helps. In fact, Stevie still uses that mic to this day, and it has become one of her trademarks.

This was my plan with Christine on that day, but for this song I wanted a mic that could blend the elegance and intimacy in her soft contralto delivery, if I could find such an animal. I decided to give Christine only three choices, one ribbon mic and two condenser mics: an RCA 77, an AKG 414, and a Neumann U47 tube, respectively. Christine picked the Neumann as expected since it was the famous mic used by the Beatles, worth thousands of dollars both then and now. By this point, Christine was an old pro, and we spent the next two hours singing through her song.

I typically like artists to sing the whole song from beginning to end, top to bottom. Then, we start singing section by section, from easiest to hardest, slowly warming up their voice and letting them extend their range. Another trick I've learned is that many inexperienced vocalists sing in too high a key, so if an artist is having a hard time reaching all the notes of hitting the low notes, try dropping the key of the song one or two steps down the scale. I'll work like magic and restore his or her confidence.

Each time we do a complete pass from beginning to end, we build a complete take of verses, pre-choruses, choruses, or bridges, to use up one full track on tape, depending on how many tracks we had available. Usually, we have a minimum of four to six empty tracks, which is why we do lead vocals midway through the song's growth, while the artists have enough music to sing to but before all the available tracks have all been used. We will go line by line, section by section, and listen to each word and phrase, noting which were keepers and which were not. Then we will bounce the best vocals onto one complete track, so that the end result was a vocal performance that was the best of the best.

Sometimes artists will not be satisfied with a word or two, and we will have to go back and have them re-sing or "punch in" those words until they are satisfied. It is very, very rare that an artist will get a perfect complete take all the way through. But it can happen. Stevie sang a work vocal live with the band on "Dreams" that she could never better in successive performances, so we had to use that track, even though it had drum leakage in the recording. You always have to be prepared to go with your gut and accept imperfection over gloss.

Dennis Wilson was, what we say in Spanish, a loco lindo, *which translates to something like "a likeable, crazy guy," or in other words, Steve Martin, a wacky person with a charming, good-natured demeanor, funny, and not causing trouble or damage to other people, and someone who is fully authentic with no filters when giving an opinion, even when moving between light and darkness. He was one of the few outside people, together with Lindsey's girlfriend, Carol, to hang out regularly at the sessions in Studio D where I had a chance to talk to him and hear his anthology of Beach Boys stories. Later on, I had the opportunity to befriend him better when going out with the girls.*

He received plenty of slack and flak from the Mac for his opinions on music and sound, and for his unique sense of humor. I liked the fact that he didn't behave like a rock star, and was open for conversation with anyone and sharing himself with whoever was around. I knew his life had been tough growing up with his brothers under an abusive father who sold all their publishing behind their backs, plus all his personal turmoil that included a brief stint with Charles Manson, so I was able to empathize with his conduct.

One of the craziest stunts he performed while together with Christine happened was when we were mixing in Studio D. We got an urgent call from Christine's house that Dennis had climbed the two-story roof of her house dressed as a woman, with a wig and makeup, screaming and threatening that he was going to jump from those heights into the swimming pool. He was completely wasted and her house was next to his mother, Audree Wilson's, so there might have been some serious Freudian issues going on there. Christine was with us and obviously freaked out, and had Ray Lindsey rush her home to help get him down without causing an incident. This surreal situation, luckily, ended peacefully and with Dennis out of danger Dennis, for better or worse, was unforgettable.

4

INTENSE SILENCE

> What made Stevie so great is that she came out of nowhere. You can't really say that she was trying to sing like Joni Mitchell or Linda Ronstadt or anybody; she was very much her own voice, which is partly why she got her own niche.
>
> —Walter Egan

I always have mixed emotions about October in Los Angeles. On one hand, the heat of September drops off, but then the Santa Ana winds come in with an offshore flow bringing dry desert heat, wild winds, and usually a fire season. You also get the occasional weirdo seeing whether a fire he starts in Woodland Hills will actually get across the Santa Monica mountains into Malibu and make headline news. The winds in LA were already crazy, swirling all over the LA basin, reaching 40 to 75 mph. Wind-tossed big rigs were blowing over and blocking the already congested freeway system. Small fires were already being reported because of sparks and embers that were spreading, and the gusty, dry winds also brought static electricity, zapping you every time you touched something.

We were also falling back out of daylight savings time into winter temperatures. I refused to let the cold temperature be a reality. You see, roughly 77 percent of LA days look the same: cloudless and warm, which is a little boring for my taste. I would often find myself saying, "Could we just get a couple of clouds once in a while?" The eerie, early darkness descended out of nowhere and sent us scrambling for warmer clothes, digging them out of a closet somewhere.

Meanwhile, at Studio D, it was time to work on one of Stevie's new songs. I walked into the control room while Stevie's demo of "Sisters of the Moon" was playing loudly. *"This song is going to be fun to record!"* I yelled over the blasting music to Hernan, who nodded in agreement. "Sisters of the Moon" was a classic Fleetwood Mac up-tempo tune that would take advantage of the group's deservedly famous rhythm section providing the backbone of the song. Over the driving drums, bass, keyboards, and guitars, Stevie would have plenty of opportunity to display her "Rhiannon"-style power vocals. The song meant a great deal to Stevie as it represented an anthem of friendship for her sorority of girlfriends.

Hernan was way ahead of me, already setting up the drums with the 26-inch kick and leaving Mick to choose his own snare when he arrived. I heard a cough and John McVie was sitting on the couch behind me, head down, nodding to the beat, which gave me a scare. He had the strange talent of being able to enter a room without a sound. John's sudden appearance was attributable to the fact that he'd usually go home and pass out well before anyone else's bedtime, and then, being an early riser, he would head in before anyone else to an empty studio. He would make arrangements for either Richard, Hernan, or myself to meet him, splitting the engineering team into two shifts, one early and one late. Most of the time, John and Lindsey would always leave

INTENSE SILENCE

first while the remaining party animals would stay and play, so John would usually arrive around ten a.m. to review his recent bass parts, and Lindsey would always come in just before noon to listen to whichever of Stevie and Christine's songs he was expected to play on that day and come up with parts. Depending on how successful the late-night team was in convincing everybody to go home early, this would stipulate how the rest of the next day went. This is how a rock album work calendar really works.

When everyone rolled in, it was show time and the band all took their places to play for an audience of three. Mick chose his fattest snare for the song and Richard gave Mick's entire drum kit a quick tune-up to make sure they were record ready. Mick took his position atop his throne, anxious to get going since, thus far, the songwriters had given him very little to sink his teeth into. John initially used his classic Fender P-Bass, but ultimately he replaced it with his new Alembic, which had a large body that often covered his chronically supershort jean cutoffs, which sometimes gave the illusion that he was playing naked from the waist down. Christine had a new endorsement deal with Yamaha, so she was switching up her sound with more modern-sounding electric keyboards, which we would then blend with the older, vintage ones. Stevie took up residence in her stained-glass vocal booth that we called the Tiki or Hawaiian Room, and sang a live guide vocal and played her tambourine. Only later would Stevie and Christine overdub the coven of witches howling in the background. Lindsey chose to play an ominously distorted rhythm part on his Fender Stratocaster, playing lead fills between Stevie's lyrics.

"Sisters of the Moon" was one of the first *Tusk* songs the band had worked up months earlier and had even played live on its summer tour, and the Mac was ready to lay this one down. Hernan played the demo tape in the band members' headphones as they got loose and got their head arrangement together.

"Okay, shall we try it for real?" I asked.

Richard added some words of encouragement: "Sounds fucking great, you guys. This could be the first hit song off the record!"

"How is everyone's headphones?" asked Hernan.

They all simultaneously wanted to hear more of themselves and less of everyone else, which is not uncommon. Not being able to hear what you are playing makes it hard to make adjustments on the spot and affects your performance. This is one of the main reasons that the Beatles quit live performance; they couldn't hear what their Vox amps were putting out just a few feet behind them. Now, to avoid this problem, performers use monitors to project their sound back at them when they play live.

Hernan made the necessary adjustments to everyone's headphone mix, and when he was ready, I put the tape machine into Record and held down the talkback button on the console, speaking in everyone's ears and directly to tape: "Okay, this is 'Sisters of the Moon,' Take one." The big 2-inch reels began to roll and the Studer tape machine lit up red.

"Do you want to count it off, Mick?" Richard quickly interjected. Mick nodded yes and held his drumsticks over his head, clicking them together while saying, "one, two, three, four," then he started to play the kick drum only on every beat, "four on the floor" style. John began playing a pedaled bass part locked in with Mick, playing one note with two fingers on each beat. Christine noodled on her electric keyboard, which emitted fat, deep, sonorous notes that rippled from the left hand and mysterious sounding chord inversions and reverb-drenched runs in the right hand.

INTENSE SILENCE

We played through the song over and over, making minor changes as we went along, stopping occasionally to listen to playbacks and discuss what we were each hearing or not hearing. The hours passed, and to my surprise, we still hadn't gotten a final take yet. We took a break to eat in the lounge behind the control room. We naturally arranged for Dan Tana's to deliver a magnificently lavish meal of lobsters, oysters Rockefeller, and fine wine. After finishing, we were all falling into a food coma.

To wake up, we had another ritual in the studio that involved high poetry. It was Richard, the chosen bard, who had the mission of delivering the Robert Frost poem titled "Stopping by Woods on a Snowy Evening" to Mick as a signal that the team wanted the white goddess powder of the Andes.

And, of course, the whole charade was played with high theatrics worthy of Oscar nomination, with Mick responding as if he was in the woods: "Oh ye good man . . . what is it that you search for?"

"Your magic powder that allows us to reach safer lands, my master," continued Richard. Sometimes these theatrics could go for a while, with all of us laughing wildly. Mick reached his left-hand into the infamous watch pocket of his vest and pulled out yet another bottle of cocaine. One by one, he went around the room, dipping his small silver spoon into the bottle of white powder and filling each of little nose of ours with inspiration and enough energy to get through to that last final take.

"All right, my children, out with you; make music now," Mick commanded, playing the doting Victorian father. And off we went, back into the studio. When everyone was ready, I put the tape machine into Record and pressed the talkback: "'Sisters of the Spoon,' Take twenty-nine." After a little laughter, Mick proceeded to repeat his count in and began to play the kick drum at a faster tempo than before. Lindsey was all excited and he didn't wait for John's bass part to begin, instead the two played at the same time, and the band was off to the races.

"Sisters the Moon" was now running about six minutes long, building in pent-up intensity before climaxing into the monster chorus hook two minutes in. Two more choruses arrive in quick succession before Lindsey exploded into one of his bone-chilling solos, with a one-note vibrato worthy of B. B. King, full of all the emotion he could squeeze into it. Lindsey taught himself lead guitar when he joined the band, and, like everything he played, it was completely different from everybody else and utterly himself. *Tusk* didn't present as many moments as *Rumours* for Lindsey to cut loose on lead guitar, but he was a gourmet of all sounds, and if you wanted a lead guitar solo as thrilling as "The Chain," it's right here.

Ultimately, we cut thirty-six takes of "Sisters of the Moon," listening to all of our favorites until we collectively decided which one best captured the vibe of the song. This was the Fleetwood Mac think tank at its best, which is exactly how we arrived at the right answers on the previous album, almost as if we were in an escape room and had to work together to free ourselves. With equal measures of pride and relief, I asked Hernan to mark Take 35 as the master. He took a razor blade and made a precision cut right before my announcement of Take 35 and attached about 10 feet of plastic leader tape to both ends of the recording tape with specialized Scotch tape. This allowed us to look at the reel and clearly see where the master was located. We all celebrated with another round from Mick's magic spoon, and that familiar vicious cycle began again.

The band was feeling pretty good because "Sisters of the Moon" was sounding really phenomenal. Everyone refreshed his or her drink, and I thought, *It's now or never*, so I stood up and said, "Perfect day everybody. This is going to be a great record. I have to go because I have a friend in town. Take my advice and don't stay up too late and hurt yourselves!"

With that, I vanished in a cloud of smoke before anybody had a chance to swallow their drink. I dashed out to my little Dino. It was still comfortably warm outside. We had been playing the speakers very loud all day, so I drove home in silence accompanied only by the ringing in my ears. The moon was beautiful that night and it shone across a calm, glassy ocean as I drove home. I couldn't wait to get home and out of my clothes into that swimming pool and see how Cheryl's suntan efforts had gone. I thrust my foot deeper into the accelerator.

So, there I was at Studio D that Monday, getting an early start, fresh and recharged, standing ready to face whatever challenge was churning for that session with one of the most complex group of rock stars and their team. I made sure all the multitrack and stereo tape machines were aligned along with the double 24-card Dolby racks. I fired up our beautiful Neve console ready to receive musical voltage from the band, and arranged the various microphones we preferred from AKG, Beyerdynamic, Neumann, Shure, Sennheiser (Stevie's favorite), and a collection of Direct Boxes for extra kick.

John McVie showed up way ahead of the band and I enjoyed chatting with him, especially listening to his stories as a privileged member of the British blues revival as the bassist for John Mayall's Bluesbreakers. I knew very little and John taught me about the Delta or Chicago bluesmen that had given birth to rock, such as John Lee Hooker, B. B. King, Howlin' Wolf, Etta James, and Muddy Waters. This was why it was so tragic that by October, John already showed the scars of Lindsey's beating, acting shier and more insecure than usual, and asking me about takes or parts he had done before. If he had more than one vodka and tonic before noon, the conversation led to his frustration of the situation he was in, left out or heavily pushed to play in a style that wasn't his forte.

By eleven a.m. John was holding good, and to our surprise, Stevie showed up earlier than usual to take the lead in recording "Sisters of the Moon." Stevie sat at the sofa at the back of the control room with Sara Recor, Sharon Celani, and Robin Anderson, all close friends of hers and members of the sisterhood to whom she gave a golden half-moon pendant. These three sisters were about to witness how their anthem, which had been previewed on the road during the mini summer tour, was going to take form and become a living musical statement of their bond.

That morning, I could see through those blond curls that Stevie's eyes were pouring out pain and sadness, and noticed her slim body, hidden by a stylish hippie-chic dress and the bouquet of trademark scarves that she carried everywhere, moved with frailty and fatigue. She looked straight into my eyes and said my name with a near-perfect Spanish accent, "Hernan, can you please drop this cassette in the player, so we can hear my new song that we're recording today?"

"Cool, Stevie; looking forward to listening to 'Sisters,'" I said, with a slight Latin accent that later on I would find attracted her, which she made me repeat or invent phrases to charm her, which made me feel like Gomez, the Latin lover patriarch of the Addams Family with his Castilian accent. I found it preferable to Mick's Christianizing me with the generic "Hernandez."

The mystifyingly beautiful Sara spoke next to me in Spanish, "¿Hola, que tal . . . de donde eres?" She looked at me with flirtatious eyes while running her hand through her hair.

INTENSE SILENCE

"From Chile, born in Santiago, and raised on rock and roll!" I answered, catching Stevie's attention; she laughed. We started to listen to the song a few times, while Robin made comments to Stevie. Little did I suspect at that point that I, too, was going to be part of the Brothers of the Moon. The initial hellos and music comments with Stevie moved little by little beyond small talk until she opened up during the succeeding weeks into her personal world. Her superstar category was not an issue, nor did I treat her as such, something that I think she liked.

Eventually, Ken, Richard, Mick, Christine, and Lindsey arrived at the studio, so we had full crew to go to the live room and start cutting. After conferencing about how many verses and choruses were going to finally end up on the song—most of the time, Stevie's demos went way beyond a normal three- to four-minute song—the band agreed on a longer version that would clock in close to six minutes, so that we could edit it later in case the Mac decided "Sisters" had single potential.

Fleetwood Mac's well-oiled rhythm section started its strut with Mick's working the kick and waiting to add the snare after a few turns to match John's syncopated bass eighth notes. Christine's sinister low to midrange chords evoked the ghostly sounds of the song's title and Lindsey's Stratocaster subtly accented it through the fuzz of his Marshall stack like a caged demon. During the following months, Lindsey would add some more guitars that would get the song to its full potential, including two tracks of electric volume swells and reverbed arpeggio guitars, three tracks of high-power grungy Strats, and a set of two acoustic guitars that heighten its mysteriousness.

The intro of the song is quite long, pregnant with tension, building slowly before Stevie's chest voice enters and we hear the Welsh Witch poetically addressing the sisterhood and herself.

Stevie's reputation as the best lyricist in Fleetwood Mac is well deserved.

GET TUSKED

Lindsey and Christine could never be bothered to paint a scene or create characters in such a fashion. Stevie's lyrics were very '70s and somewhat proggy, in this regard, drawing the listener into a story, which she would then act out onstage with specific costumes for each of her songs. Stevie could have easily replaced Peter Gabriel in Genesis if Phil Collins wasn't up for it.

Stevie had even written a big heavy metal hook for the song and we were hoping Lindsey would be inspired to deliver a hot track of riffing and power chords that would build up to an orgasmic guitar solo reminiscent of "Go Your Own Way." Eventually, after the bridge, Lindsey gave us a fiery, unhinged guitar solo, a relative rarity on Tusk, his wailing bends trading blows with his trademark staccato notes that pierced through the long vamp fade and brought this witches' sabbath to an end. When played live, "Sisters" became a beast, with Christine opting for a more gothic organ sound to underpin Lindsey's extended soloing and Stevie's ad-libbed screams.

Stevie's mood during those initial sessions after the tour tended to be melancholy. She didn't seem grounded enough to fight for her songs and inspire the band to give them its best. To complicate matters, her duet with Kenny Loggins, "Whenever I Call You 'Friend,'" was climbing the charts and had already broken the top 10, reminding the band, which didn't have a song in the charts, that she didn't need it to be successful. In spite of having the company of her sisterhood at the studio, she was not her full lively self, and consequently her wailing powerful vocals were her only recourse. We could see all the members of the band doing their thing in the main live room, trying to connect as they had done so powerfully in the past, with Stevie howling her big note into her Sennheiser to signal the big chorus riff and an outpouring of energy.

Another important trick we used in Tusk was to record Stevie's, as well as Christine's, vocal live during the basic track sessions, to capture the primal *feeling they put out, which was never was the same afterward. In the case of "Sisters," and many others, we would combine these original live vocals where Stevie was belting it out with her head voice with the ones they overdubbed at later dates for a perfect mix of moods, the raw and the refined. One special feature of "Sisters" was the fact that Stevie wanted the background vocals and harmonies to be all female, which led us to record her and Christine doing all the work, including those haunting "Ooohs" that Stevie nicknamed the "Ooohs for Bucks"! The sound of those background vocals in "Sisters" became a sound stamp for much of what she has done since.*

As we dug further into the session, by Take 29, we couldn't agree on a take that satisfied everyone. One of the rituals we had when cutting basic tracks on a song that the whole band played together, especially the rhythm section, was to take the time and go into the control room to listen carefully, soloing the kick and snare tracks from the rest to detect any deviations in pulse and feel.

Pulse consists of repeating beats in identical, yet distinct, periodic durations in music, at a given speed. It's the thing that makes us tap our foot to. The speed of the pulse or beat is called tempo, and is expressed in beats per minute, or bpm. The pulse in music is directly related to the heart. The pulse is not static—it changes speed according to different physical and emotional circumstances. The way pulse changes is what groove and feel is all about. It's the preciseness or looseness that notes are played to the mechanical pulse or click track that we feed the musician to reference. Listeners feel these changes, and when done with grace and at the right time, it can draw their attention deeper into the song. We decided later to speed up the song by two bpm, subtle, but effective.

English drummers made their mark in rock's history as they played the kick in the pocket, as it was known, meaning "right on the beat of the pulse," and the snare slightly behind the beat to convey and unrushed feeling. That was one of the great musical attributes that distinguished Mick's playing, and that was what we were listening for during the playback ritual while soloing his drums.

The first time I experienced that ritual, I thought, These guys are crazy! Eventually, I taught myself to listen for minimum deviations of the pulse and feel of the drum track, and appreciating the importance of getting a take that the basic foundation of the song was solid and felt good to build on top of with whatever was needed. Many times, bands struggle to understand what is wrong in a song, as they try to build the arrangement and overdubs, and something doesn't feel good, creating insecurity and second guessing. The answer is always in the basic foundation of the track.

After we broke for dinner, it was time to get back to "Sisters" and recreate the magic in the studio that would give us that special take. But we needed rocket fuel to lift off from the gravity of such banquet. And, of course, that night, the team got the necessary refueling powder to continue on to Takes 30, 31, 32, 33, 34, 35, and 36, after which Richard pushed the talkback and asked the band with his best British accent:

"Captain, have we gone a bridge too far?"

Magic words that brought the band back to the control room to listen and check whether we had the magic take that would satisfy all. It was past three a.m. and everyone's mind had worn down in spite of the Andean fuel. Still, we managed to screen through the seven takes to decide on Take 35 as our master, and called it a night with the satisfaction of mission accomplished.

5

DO YOU HAVE TO HAVE ME?

> *Rumours* is perfect. *Tusk* is interesting. People listen
> to *Rumours,* but they talk about *Tusk.*
>
> —David Fricke, *Rolling Stone*

It was the fall of 1978, and for me, life was bright and shiny. I lived only a few blocks away from Village Recorder with a beautiful, fun Minnesotan girlfriend named Kris and her sweet four-year-old daughter Katy, whom I cared for as if she were my own. Our house was located on Beloit Avenue in West Los Angeles, a typical stucco, Spanish-style unit that hugged the side of the 405–San Diego Freeway. It had a nice yard and a room for a mini-studio that I built to make sound experiments and mix tapes for our famous parties. It was a real challenge since the noise of the freeway, the busiest in the country, was unceasing.

By then I was totally part of the SoCal mind-set of eternal sunny weather, and the "have a nice day" vibe definitely gave a trademark sound and feel to the music of the artists and bands that made LA their home base. The original West Coast sound, "yacht rock," characterized by perfect sound and a smooth aesthetic, was in full bloom. The larger and better equipped studios and big recording budgets allowed for lush and detailed production and engineering for the ear-catching vocal and instrumental arrangements. The Beach Boys were the uncontested founding fathers of the SoCal sound. A select group of studio musicians that included the '60s leading hit makers, the Wrecking Crew, had become the city's backing band, creating a sound all their own that was characteristic of the songs they recorded. LA's music machine was every bit as streamlined as the studio system during Hollywood's famed golden age: it was entertainment made to order.

But my musical heart was close to the underbelly of the LA scene represented by such bands as the Doors, Love, the West Coast Pop Art Experimental Band, and the Mothers of Invention. Frank Zappa, it seemed, was sent specifically to break the spell of the flower children and their fun-in-the-sun ideals with his sarcastic wit. His deeper and darker content subverted the hippie California lifestyle on such albums as Freak Out! *and* We're Only in It for the Money. *He delighted in spoofing the sound of psychedelic rock that every band played at the time. These were the undercurrents that either eagerly informed or were purposefully ignored by the music scene in the '70s.*

Just prior to Tusk, *I had the privilege of assisting Joe Chiccarelli on the recording of Frank Zappa's most successful album,* Sheik Yerbouti. *Zappa's musical and sonic directions, such as "xenochrony," were innovative and inspiring to all of us in the studio, adding to my bag of tricks, which would come in very handy with Fleetwood Mac. In fact, Zappa would return to Village Recorder soon after to record* Joe's Garage, Acts I, II, & III *down the hall from us in Studio B, which would see release around the same time. And they thought* Tusk *was too radical . . .*

Up until that point, most of the recording projects that I had worked on as an assistant engineer had been with top artists, who brought in their own producers and engineers. This gave me the opportunity to learn and grow with the best. I worked with Robbie Robertson on the Band's last studio album, Islands, *and on* The Last Waltz, *which was the soundtrack of the Band's farewell concert made into a feature film by Martin Scorsese. During that period, I had the pleasure of working with many of my favorite female artists, including Carly Simon, Joni Mitchell, Flora Purim (the "Queen of Brazilian Jazz"), Toni Tennille, and Jennifer Warnes, learning how to capture the nuances of the female voice.*

Second engineers made a modest salary in those days (they still do), so you learned to take on whatever projects you could to make a name for yourself. I was promoted to first engineer for a series of disco albums by the LA-based disco label Butterfly Records. It was another situation where serendipity had stepped in. The project was Two Hot for Love! *by the THP Orchestra, which was a typical disco concept of that era with a cover shot of an attractive blonde in a bathing suit standing in a cloud of steam in front of a cherry red fire engine. We had recently installed a new Harrison inline 3232 console that had revolutionized the industry. It was an amazing console with VCA automation, variable parametric equalization, and many other audio refinements that would soon embrace digital. As a staff engineer at Village Recorder, I had been trained to use all our consoles at their full capacity. The original engineer brought in by Butterfly Records didn't know how to work it, especially when he was on substances, so I was the natural candidate to take over his duties, which I happily did.*

The staff producer liked the sounds I was getting out of the Harrison console. The fact that disco music relied heavily on deep bass and crisp high end was a key factor, allowing the console's equalization modules do their magic. In addition, many of the songs lasted well beyond the three-minute average running time, which required sophisticated and complex mix-down moves that only could be achieved through the use of automation. This is what the hottest dance floors demanded of the music industry. DJs in New York were taking our records and cutting them with others to make them even longer, so the party never stopped.

These sessions with Butterfly Records were my first real professional recognition and I finally tasted some success, which changed my standing radically. As fate would have it, one of the reasons Ken and Richard chose to use the Village Recorder for remixing the Rumours singles was because we had the Harrison console. Unbeknownst to me, Ken and Dave Harrison were friends. Ken explained that Dave was a burly and bearded sax player out of Cincinnati turned engineer and inventor who had spent time at King Records, recording the Platters, John Lee Hooker, and James Brown.

I felt very lucky to have moved up the music industry ladder so quickly by doing disco, but it wasn't something you'd brag about since, even then, disco was seen as cheesy and not artistic. Rock was very much the respected genre of the time, and it was what I enjoyed most. Even some of the maintenance engineers at Village, such as Frank Wolf, gave me the derisive nickname, the "Disco King." So, I didn't pursue this new career title; instead, I chose to remain an assistant engineer waiting for a new break in rock music, and I'm very glad I did.

The Village had an equal opportunity employment policy, so half of the engineering staff were young women, who were all cool and fun. Terry Becker, Lenise Bent, Barbara Issak, and Carla Frederick all worked on some of the best albums of that era and had to work even harder to gain respect as the outstanding engineers that they were. Carla assisted me on many of those disco albums, working into the wee hours since the producer was a night owl. And as Butterfly Records was no Warner Bros. or Columbia, the informal drug budgets were slim. Instead of cocaine, we had to rely on amphetamines, such as black beauties, to stay awake, and Carla's never ending supply of cigarettes. Carla would fill in for me at various times during Tusk.

DO YOU HAVE TO HAVE ME?

In those days before the violence of drug cartels was headline news, the provision of marijuana, hash, and cocaine were handled by house friendly dealers that had the trust of the studio to purvey the best at reasonable prices. It was so casual and tacitly understood, that we included them on the session work orders; such items as "quarter-inch reel-to-reel copies" or "cassette copies for the artist" were code to get paid by the record company so as to pay the friendly dealer.

For many music fans, the Fleetwood Mac era with Lindsey Buckingham and Stevie Nicks was a quintessential part of the California sound, practically its crowning achievement. So, by the time the Mac made the big leap into superstardom with Rumours, *it had completely outshined and surpassed the scene where big-name producers and hired studio guns were needed to create hits. Fleetwood Mac had been able singlehandedly to achieve gold on its own terms, combining top songwriting craft with distinct and polished playing and arranging. Much of the ink that was spilled concerned the band's romantic turmoil without paying much attention to one of the key elements of its hit sound, namely its recording engineers, neither of whom was a producer. To cap it all off, the band managed itself, which at that level was unheard of.*

LA made this success possible and always moved in to eat its young with its insatiable appetite for all things new. The impact of Hollywood through its motion picture, television, and music recording industry in shaping the country's view of itself cannot be overstated. It's common knowledge that this oceanside wonderland has created superstars and millionaires of the lucky and the talented. LA has always been a magnet that has trapped countless poor souls who just wanted to be in the mix. Many of the band's organization, crew, and entourage lost their way during those days and never recovered. Many of them thought that the fact that they were partying and hanging out with the band would give them a share of the glory, and because of this, never made a life for themselves. Fleetwood Mac's live sound engineer for the Tusk tour, the famously outspoken Trip Khalaf, summed up these folks perfectly as "dead bodies lying on the curb." The sex, drugs, and rock-and-roll credo took a toll on them, and they were left behind, but those were the times we lived in. That was the Hotel California.

During the months that Fleetwood Mac was away on tour, my schedule remained hectic. I returned to engineering disco concept albums for Butterfly Records and assisting on some of the most exciting projects that were happening at the Village, including patching in for Lenise Bent on Supertramp's historic sixth album, Breakfast in America, which it was recording in Studio B. It would become the band's highest charting and best-selling record, recorded over eight months and winning the Grammy for Best Engineered Album. The similarities and differences between Supertramp and Fleetwood Mac were instructive.

After releasing several fine albums, Supertramp had hit its stride and had the clout to book the studio open ended, meaning that no other artists could use it. This practice could be construed as egotistical, but in actuality, it was a strategy that was crucial for bands that spent a good amount of time in preproduction, writing and rehearsing the songs enough to enter an expensive studio to dedicate themselves fully to cutting all the basic tracks in a linear fashion. The process of overdubbing the rest of the instrumental arrangements and vocals was done relatively quickly with the confidence that the drums, bass, guitars, and basic keyboards were solid. This was the polar opposite of a band like Fleetwood Mac, which both built and leased its own studio for Tusk and took its sweet time with nothing planned ahead of time. As always, Fleetwood Mac was the exception.

DO YOU HAVE TO HAVE ME?

The paradox in the history of popular music is that no amount of preproduction, musicianship, budget, studio technology, or marketing can ensure the artist or band will be a hit. Whether it's Fleetwood Mac's self-indulgent, experimental method, or Supertramp's and Steely Dan's lengthy quest for technical perfection, both approaches work as long as they write songs that touch hearts and minds. Listeners don't discriminate about how a song came to be. They're happy as long as it exists and can be adopted as part of their life's soundtrack. The song could have been recorded with a closetful of mics over a year or in a single take with a mic hanging from the ceiling. You just never know how it will be received, and that's part of the fun, the feeling of suspense every time you hit Record.

During that time, I did catch myself missing the no-routine, do-as-we-feel call of Fleetwood Mac and Studio D, the door at the end of the hallway where we could do whatever we wanted. In spite of the implications of Lindsey's complete change of character and the outside-the-box recording process that was churning, there was some part of it that really rang a bell inside me and made it very attractive to be part of it. A Lindsey session could go anywhere. If I had to pick which member of Fleetwood Mac I felt close to after those initial sessions, Lindsey was definitely the guy. Not only did we talk studio stuff, but we also shared personal tastes in music and influences. During those conversations, I learned more about his fondness for proto-punk, roots rock, Mexican folk, classical, movie soundtracks, jazz great Django Reinhardt, and such disparate outsider artists as Captain Beefheart or pop crooners as Frank Sinatra. It was all up for grabs.

The Brits behaved as such, preserving their rank-and-file demeanor toward me. I guessed, correctly, that they were measuring my worth, waiting for me to prove myself deserving of their acceptance and trust. Stevie was a different case altogether to the rest of the band. Since she was not as present during the first days of Tusk *in Studio D, and because the talk around the control room was that she was quite a prima donna, with me she had shown flashes of what eventually became an open door to her troubles and dreams.*

One of Christine's first new songs for the album was "Brown Eyes," a darkly seductive song that talked candidly about sex but also struck a note of mistrust at her lover's deceitful ways. It was short and sweet with two verses, three chords, and a wordless chorus. Christine always told me it was about her dog, and I think initially it was, but then she opened her heart and it may have been about Dennis Wilson, who actually had green eyes.

Lindsey stepped into his old role as producer and arranger without insisting on making Christine's song a New Wave tune, which it could have easily become, and instead kept its moody full-band vibe. Lindsey was always attuned to what a song was giving off, and he would make all of his decisions based on what it was trying to convey to the listener. Giving Christine's song a spray-painted Mohawk like his own songs just wouldn't have made sense.

In my opinion, Christine and Stevie's songs on the *Tusk* are some of their finest work, surpassing their *Rumours* songs, and arguably even their songs on *Mirage*. The sensitivity, warmth, and sultry mystery in "Brown Eyes," "Honey Hi," "Over & Over," "Sara," and "Storms," among others, was superb. If Lindsey had attempted to better his previous work doing what he already knew how to do, *Tusk* may have very well have been the band's best-selling album. For some reason, he wouldn't allow his own songs to follow in the same footsteps, but with the girls' songs, he was free to be more himself, and he was magnificent.

The "Brown Eyes" session was set up in traditional Fleetwood Mac style similar to "Never Forget," although we decided to mic John's bass amp, which I rarely did, preferring the fullness from a direct bass channel. This was one of John's best bass parts on *Tusk*, classic McVie all the way. He knew his parts and could take his time and perform his musical magic for Chris. Mick played his full drum kit; however, he played rimshot on his snare so it sounded like light clicks. Christine played her Yamaha electric piano in typical blues style. Lindsey played his white Alembic electric guitar through a volume pedal. Stevie would only be singing background along with Lindsey and Chris, so for its first actual tracking session Stevie just danced in the control room with us and created harmonies. Much like "Dreams" on the last album, "Brown Eyes" was a simple song with lots of space that made huge demands on the rhythm section and the melody instruments to fill it with color and ambience.

Instruments filling in space is my specialty, especially with a console's "sound-shaping" capabilities combined with our analog toys. My palette consisted of two electric piano parts, five guitar parts, a deep and lush bass, rimshots and cymbals, and approximately sixteen combined vocal parts to spread and fill the song's sound-field. Plus we had real reverb, a real rotating Leslie speaker, and tape delay, creating a hypnotic, ethereal feeling sounding track.

The band was pretty familiar with this song because it was the first one that Christine had brought to the rehearsal house on Mulholland way back in April. We ran the track down until everyone knew their parts and the tempo. Chris had a mic set up so she could sing and play piano at the same time. We decided to try and get a few takes recorded before lunch. We got the master in only thirty-seven takes. Christine delivered a breathy lead vocal that oozed sex, with Lindsey and Stevie again stacking their voices on hers for the wordless chorus of cherubim.

Mick suffered no performance anxiety, delivering perfect time on the heartbeat kick, rimshot, and sizzling ride cymbal. Mick's less-is-more restraint was inhuman, waiting a full minute before introducing even a snare-crash fill or a hi-hat flourish, and giving away very little afterward. Stevie was equally as tasteful with her tambourine. Lindsey was a true chameleon on the track, playing a low swelling tremolo'd guitar part that both mirrored and accented what Christine's left hand was doing on the Fender Rhodes while also playing a high-string rakes to complement the tinkling of Christine's right hand on the Yamaha. I can think of no better example of the pure concentration of these accompanists on their singer.

"Brown Eyes" would later benefit from a stellar guitar part a few weeks later played by the Green God himself, the original Fleetwood Mac leader, Peter Green. Unfortunately, Lindsey felt that Green's bluesy soloing didn't fit with the final mood of the song, so it was muted. As wonderful as Green's cameo was, Lindsey ultimately made the right call as we agreed the track needed a different kind of style of playing, one that didn't distract the listener from the singer.

We did manage to sneak some of it onto the end, though, and it can be heard in the fadeout, so if you listen closely, you can hear Green closing out the song with some tasteful licks. The next thing I heard about Peter Green was that he pulled a gun on the Warner executive who was trying to sign him, bringing an abrupt end to Mick's attempt to rejuvenate the career of his mentally ill friend, the man who had started this band and was responsible for it all. I couldn't help thinking, *Is everybody in this band crazy?*

"Brown Eyes" would become every bit as lush and rich as "Dreams" and benefited from our original decision to make this an album with a rich bottom end and a sparkling top end, which we would perfect during its final mixing almost eight months later.

Engineers and studio techs had a funny name for our unique pale faces, especially when projects lasted long and we spent most of our time indoors, barely seeing the light of day: studio tan. So, whenever we had a chance or break, we would sneak out through the inconspicuous side door to line up on Butler Avenue like lizards to get some sun hoping we would regain our California color. After setting everything up and making sure it was ready for the Mac, I took a sun break at the precise moment that Dennis Wilson was driving Christine up in her Rolls-Royce Silver Shadow. They would carpool between that and his Shelby Cobra race car, which I hoped someday he would allow me to drive.

They walked into the side door of Studio D like teenage lovers, laughing and smiling conspiratorially. By then, Mick, John, and Lindsey had arrived, and were listening to the cassette of the "Brown Eyes" demo in the control room with Ken and Richard. Most of the time, Dennis would just leave Christine and drive away, sometimes dropping in during the evening. But that day, he stayed awhile, joining us in the control room. He was not the kind of person to refrain from commenting on any given situation, especially if the subject was music and sound. So, Dennis ventured some concepts and opinions on how the song could be approached—a brave act, considering his new status in the Penguin Brotherhood. Of course, John was the first to open fire, probably still motivated by his former marriage with Christine, followed by Mick and Richard. Dennis made some attempts to salvage his honor, but decided discretion was the better form of valor, and left with a bruised ego. Studio D could be a tough room.

Initially, we tried some double unison lead vocal with Christine and Lindsey, as they had done before on "Don't Stop" and "Think About Me." Their vocal timbres matched so well that they blended as one, but in the end, we decided against it. Lindsey also laid down more exquisite guitar work that included one of the most understated solos on the album, building from three different tracks of Alembic and Stratocaster electric guitars played through a volume pedal.

Christine's vocals on "Brown Eyes" had that velvety quality that I believe is her best and most touching tone, soft and laid back. That range and vocal style is empowering when she sings such ballads as "Never Make Me Cry" or "Oh Daddy." For this reason, I always thought it would be a dream come true if Christine and Stevie got together to make an album of old jazz and blues ballads, à la Nina Simone. It amazed me how this band was able to take a pretty spare track like "Brown Eyes" and, layer after layer, take it to another dimension. The "Sha-la-las" chorus was so mesmerizing. Sometimes, basic wordless chants work as powerfully as words in transmitting emotions and context, as old a practice as the art of song itself.

During the dining break, Dennis Wilson came back to Studio D to see how his sweetheart was doing on that special day when "Brown Eyes" was being recorded. Christine never opened up as to whether the song was about him, but we can surmise that singing about seduction and the fear of another broken heart had to with him in those days:

Do you have to have me / The way that I want you, I want you?

Dennis had come with a mission, to take revenge on the dark knights that had made fun of him earlier, and he did it with a full audience, to make sure that nobody was left out. As we were all eating, he suddenly burst out of one of the two bathrooms that faced the lounge with his pants down, walking with slow baby steps until we all realized as he got closer to all of us, that a long toilet paper trail, like the tail of a lizard, was unwinding from the wall roller. When he was halfway into the lounge, he proceeded to declaim:

"I want you people to know that I finally got my shit together! I can dance, chew gum, and play drums at the same time!"

He turned around to show his naked ass with the beginning of the toilet paper roll tight between his cheeks. That performance gained him points and respect from most of the band and crew, except obviously John, who just mumbled: "Shit together? My Brit arse!"

Humor was essential to our survival all those long months in Studio D, so Dennis's act had us laughing throughout the rest of the "Brown Eyes" session. We finally settled on Take 37 as the master. The rimshot-driven track had a wonderful feel, and was ready to receive the some of the most ornate guitar and vocal parts on the album, which to me is one of the most underrated aspects of Tusk. To cap it all off, Peter Green's surprise visit, reminiscent of Syd Barrett's unexpected appearance at the *Wish You Were Here* sessions, and his playing, adds to the album's many deep-listening, gem-filled moments.

We wasted the rest of the time in the studio triumphantly drinking and drugging and listening to "Brown Eyes" and other tracks in various states of completion, taking notes, and brainstorming. When we were finished, I walked out to my car and noticed something was amiss. My Ferrari's windshield had been completely covered in long strips of duct tape! In an instant, I knew this stupid joke could only have been hatched in the mind of Frank Wolf, the jokester maintenance guy at the Village.

It had also started to rain.

I threw Scooter inside the Dino, hurling curse words everywhere and pulling strips of duct tape off my windshield. With both hands, I just barely managed to pull a complete strip off the glass, leaving behind plenty of crap all over the windshield. Well after two in the morning, I removed the rest of the duct tape and got in my car. Thanks to the rain and the horizontal lines of goo, everything was a complete blur. The wipers had a hard time navigating the debris field. I could barely see, so I decided to take surface streets home, which conveniently took me through the Pacific Palisades and by Frank's apartment on Sunset Boulevard. I located his classic VW van nicknamed "Ludwig," which was also on the license plate (Frank was a classically trained pianist turned engineer and equipment tech). I thought, *This means war*, and I walked up and stole his windshield wipers, ripping them straight off the car. It wasn't exactly tit for tat, but it would have to do. When I got home, I threw Frank's wipers into the trash, dried off, had a drink to warm up, laughed at the lunatics I worked with, and went to bed.

6

TRANSCENSION

> The studio contract rider for refreshments was like a telephone directory. Exotic food delivered to the studio, crates of Champagne. And it had to be the best, with no thought of what it cost. Somebody once said that with the money we spent on Champagne on one night, they could have made an entire album. And it's probably true.
>
> —Christine McVie

Today was Lindsey's day at Studio D. I was filled with apprehension on my way to work. I eased my mind by looking out over the beaches as I drove. They went from narrow rocky, shoreline to 500-foot-wide stretches of smooth sand. I shot through the McClure Tunnel as the famous Santa Monica Pier and Amusement Park whipped by my rearview mirror.

Walking into the Village a few minutes later, I was greeted by that twenty-two-year-old knockout and animal lover, Diane, who always had her head in a book. This time it was *All Creatures Great and Small*. Diane had begun to hang out with my Village crowd, and had come to one of my pool parties. I found that she had a boyfriend and had declared herself currently off the market and completely unavailable. I vowed to myself that I would be patient and wait for her.

Trying to put off the inevitable, I stayed at the reception desk and chatted with Diane about how we both spent our summers and the work ahead before taking my leave. "Oh, Diane," I said before walking away, giving her a running reminder, "I've been thinking about you a lot lately and I just want you to know, if your boyfriend makes one mistake, I'm right there for you."

She smiled the most adorable smile and said, "Why, *thank* you, I'll be sure to let you know!" She said the word *thank* with a raised pitch, which, as I headed down the hall, assured me that I might have a shot here.

Savoring this Bogart-Bacall moment, I walked into the lounge where, to my surprise, Richard had brought in a friend. She looked very familiar. "Ken, I want you to meet my new friend, Morgan Fairchild. She's an actress. You might have seen her on *Dallas*," Richard added boastfully. "We just met at a new restaurant that opened down the street. It's called Central Park." Morgan appeared to be in her late twenties and way out of my league—she was actress beautiful, not to be confused with girlfriend beautiful. It struck me right off the bat that she was in full makeup, as if she had just come directly from the set. It was strange sometimes working in the Land of Make Believe, fact and fiction blurred on a daily basis.

Richard continued, "I met the owners, too. They told us to come on in and they will treat Fleetwood Mac like royalty."

"Wow, that's a big of them," I said sarcastically.

"Anyway, *Cutlass*, they have an amazing surf-and-turf menu, like lobster and steak, and they said they would be willing to bring us dinner here at the studio anytime we want, including the best wine and Champagne!" His excitement had put him a little out of breath.

"Well, if they're any good, they could easily make a million with this band over the next year. We should start a restaurant."

"Very funny, Cutlass." He laughed.

"But we could make M-O-N-E-Y the way these guys eat and drink!" Actually, it didn't sound like such a bad idea, catering recording studios. "I'll bet the band eats and drinks a million dollars of food and booze while we are doing this album."

Christine walked in the room just as I was finishing my sentence. "Oh, shut up with your talking and somebody get me a glass of Cristal," she joked, proving my point.

The rest of the band arrived soon after. Lindsey reached into his pocket and pulled out a cassette demo of the song that had the title "Lindsey's Song #2." Again, it was indicative of Lindsey's working habits that he hadn't written lyrics or titles yet, preferring the music to suggest its message or poetic content. Most writers have a title for every one of their songs, but Lindsey only had melody ideas, which is why for the first few months, his songs were referred to by only numbers.

He handed the cassette to Hernan, who popped it in and played it over the control room speakers. Everyone shut up and listened intently. We checked the tempo; it was about 117 bpm, which was pretty slow. The band went out into the live room to jam with it. We played the song down a number of times in a number of ways with the standard setup of Mick playing drums, John on bass, Christine on electric piano, and Lindsey on electric guitar. Lindsey's scratch vocal surprised us by consisting of some deeply confessional lyrics that didn't yet include the title hook of the song. Once Lindsey had the title, he would jettison the working lyrics completely, cutting them down to coalesce around the title phrase so that they became more of a billowing mantra. We all liked the song, but it lumbered to get off the ground.

What still resonated in our ears from the last Lindsey recording session was the initial attempts at "The Ledge," his raging proto-psychobilly song that he deliberately used as a battering ram against Ken's engineering pride, as well as what he saw as his band's complacence. This ignited immediate tensions among everybody. But when Lindsey handed in the demo for "That's All for Everyone" for playback, we were surprised. The song struck me as the polar opposite to "The Ledge," with its midtempo, laid-back pulse, and a revolving atmospheric set of chords with an interesting call-and-response melodic structure.

It was hard to believe it was from the same songwriter. Lindsey just sat there during playback, rolling extra-large sets of joints that he would burn through in sequence in what become a routine ceremony at the start of every session. "That's All for Everyone" and its sister song, "Save Me a Place," would become my two favorite Lindsey songs. He wrote "That's All for Everyone" with its harmonic progression rooted in the tradition of blues and folk, but interjected some clever twists that created anticipation as it modulated into the line "Must be just exactly what I need," resolving back to the root tonic of the title. These lyrics only showed up much later, as it was Lindsey's method to first hum the melody, eventually putting words to it as they came to his mind.

The lyric to the song and others changed as Lindsey's mood and state of mind "transitioned." Lindsey's songs on Tusk were a swooping roller coaster of naked vulnerability and caustic insults.

TRANSCENSION

▼

Despite many attempts, we wouldn't have the final master of "That's All for Everyone" for a while yet. Lindsey acknowledged that recording the song traditionally may not be the final approach and was clearly frustrated that one of his favorite compositions had tripped out of the gate. Over the months, we would pull out "That's All for Everyone" almost as a puzzle that had to be unlocked. Lindsey's eternal question to the control room was always, "What's the music giving off?"

We would gradually add pieces to it, notably Lindsey's experimental triple-tracked lead vocals, slathered with lush reverb and slapback tape delay, which up until that time was rare for one of his songs. The vocal lines of "That's All for Everyone" evoke a personal dilemma, relating the back and forth of an interior monologue. Lindsey layered his vocal lines so that they crisscrossed over one another, one finishing as another started, going from one ear to the other, as a chorus of doubts and insecurities well up from the middle. Instead of a soaring guitar solo for the climax of the song as in "Sisters of the Moon," Lindsey chose a rising, wordless note that he harmonized into the ether, repeating it again into a fadeout, floating above the fray of concerns, hopefully suggesting some kind of release.

For a song as emotionally sophisticated as "That's All for Everyone," we decided musically that less is more. Thus, Christine's piano accompaniment was kept to bare-bones block chords on top of John's fluid bass, which was lower in the mix, propelling the song subliminally like an undercurrent. Mick separately recorded a kick drum, a snare, a shaker, and a clave. Lindsey added his trademark doubled Fender Stratocaster volume swells to buttress the acoustic guitars. Doubling is an old recording trick where the musician plays or sings a part he likes; then, when he's perfectly happy with it, he goes back and performs the same part again exactly the same way. But the minuscule differences between the two parts when played together, especially when panned to opposite speakers, sounds amazing. Many artists, from the Beatles to Taylor Swift, have crafted their hits using doubling.

We realized that the standard way that we used to record was not going to be good enough anymore. Lindsey increasingly wanted "found sounds." Things around the studio, such as chairs, cans, Kleenex boxes, or pillows, were some of his favorite drum replacement ideas, anything that would provide some Dadaist breakthrough. Lindsey never forgot the sound he got in "Secondhand News," when we used a Naugahyde padded chair, doubled and low in the mix, to provide a haunting energy source to the song. In this case, the found sound that would provide the key element to "That's All for Everyone" would be supplied by Hernan.

What was also a complete departure for rock or pop music, Lindsey accepted my gift of a charango. A charango is a South American folk instrument similar to a lute, with ten strings in a special open tuning and an armadillo shell–backed resonator. For completely different sound tonality, the charango hit the spot, and Lindsey was smitten. Like the musical genius he was, he proceeded to retune the instrument to his needs and figured out an arrangement. After Ken miked it up, Lindsey went out into the studio and played to the track, which gave the track an exotic shimmering tone. We doubled the charango to use as the basic harmony builder for the song, emulating and replacing the high strums of a capo'd acoustic guitar. I believe that beyond Simon & Garfunkel's intentional evocation of an

TRANSCENSION

Andean folk band with their cover of the traditional "El Condor Pasa," Fleetwood Mac was the first band to use a charango for a mainstream pop song.

Several months would pass as Lindsey kept us experimenting with layers of nontraditional instruments and sounds. He was on a quest to continue down the road of two of his musical heroes: Brian Wilson and John Lennon. Basically, what this meant was replacing the basic set of instruments on a four-piece rock band, and changing them to alter the tonality so much as to render the original group unidentifiable, to reimagine what a pop song could be.

The deconstruction of Fleetwood Mac's sound literally started that afternoon with "That's All for Everyone" as he invited Mick to get rid of his toms and cymbals, leaving only the snare and kick. Mick obeyed with a look of complete disbelief despite the sacrilege of that moment. This band was no longer Peter Green's Oldsmobile. With that first instruction, Lindsey gradually started a process whereby the band would never return to the old ways on his songs. He exhibited total confidence and conviction in what he was hearing in his brain for his songs.

From the first takes of that session, no original instruments were kept, including a muted rhythm Stratocaster that Lindsey played to build the song, coupled with Mick's cymbals. Eventually, Lindsey would overdub his own bass and piano over the McVies and play along to Mick's kick and snare separately. The famous Kleenex boxes that Lindsey played were highly compressed and equalized to respond to the snare. Since there was now a lack of hi-hat on most of his songs, leaving the eighth-note feel to be handled by the guitars, maracas, or other odd instruments.

For the song's evocative countermelody, we pulled out Lindsey's bag of tricks to find a new sound—toy piano, harmonica, and modified electric guitars—but none of them was quite right. Again, I offered up my kalimba (an African thumb piano) that Kris had given me for my birthday. Lindsey was intrigued and played around on the kalimba with an amazing dexterity until he had the cascading melody he wanted. We doubled it against the charangos, which gave the song its magical and unique sound you hear on the finished mix.

The beautiful yet haunting Stratocaster volume swells interacted with all the call and responses of the multiple layers of instruments and vocal parts by Stevie, Christine, and Lindsey, completing a sonic portrait of immense power, which augmented the emotional impact of the lyric. While the charts were dominated by disco, Fleetwood Mac was recording a gorgeous Andean-African confessional ballad that's more about despair than dancing.

For a song like "That's All for Everyone," which was a chanting drone that was neither upbeat nor had any changes to speak of, the way we layered the different instrumental and vocal textures and timbres was the key to bringing out its inner beauty. Its tempo now rolled and swirled rather than plodded along, which is what production and being open to new ideas is all about. Sadly, Hernan never got his charango back. It was last spotted on Lindsey's first solo hit, "Trouble."

Several bottles of Champagne and packs of cigarettes later, folks were starting to get hungry and in dire need of a break, so Richard volunteered Central Park again. He guaranteed we would love it and convinced us all to go. The restaurant was about five minutes' drive away and it wasn't too bright, with about thirty tables of various sizes spread through the large, open room. Each table had a nice linen tablecloth and several flowers in a vase; the chairs had round, carved wooden backs, almost as if they had been bent out of grapevines. Richard introduced the band to the owner, a very attractive woman named Carla who worked the front while, her husband, Bob, ran the kitchen.

The food was excellent and Bob and Carla treated us like family. There was something magical about this place and the wine flowed to the point that we were having too much fun. After a long day in the studio, everyone was coming alive again. Christine needed a toot and asked Carla, her new best friend, whether there was a place she could go for privacy. Carla showed Christine to the large, open bathroom at the rear of the building overlooking the parking lot. We didn't see them again for nearly an hour.

Carla and Bob were from New York and felt like one of us, so we trusted them. After dinner, we went back to the studio and agreed that from now on we would just have them deliver food to us so we wouldn't lose so much time. When we got back to the studio, we noticed that Lindsey had ditched us. All that alcohol wasn't optimal for him to create music. Morgan Fairchild turned out to be quite a trouper and came back to the studio with us to party awhile. With Lindsey gone, we could have fun and indulge in our first transcension of the album.

The term *transcension* started during the last album, when the band was too tired of working day and night and a substantial quantity of cocaine would be called upon to fuel a midnight mania musical event where everyone would play and absolutely nothing got done. Eventually, as this became more frequent, the production staff would leave early. Technology had improved enough that we found we are able to play two tape machines together in sync at the same time. This would allow us to give the transcenders the ability to record on a safety tape without erasing any of our masterworks, so it would become a game between Richard and me as to who could sneak out first, leaving the other guy holding the bag of coke. Many times, it would be poor Hernan who would be left to safeguard his boss's studio from the crazy millionaire rock band.

I convinced everyone to leave at midnight by reminding Stevie that we were recording her new song tomorrow. After spending the entire day sitting next to a huge stuffed bunny on the couch and scribbling in her journal, sullenly watching the band try to commit "That's All for Everyone" to tape, Stevie decided at dinner to call dibs on the next day's session, announcing that her song "Storms" would be the first order of business. So, when I reminded her of this, she stood up and forcefully told the other revelers that they all had to vacate the premises and go home. I glanced over at Richard and gave him a satisfied look.

Mick had been quietly listening in the corner to Ken and Richard's good-natured recommendations for everyone to go home so we could all be rested for the next day's session. As the control room emptied, he looked at me with his twisted smirk, saying, "Oh, Hernandez, what a pity that they are all gone. We will miss them!"

"What do you mean, Mick?"

"Yes, my faithful Fernandez, there will be no Chilean uprising tonight! We shall transcend instead!" He pulled a vile of Andean snow from his vest fob pocket. "So, let's get those amps on and some microphones on the congas. It's transcending time!"

This happened a lot.

7

SLEEPLESS CHILD

> But I am only—one small part of that band, "the baby sister,"
> the one to be jealous of, the one to come, undone,
> over . . . if they only knew . . .
> —Stevie Nicks, diary entry

Several months into the *Tusk* album, I couldn't help thinking about how much life had changed for all of us. A year and a half earlier, we had all been renting small homes and apartments, living with each other or with friends, and trying to make ends meet. Richard and I were barely five years out of college and into our professional careers and drove to work in used cars, grateful just have a job in a recording studio. The band, for its part, was about to fizzle out in the '70s like the rest of its contemporaries. Fleetwood Mac was happy that it still had a record deal because it was all it did have.

Until recently, Mick, John, and Christine had no access to their past earnings, thanks to a pending lawsuit. Lindsey and Stevie were often unemployed and virtually penniless. The first album by this fourth version of Fleetwood Mac took a year to catch on and make any kind of money. They had to tour hard across the entire country by station wagon to pay the bills. When we recorded *Rumours* in Sausalito, all the guys crashed in one rented house while the girls shared a semidetached cottage. When we weren't sleeping, we practically lived in the studio like squatters. All of that would change to an extreme degree.

Now, Lindsey had moved from a shared house on Pico Boulevard next to the Miracle Mile in a posh area called Hancock Park next to the Wilshire Country Club and the La Brea Tar Pits. It was an affluent, palm tree–lined residential neighborhood built in the 1920s, where the elite of old had lived and ruled. Lindsey's home was one of the many European revivals along the private golf course, with a spectacularly large staircase taking center stage upon one's entering the home. His pride and joy was the upstairs bathroom with such amazing natural reverb that he would use it to record many guitar and vocal parts.

Christine had bought Anthony Newley's home off Coldwater Canyon next to Dennis's mother, Audree Wilson. Parked in front of the house were two Mercedes-Benzes with personalized license plates of the names of her Lhasa apsos. She spent all of her time away from the band, either at her new home or with the Beach Boys' drummer on his new 68-foot ketch. When they weren't enjoying their lovely view of Beverly Hills, they were speed boating and waterskiing around Marina Del Rey. There was even talk of marriage.

Stevie moved out of her big pink house in Hollywood that she called "El Contento," and bought "Fantasy Land," a mock-Tudor mansion above Beverly Hills, with her newfound wealth. Stevie would talk your ears off, but she was always very discreet about who she was seeing privately, summoning people to visit her rather than being photographed at every club in town.

Mick had bought another giant mansion near the studio in Bel Air, where he lived with his mother, and for a short time, his family after he had reconciled with Jenny. Although Mick was always in fine feather in his immaculate suits and vintage sports cars, he made a series of questionable investments, which along with alimony and child support payments, kept him comparatively broke. So, Mick always needed to work, to tour, and to sell albums because he and John drew a percentage as Seedy Management, handling all of Fleetwood Mac's varied business affairs. In his mind, Mick thought he was a rich rock star, the manager, leader, and drummer of one of the biggest bands around, spending his money just as the songwriters did, who made ten times more from their publishing. Aside from his mansion, Mick purchased a second home in Topanga Canyon and a black Porsche 911 Turbo Carrera with a phone in it to get between the two.

John, on the other hand, could handle his money quite well. Never one for flash, his retiring personality lent itself to sound investments. He had hired an excellent business adviser to invest his money wisely. John was living between his boat in Marina Del Rey and his hilltop home in Topanga Canyon with his new wife, Julie Rubens.

My buddy, Richard Dashut, had just bought his first home and we were all happy for him. It was in the hills above the studio in Brentwood, which would become notorious years later during the O. J. Simpson trial. Richard had a modest home compared to the band, but he was the first of our engineering team to buy one. Dashut had a Jacuzzi installed soon after he moved in and began entertaining the eligible young models and actresses of LA, including Pamela Sue Martin, who played Nancy Drew on TV. Because Richard's place was ten minutes from the studio, it would often become my home away from home when the party moved or when we just needed to crash.

Richard invited Hernan and me to take a quick drive up the winding streets of Brentwood to visit his new property just north of Sunset Boulevard. He pointed out the house that Marilyn Monroe had died in was just a few doors down. Richard's home was bright and sunny and modestly spacious with two bedrooms, two baths, a bright living room, and a quaint kitchen. The big bonus was the newly installed hot tub. Richard was always a ladies' man, but as he got some money and a little fame, he and made good use of his charm and humor. To all of our surprise, he started dating models and movie stars. You never knew who you'd meet in Dashut's magic Jacuzzi or how many dates you might end up with after.

"I have an announcement," Richard declaimed. "I ordered a new car. It's a replica of the classic 1930s Excalibur. It barely fits in my garage!" He led us out to the garage to admire his new toy.

"*What?!* Awww, Richard, that seems like something you're going to get tired of right away," I said, feeling slightly paternal.

"I saw one rolling down Ventura and I had to have one. They're beautiful," he explained, beaming.

"Dashut, you never cease to amaze me!' Hernan said in disbelief, as we all gazed longingly in a way that only engineers do at the miraculous machine in front of us. We went inside and met another exotic foreign model, a friend of Richard's from Australia, named Lindy. She had classic features, high cheekbones, a slender waist, and an Aussie accent that was sexy as all hell.

"Richard, dear, my friends are coming over and the hot tub won't turn on," she pleaded. "Fix it, love, before they come." Richard went outside, flipped a switch, and it immediately roared to life. Lindy squealed and then thanked him.

"I'll be home later," he said. "I just had to get out of the studio for a minute." He kissed her and we headed out the door.

"Wow, how long is she staying here?" I asked.

"Just a couple of weeks," he said, smiling broadly.

"You're the luckiest bastard I know!" Hernan said, shaking his head.

We headed back down to the studio and the winds were acting up again. The Village studio's entrance was at the southwest corner of the building, and entering it from the parking lot was always a violent experience on windy days. The studio was built and modified to be soundproof, so it felt like entering a large bunker, but as we passed through the front into the protection of the building, the door took on a mind of its own, breaking free from my hand and slamming shut.

"Holy shit!" I said involuntarily and heard a laugh from the front desk. My favorite receptionist, Diane, the hottest girl at the Village, was smiling at us. She was a model for several magazines and newspapers, which only made me want her more.

"Hello, my darling," Dashut blurted out to my future love, and then, bowing partially, "I must say you're looking ravishing today."

"Thanks for noticing, Richard. I'm glad you guys weren't scared too much."

"Us? Scared? Impossible," I protested.

"It's all right; it's been happening all day. It's hilarious."

"Diane, will you be here a while longer?" I asked.

"Yes, I will . . ."

"Great. I'll be back in a bit to talk."

Our roadies were in the lounge, watching the Dodgers playoff game. There was a close-up shot of the Dodgers third baseman, and the FM All-Stars coach, Ron Cey, who looked like Tom Skerritt and Nick Nolte's love child. By a very strange coincidence, Cey's nickname was the same as Fleetwood Mac's mascot, "the Penguin,'" because he suffered from tiny shin disease, which meant his knees were only 4 inches above his ankles. His coach in college gave him the nickname because it looked as if he waddled when he ran. He was just shy of 6 feet tall, a big, stocky guy with huge thighs and a great baseball player. I couldn't wait until our grudge match against the Eagles; they could fly, but we could bat.

It was a roomful of hungover and haggard faces that greeted Stevie's new song, "Storms," which was fitting, I thought. I didn't like the song very much. It felt very sluggish me, and her rudimentary piano part only exaggerated the loneliness. By contrast, Lindsey was feeling surprisingly buoyant today and fell right into his old partner's song. Historically, Stevie would write a song on the piano, but then Lindsey's brilliant playing would transform it into it a luscious guitar piece. Although both Stevie and Lindsey claimed sole songwriting credit for their songs, they were more of a songwriting team than most people realize. Each of them could write their own tunes, but what each brought to each other's music was that special magic that often eludes solo artists.

Lindsey was not the only member of the band that was going through deep emotional changes, not by a long shot. From what I learned later, Stevie had come back heartbroken after a brief love affair with Mick during the Rumours *tour. Not surprisingly, the first song she presented to us to record was "Storms," a confessional ballad sung by a broken-hearted woman trying to alleviate the pain of a romance that was dead on arrival. It took a few weeks after she first played us the demo before we were set to record it. Meanwhile, Stevie just hung out in the studio as we were cutting "That's All for Everyone." She was quieter than usual, and would ask us every so often* when she would get her turn. During the long hours that passed, she would sit on the couch and write poetry to soothe her heartache, much of it showing up as lyrics over the years.

I was a sensitive guy, and I felt her pain. I took the chance to talk to her during some of the breaks. Of course, being the no-filter person that she was, she poured out her heart to me. She would gradually share her grief on how the band treated her, especially Lindsey and Mick. She felt punished for being the center of attention for the press and left out of the recording process. When she proposed a song to record, she felt it was criticized too harshly. Among our team and the crew, the general opinion was that she was a drama queen, which was a view I didn't share with them, although I was a newcomer to the scene.

So, when Stevie passed me the demo cassette of "Storms" for us to hear, the first thing that I noticed was the different sound quality of it, the stark arrangement with only her voice and a basic piano part played by her. It confirmed to me that the secret weapon Stevie and the band had was Lindsey's near-genius capacity to unfold himself and switch into full producer mode to get the best of that rudimentary piece of music and turn it into gold, like an old alchemist. It wasn't that Stevie's songs weren't good, just that they presented more of challenge, not only to arrange the song structurally, but also give it a brighter mood, since her lyrics often meandered into a tormented, dark night. Stevie didn't do sunny pop songs with fluffy clouds.

I took a mental note then how surprising it was that Lindsey was willing to commit his best creative musical effort despite a decade of shots exchanged in their songs. The history between the two of them seemed to be a vein that always yielded creative gold. This is a textbook case of how a demo builds and builds into a finished track through addition and subtraction. Lindsey set to his work patiently and methodically, building a basic track with a strummed acoustic guitar on top of a click track for reference. The steel-string acoustic was eventually replaced by a fingerpicked, nylon-string acoustic guitar finger, sliding across chords as a way to add more dynamics and movement to the vamp of the song. From there, he added an assortment of electric guitars, one clean and one crunchy, arpeggiated to weave a canopy of crisscrossing notes.

Christine passed up her Yamaha to play her favorite keyboard, the classic Hammond B-3 organ amplified through a rotating Leslie speaker, which remained true to the song's feel as a lament or a requiem. She would also add a velvety Rhodes electric piano to complement Lindsey's suite of guitars. We privileged her Rhodes track on the final mix to add some more movement, supported by John playing a simple, walking acoustic bass that didn't clash with the amplified instruments.

Mick's role on "Storms" was to play a moving, muted floor tom that starts appearing in the middle of the song, taking on more presence toward the end. On the final mix of "Storms," we used some Beatle tricks to accentuate Mick's performance. One was a variable speed oscillator (VSO), which was built into the Studer to slightly increase the pulse of the song, from the original 104 bpm to 109 bpm, giving it more life and shine. The other was partially a result of Mick's search for different percussion instruments that would carry the beat of the song without taking center stage. Initially we had a reverbed snare and shaker cracking in the distance like thunder and lightning, but instead opted for a light, propulsive tambourine, and by equalizing the click track, we turned it in a kick drum to Mick's disappointment and our amusement.

For the sound fanatics, I can disclose some of the studio tools we utilized in getting the fantastic guitar sounds that permeate Tusk. Most of the tracks with electric guitars were first sent through Ken's Direct Fat Boxes, as well as *through outside amps to capture some ambient acoustics, using close and far microphone placements. In some cases, we would tape a very small, lavalier microphones to the inside an acoustic or under the bridge of an electric, for another parallel feed. Sometimes, these feeds would go out to other amps, or to the rotating Leslie speaker. Once in the control room, some of these parallel guitar signals would be filtered, equalized, compressed, and treated for their tonality and dynamics to achieve the best sound quality for the song we were recording. This was definitely the case for "Storms," which has lots of string and bridge action. Finally, Lindsey's fingerpicking action on the guitars was the most important sound characteristic of his particular sound, so getting those textures and subtleties on tape was very important to us.*

I would like to state something obvious, yet somehow overlooked: The key to a great-sounding record is great-sounding instruments, and of course, great players. Recognizing the particular strengths of a musician, whether it's Lindsey fingerpicking or Stevie's dynamic vocal range, and accentuating them is a fundamental responsibility for any producer or engineer. For example, Stevie was at her best when adding her mysterious background vocals and harmonies. She always had so many vocal ideas that we had to put them on separate tracks on the tape before we painstakingly went through and evaluated them one by one. The relative lack of group singing compared to the two previous albums is a charge that has been leveled at *Tusk* time and again, but it's there, if you care to listen, as Christine and Lindsey's voices float subtly right alongside Stevie's passionate confessions. Sifting through vocal tracks was another time-consuming Fleetwood Mac obsession that was rivaled only by checking drum tracks and tuning.

It was evening by this point and Hernan took my lead and suggested that we not spend another long night partying, and instead go home and enjoy our Friday night with our loved ones and be ready for a new song in the morning. We called it an early night, and everyone was happy with the work we did. Days like these were beneficial for the band because it working as a team and making progress, each member contributing something special and uniquely his or her own to the group's sound. No drug was better than good work. Drugs wear off, but good work endures and fosters morale, which we all needed. There were hidden pressures bubbling under the surface that we didn't acknowledge when we started this album, namely, making a ton of money, being told daily that we were a superstar (a god of sorts), being told we were the reason for the band's success, and doubting whether we were really that good and could repeat the miracle again.

This burden rested most heavily on Lindsey's shoulders. The three British members had been to the top and back again. *Tusk* was their twelfth album, and they knew it wouldn't be their last. Stevie, for her part, was the darling of the music press, who had a bright future no matter what. But nobody was turning to Stevie to take the lead and produce another mega hit record. Her enthusiasm and energy was saved for writing at home and live performance. She was so incandescent onstage that very little was expected of her in the studio. The role of the middleman, who got the song from demo to finished product, was left to Lindsey, who was growing increasingly irritated with his lack of recognition. He felt that he was using all his best ideas on the others' songs, and he may have been right, because no one remembers the middleman.

Lindsey was an introvert, and his discomfort with other people meant that he immersed himself in his work at home and his girlfriend, Carol. She had her own massive insecurities that made cocaine an attractive means by which she could assert herself and make friends. The two of them became a mutually supportive yet destructive couple. She didn't protest when he decided to transform himself and his band entirely; instead, she supported him unquestionably, amplifying his ego. Lindsey was single-handedly responsible for all the beauty and intricate guitar sounds that made *Rumours* the hit it was. And what's more, he knew it. He began to assert himself more like his hero, Brian Wilson, by taking leave of his famous band and helming whole albums and hit songs for Walter Egan, Bob Welch, Leo Sayer, Danny Douma, and John Stewart. Those forays were productive and bore fruit. We were just afraid that he would retreat from Studio D into his own sandbox and never return.

The hidden pressures were whispering in his ear not to take the easy road, not to do what everyone expects you to do, not to be merely "radio-friendly." As I look back on it now, he didn't have a clear plan and he didn't know how to say what he was feeling. He didn't know how to include all of us in the studio. I wish we all could have got together and said to Lindsey, "We understand what you're trying to do and we want to help. How can we help you accomplish your dreams and your own ambition?" But unfortunately, that did not happen and we chose to take the less-traveled path with a dark cloud in our soul. We would make it through this. We would sell millions of records. We would find a way to work together. We would find some measure of happiness. Besides, there was always cocaine, alcohol, and pot to shine a light on the road ahead. What could go wrong?

As we were leaving for the night, one of the studio's runners came in and frantically told us that there were strange noises coming from upstairs in the empty auditorium, and he thought he heard Mick calling for help. Biting our lips, Dashut said "My good man, let's go see what's wrong with the poor bastard."

Outside Studio D was a large marble staircase built in the 1930s to access the second floor auditorium of the old Masonic Temple.

"Listen!" Dashut demanded and dramatically pointed up the dark staircase. Suddenly, we heard the eerie sounds of a harmonica almost weeping. "It's him! He's returned from the dead!" Dashut warned dramatically. "The Harmonica Killer has returned!"

Out of the shadows came Mick down the stairs with a blood-soaked towel around his neck and a knife sticking out of it. Dashut met Mick halfway up with mock concern.

"Run for your lives, fools!" yelled Mick. "The Killer is loose! But first, for god's sake, pull the knife out! Hurry, you idiot!"

"I shall! But first I will need all of your cocaine!" Mick reached into the watch pocket on his silk vest, and pulled out a small half-empty amber-tinted vial. "Now, that's more like it!"

Dashut then pulled the fake rubber knife out of the towel and stabbed Mick in the chest to the whistling and applause of all of us gathered around the bottom of the steps. Christine and Stevie always enjoyed the antics of Dashut and Mick, and I remember Christine laughed loudly like Dame Edna.

"I'm out here, guys. I got a date," I said, to more hollering, "Umm Mick, could I borrow some of that for my lady friend tonight?" looking at the blow. Mick gave me a big smile and a wink and donated a little bit to my evening's entertainment. Thankfully, humor and practical jokes would lighten up most of our days and nights, even if we sometimes felt like killing one another. In the months to come, Richard, Mick, and the crew would pass the time by making a homemade horror movie called

SLEEPLESS CHILD

The Harmonica Killer, shot with one of the first commercially available VHS cameras around the Village. It can now be viewed in all its low-budget, dry ice, gory glory on YouTube.

The following day, Fleetwood Mac displayed its versatility further by exploring its soft side. Stevie's ballad "Beautiful Child" is my pick for the most gorgeous song on the album and displays lustrous ensemble playing by John and Lindsey and a delicate piano figure by Christine that always reminds me of a music box in a child's bedroom. In addition, the heart-wrenching harmonic interplay by all three singers reminiscent of "Dreams," which makes this song a highlight not just on *Tusk*, but in the entire Fleetwood Mac catalog.

We took some time to adorn the ballad with some audio tricks, such as the slight chorus effect on John's bass to make it shimmer a little more, and then we added a synth bass under it to extend the instrument down another octave. The bass and the snare come in together at the end of the first verse, and I employed a trick called reverse echo on the snare where we literally turned the tape upside down so that the tape recorded backward. We then added echo to the snare hits and printed the echo on two separate tracks. When the tape was turned back over and played normally, the echo on the snare actually preceded it, giving each snare hit a minor crescendo before it was actually struck with a "wooo0OOOSh." It's a very dramatic effect, and you can hear it thirty-eight seconds into the song. That was one of my special tricks that I stole from the Beatles and the Yardbirds.

When it came time to lay down the background vocals, instead of having them all sing together, we had Stevie, Christine, and Lindsey sing their lines one at a time in the gorgeous live echo chamber we had.

We ended up with two vocal tracks for each of them, which we were then able to fade in and out on the console to make their parts swell and recede throughout the song. "Beautiful Child" was the kind of song that Studio D was built to record. It was moments like these where a producer could easily feel as if they were Phil Spector recording the Ronettes over a decade ago.

The compelling and risqué lyrics to the song "Beautiful Child" invited speculation almost instantly, as many of Stevie's songs did. While we were recording it, we didn't ask Stevie to explain, feeling that it was too intimate a question. The song's inspiration wouldn't be revealed for many years until recently when Stevie admitted that the lyrics were about her illicit affair with Derek Taylor, the urbane and dapper press officer for the Beatles, the Beach Boys, and the Byrds, to name a few. Taylor was not only a married father at the time, but also much older than Stevie.

The psychodrama of that relationship, and others, as recounted in the lyrics of her songs on *Tusk*, make the ones on *Rumours* appear almost quaint by comparison. The lyrics of "Beautiful Child" describes Stevie's last night with Taylor at the Beverly Hills Hotel and frames her love for an older man in father-daughter terms. It says a lot about Stevie's lyrical gift that she can control such provocative imagery and make it somehow touching and universal, which is what Fleetwood Mac, at its best, does so well.

Shortly after we cut the song, UNESCO, which is a special agency of the United Nations dedicated to international cooperation to promote justice, education, and human rights declared 1979 to be the "International Year of the Child." In addition, the "A Gift of Song—the Music for UNICEF" was created to raise awareness and money to combat malnutrition, promote access to education, and help mothers in developing countries. Stevie wasted no time in donating "Beautiful Child" and its royalties to promote and fund the cause as well as appearing on the Easter Seals telethon to raise money for the disabled. That was the type of person Stevie was, and still is today, very much a free spirit, outspoken and unapologetic, looking to help others through her widely recognized humanitarian work.

8

THE HILLS ARE FILLED WITH FIRE

> Dennis awakened things in me I'd been scared to experience
> and made me feel the extremes of every emotion.
> —Christine McVie

Work on *Tusk* was beginning to pick up steam with new songs being brought in by each of the three writers every week. It seemed at the time as if we would have a full album's worth of material before the end of the year. Even Lindsey appeared to be softening his attitude ever so slightly. Unbeknownst to me, Mick had been trying to reason with Lindsey, telling him that he was concerned that if Fleetwood Mac departed too far from its fans' expectations, the fans might not follow.

Mick had intimate knowledge of this precarious path when his fledgling blues band hopped up from one successful single to the next, building a large fan base, which quickly dwindled once Peter Green suddenly departed. Both Danny Kirwan and Bob Welch did their best to fill the gap, but the band's early fans never returned in the same numbers. Mick was thrilled that its change from blues to folk rock was accepted, thanks in large part to Christine's ever-present soft rock ballads, but he warned Lindsey not to take the fans for granted, especially when Lindsey had wandered so far off from where are his talents normally took him.

Mick and Lindsey spent several days talking over what was right for the band and what was right for Lindsey's creative path with the ultimatum laid down that Lindsey was either in a band or he wasn't. A compromise was struck that Lindsey's songs were his own, but he had to come back to Studio D full time and take a more active hand on the rest of the album.

A few days later, the band chose to work on Christine's ballad "Over & Over" as smooth and sun-drenched a '70s ballad if ever there was one. Christine was clearly an accomplished songwriter by this point, but it was clear to me that Lindsey and Stevie drove her harder to be even better and contribute quality songs that could coexist between their fire and ice. Lindsey's playing was the perfect companion to Chris's warm contralto, first with understated acoustic muting, and then with quirky slide guitar, almost as if a bluesman had walked in on our session.

Slide guitar was not a style Lindsey played much at all, but "Over & Over" reminded him of Christine's "Warm Ways," so he intuitively knew it would work on this song (we made sure to bring it back on "Never Forget" so that it subtly bookended the entire album). Lindsey then dropped the slide and switched unperceived to a florid, fingerpicked lead on his Stratocaster in the bridge, which he played for the rest of the song, in and out of Christine's lead vocal.

Dennis Wilson, high on life, and possibly other things, couldn't sit still throughout the session and kept asking me to push the talkback button so he could talk to Christine and sing ideas to her. Past experience led me to believe this would not go over well with Lindsey, but Dennis was spot on and the parts he suggested were incorporated into

THE HILLS ARE FILLED WITH FIRE

the song. He had a great idea for the line "To keep me around" coming out of the last verse into the tag. He suggested the band play the descending chords from the chorus instead. Dennis, who knew a thing or two about harmonies, urged Christine to try some softer background vocals. We set up three mics in the studio and our singers went to their respective microphone and we simply put three tracks in Record and let them work. "Over & Over" had a lot of space in the track, and we ended up deciding to let the verses be open and have the choruses and tag be rich with harmonies.

One of my favorite parts of working with this band is how it went about doing its vocals. Lindsey would always sit down at the piano and have the two girls stand around the piano while he worked out the exact notes that each of them would be singing. We could hear the notes they sang forming a perfect chord. Many times a singer will improvise their notes, but when you play them on the piano, often you will find notes are duplicated by one or more people. But plotting the notes out on the piano ensures perfect harmony.

I only saw this occur one other time in my career, and that was when I was sent to Brian Wilson's house in the early '70s to help them record with Wally Heider's mobile truck. I set up some microphones on the piano and for vocals. Brian did the same thing that Lindsey did. He played the vocal harmonies on the piano and had each of the Beach Boys memorize his respective part.

The other thing that Fleetwood Mac did uniquely well was in the fade-out tag, it would always add a new hook line as a final build in the song. This was done for "Say That You Love Me," "Don't Stop," "The Chain," "You Make Lovin' Fun," to name just a few. For "Over & Over," they took Dennis's idea and joined together to sing the title in a way that simulated the revolving motion that the title implied, making it sound like it could repeat infinitely, and often they extended this part to wondrous effect when they played it live. The band ratcheted up the energy as the song faded, and if you listen closely, you can hear Lindsey having a little naughty fun by singing "Over bend over" in his highest register. We obscured that with a low gurgling bass synthesizer reminiscent of Pink Floyd that comes welling up out of depths along with Christine's Hammond organ, John's thumping bass, and Mick's switch from cymbal swells to full drum fills.

I'm always excited when that crescendo comes in, no matter how many times I've heard it. I drove home that night with my confidence renewed. I felt that there was hope for this album yet. It could come together. Lindsey Buckingham would pull this off and be just the guy to guide it into the homestretch.

I remember Game 2 of the 1978 World Series as the day we recorded another of Chris's love songs for Dennis, "Honey Hi." I also remember that day for what happened beforehand. Dennis, being a musician, usually left Chris alone when she was at the studio. This time, though, he drove her to the studio in his new Shelby AC Cobra race car and wanted to show it off to all of us. Dennis was always so open and friendly with us all, equal parts handsome and charming.

He put his arm around me and said, "Ken, buddy, let me take you for the ride of your life and show you what my car can do," before taking an unhealthy swig from his jug. Dennis always used to carry a large, half-full, translucent plastic jug around with vodka and orange juice. I demurred, but everyone told me go and have fun, and being a bit of car junkie, I couldn't pass up the opportunity. I was a big fan of fast cars,

THE HILLS ARE FILLED WITH FIRE

but my Ferrari was no match against the Cobra. The Cobra was an amazing car, weighing only about 2,500 pounds and boasting between 250 and 800 horsepower under the hood.

We walked out into the bright sun of the Village parking lot and around the little Cobra with Dennis telling me its history between swigs. He handed me the jug, and I said, "Sure; what the hell."

The mixture lit my mouth on fire.

"Whoa! That's got some punch!"

He threw his head back and laughed, his long brown hair blowing back in his face from the wind.

"Hop in!" he said leaping over the door and into the driver's seat. He took another swig and then started the engine, which with its special exhaust pipes, roared like a race car. I cautiously got into the passenger seat as he handed me the jug and instructed, "Here, hold this and buckle up!"

Dennis thrust the four-speed stick into first gear and pulled out into the middle of the sleepy residential street and stopped, looked at me, and said, "Hang on to something!" He simultaneously popped the clutch into gear and punched the great machine to full throttle. My vision was instantly blurred into violent shaking as the nose of the little beast rose up into the air and Dennis and I rocketed down the street with such force that the little Cobra was drifting side to side.

Dennis shifted into second gear and tried to control the beast's acceleration as we shot toward the end of the block and the West LA Police Department. I lowered the jug from view. Dennis was howling with laughter the whole way before skillfully downshifting to a full stop inches away from the Stop sign at the end of the street, pitching us both forward before our seatbelts snapped us back. Dennis prepared to go again, waiting for the cross traffic to clear. Realizing that I might have just managed to escape my death in a tragic accident involving a drunk Beach Boy, I said, "Whoa, Dennis, you gotta take me back. I'll take a rain check for another time!" To my relief, he saw that I was right and we calmly cruised back to the Village at a more sensible 60 mph.

"Thanks for the ride, Dennis. Great car!" I said, getting out in front of the Village and back to safety, "Are you coming back in?" I asked.

"No, tell Chris I love her and I'll be back later," he said.

"Please be careful driving, buddy; that's not just O.J. in that jug. Can I get you some coffee?" I asked.

"Ha! Funny. Don't worry, baby, I'll be careful. Thanks for thinking about me, but I have to get to a session at Brother Studios," he said over his shoulder, pulling away from the curb and disappearing around the corner onto Santa Monica Boulevard at speed. Dennis was currently cutting songs to follow up his first solo album, the previous year's *Pacific Ocean Blue*. Between Mike Love's fixation on meditation and cheesy songs and his brother Brian Wilson's mental illness and drug addiction, I thought Dennis was making the right move, that is, if he didn't James Dean himself first. I got back into the studio, and Hernan was nearly finished setting up the session to record "Honey Hi" in a traditional format.

"How was your ride, Ken?" Christine asked. I gave her a knowing look.

"You know Dennis; never a dull moment." She laughed.

"That's what I love about him," she said, smiling, while exhaling a plume of cigarette smoke upward.

I ducked around the corner to look in on the ball game with the roadies. Happy Hooton was holding the Yankees at bay, but Reggie Jackson

Studio D, The Village Recorder

Stevie Nicks and John McVie listen to basic tracks.

Harmonizing

Lindsey Buckingham overdubbing

Stevie at work

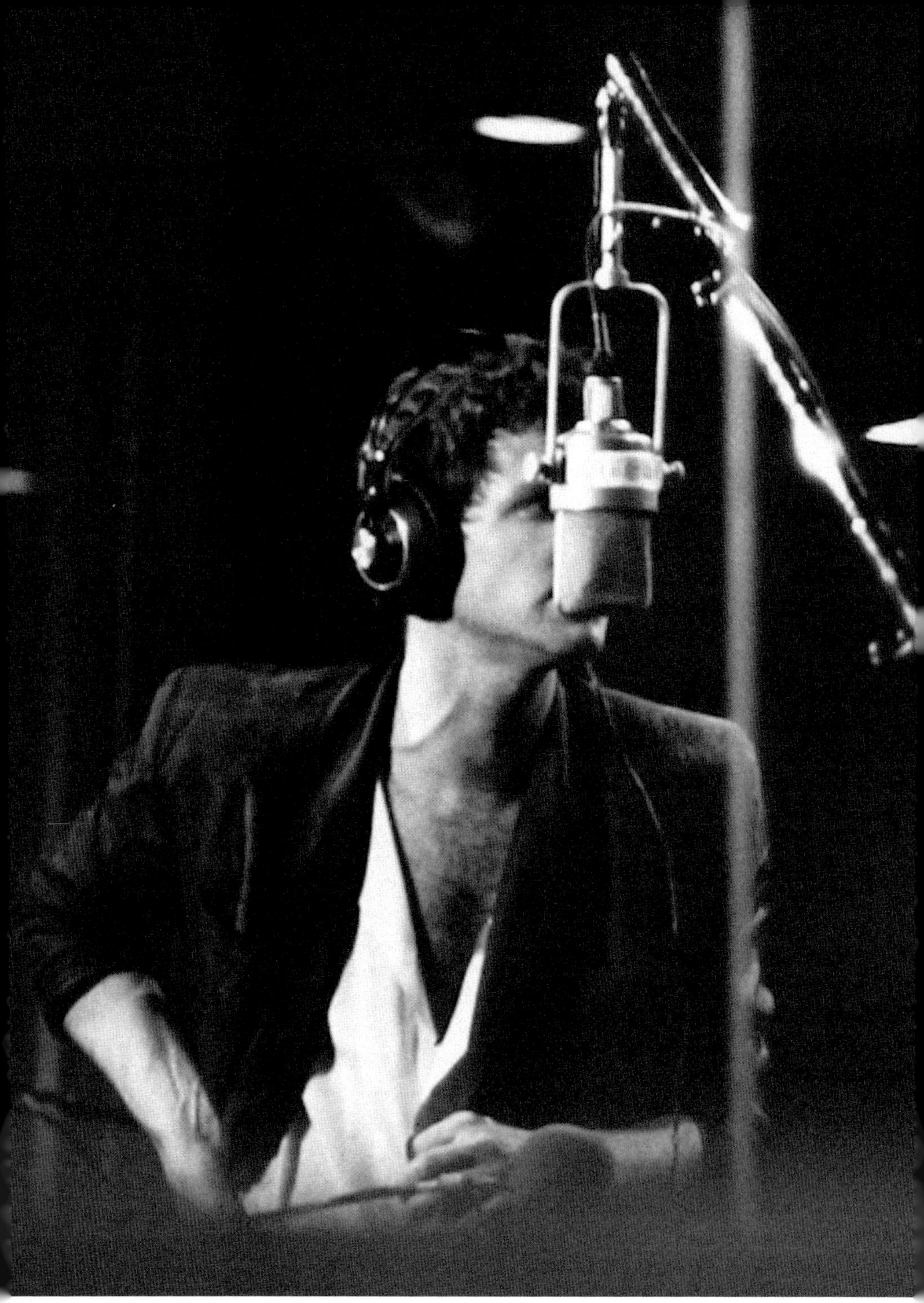

Lindsey and Christine recording background vocals

Scooter

THE HILLS ARE FILLED WITH FIRE

appeared to be unstoppable. Thankfully, Ron "the Penguin" Cey hit a three-run homer in the sixth to take the lead. We were only able to watch the game for a few minutes before Christine lost her patience and "ordered us" to come in, do our work, and make "Honey Hi" a "fucking hit," to use her words. This is why I missed seeing twenty-one-year-old rookie Bob Welch's dramatic and historic strikeout of Reggie "Mr. October" Jackson to save the game in the top of the ninth. As a lifelong Dodgers fan, this still hurts.

Wednesday October 11, 1978, had been one of those days that the band was in full presence in Studio D, spending the first part of the day doing some of the lush background vocal overdubs on "Brown Eyes" and hanging out in the lounge enjoying some of the wonderful meals that were catered daily. The Brits especially liked tasty Indian curries. Part of the conversation during lunch had to do with the movie Midnight Express *that had just been released and was the talk of the town, as it featured the consequences that a young American endured for drug smuggling in Turkey, a subject that scared international revelers like ourselves.*

As the day became night, the band felt cheerful, or as its artists put it, "no pain," in part because all five were together in the studio again after long stretches of either only Lindsey or the rest minus him. Nothing gets musicians excited more than the call of recording a new song. Christine had been insisting that we cut her delicate and midtempo ballad, "Honey Hi," which she described as her "island love groove song." The motion was seconded and carried. As we started to discuss the recording and instrument setup, we realized that it was past midnight, so the only way to complete this mission was with some Peruvian fuel, and it was urgent to devise an emergency supply.

GET TUSKED

Audaciously, we agreed that calling Geordie Hormel, the one-of-a-kind eccentric owner of the Village, was the answer. Of course, I was tasked with being the one to make the overture. I knew that sometimes Geordie visited the building during the wee hours, so I went up to his fourth-floor hideaway to politely invite him to the session, and as a token, ask him for his personal stash of cocaine. We were very fortunate that night since he had just received some shiny, round rocks of the needed fuel, which he happily donated.

With a second wind, we decided to layout the band in an intimate circular setting facing one another with Mick playing congas on the edge of the drum area to the right of our control room, Christine in the middle of the room with her Yamaha electric piano; John to her right with his bass; Lindsey to her left; playing his Martin D28 acoustic guitar; and Stevie singing harmony with her classic Sennheiser 441 dynamic microphone. It was once again Fleetwood Mac at its best, playing together and having fun. As its musicians ran through the song, it magically erased all the bad vibes that had arisen since Lindsey's revolt, if only for an evening.

The band played for a few hours until we all felt the toll of the long hours spent that day and wisely decided to keep what we had and come back the next day to listen with clean ears and heads if we got the master. And it turned out that we had; Take 4 was the master, sounding great, capturing that intimate, cozy island love song that Christine envisioned. In a way, it reminded me of the feel the Mac got on "Over My Head," from its first album. One of the keys for the song's feel and groove had to do with the fact that the beat is being accented on the upbeat, with the strong first beat of the measure not accented, lending the song an airier feel like most Caribbean music, most famously Jamaican reggae.

On top of the master track, Christine doubled her Yamaha with the unmistakable soft and smoky bell sound of the Fender Rhodes electric piano and a piano part that faintly added color in the back. Lindsey's basic acoustic guitar was left to help move the chordal and rhythmic structure, to which he added an acoustic lead that wove between the lead vocal to create a campfire conversation. The search for new ways to replace traditional rock instruments took an interesting twist on "Honey Hi."

Lindsey and Mick knew they wanted a cavalcade of percussion, such as claves, triangle, bells, tambourine, shakers, wood block, bongo, conga, bells, and a Chinese bian gu (flat drum), but the last one was the most exotic. Mick had some fencing gear in the studio that we would use during our breaks to blow off steam. Mick and I had had fencing lessons in our respective schools, so the idea was to record a match in the live room with us keeping time with the song. It was a lot of fun and sounded great, but eventually we had to erase it when we ran out of tracks while recording background vocals.

"Honey Hi" is yet another example of the wonderful, rich, and intricate group sing-alongs that lie within Tusk, waiting for a new round of fans to discover and enjoy. Those vocals sessions with Christine, Stevie, and Lindsey were probably one of the highlights for Ken, Richard and me, enjoying the singers' intuitive heartfelt work that flowed and built upon all the great lead harmonies and call and response background vocals that at one point in the song become a three-section canon, with one singing the song title; the second singing, "Daddy, all I'm trying to tell you"; and the third, "Cause I'm far away from home." The song sounds as if it was recorded live on a beach in the Caribbean and is one of the truest and purest band moments on the album. The love affair between Christine and Dennis inspired some of Tusk's most tender, playful, and underrated music. These musical love letters were serious as there was even talk of marriage between the two of them as early as the following year.

GET TUSKED

▼

On the morning of Monday, October 23, 1978, Scooter and I awoke to the sound of shrieking winds rocking the tall sycamore trees that shaded my hillside home. The violent gusts of wind reached as high as 70 mph. "This isn't good, Scooter," I said, imagining the worst, that some crazy arsonist would play the game of "How far will the fire spread today?" I turned on the news, but thankfully there were no fires reported.

Thank God.

I closed all the doors around the house, grabbed the dog, and headed to work. It was still early, not even ten a.m. yet, and the ocean was absolutely windswept flat directly out to sea. As I passed Topanga Canyon and neared Sunset Boulevard at the ocean's edge, I thought I smelled smoke. *Crap.* I'd played this game before during fire season. I nudged the accelerator down a bit and the little Dino pushed her nose into the wind. I looked over my left shoulder, and sure enough, a plume of dark smoke had begun to rise directly to the east. It looked too close, possibly in the mountains above the studio. *Jesus, I hope Richard's okay. His house is probably on fire.*

I decided to take the long way around to the studio and avoid surface streets, in case there were fire engines, taking the Pacific Coast Highway until it ended at the tunnel and turned onto the 10 past Santa Monica. When I got up on the overpass above the freeway connecting the 10 to the 405, all I could see was a wall of fire. There were already helicopters circling it. The firestorm was just north of the studio and Richard's house and heading west toward the ocean and my house.

I floored it.

As Scooter and I cruised up the 405, the smoke was getting darker with the sky followed suit. I got off at the Santa Monica exit and shot west four blocks to the studio. Of course it was empty, so I raced up the hill to see whether Richard needed help. It looked as though the fire was mile or two up the hill, but that distance is always hard to judge due to the smoke. Big fires look closer and small fires look farther away. I began to panic.

I screeched up to Richard's house and burst through the front door. Richard was smoking a joint and talking on the phone. He looked up and put his hand over the receiver.

"Cutlass! Did you bring the wieners and buns?"

"Funny. Have you been outside? It looks like the end of the world! Do you have a ladder and a hose? Maybe we should start watering your roof, in case some burning embers land on it!"

"Yeah, can you believe this shit? Don't worry, I called my mom; she's been through these things many times. She said do what the firemen tell you to do. They know what to do. They won't let her darling boy get burnt!" For the last part, he broke into his best Yiddish accent, imitating his mom.

So, there you have it. We spent the day drinking beer and smoking joints in front of the TV, watching the news coverage of the fires that were raging all around us with garden hoses out and ready. Sirens occasionally Dopplered past the house piercing the sound of the wind and the news anchors.

"Hey, where's Lindy?" I asked.

"She's out to lunch with some of her model friends. She's bringing them up here later when it's safe," he said, feet up on the coffee table, satisfied.

"I'll go fire up the Jacuzzi." I turned with raised eyebrows.

"At least we'll be safe in there . . . if it doesn't get too hot." Somehow we both found this hilarious. Scooter just snored at my feet while the world burned.

9

HERE COMES THE NIGHTTIME

> I don't feel as if I've changed at all. I'm just richer. The last five
> or six years of my life, it hasn't been tough at all. We're pampered.
> We're spoiled to death. There's nothing tough about it. All you
> have to do is come up with some good songs and you're made.
> In blunt terms, I am a star, but to say those words doesn't
> really ring true to my emotions. I don't feel like
> an arrogant, flippant bitch.
>
> —Christine McVie

After the fires had their way with our city, we went back to our process of trying to find our routine in and around the scorched earth. We had a meeting the day after the fires where Lindsey reminded us about his and Carol's big Halloween costume party on the upcoming Saturday.

"While we're all sharing, I'd like to switch the subject to something new, a great opportunity for us to be on the forefront of technology," I proudly announced. I went on to explain to the band that my friend just introduced me to a new, digital audio company, Soundstream Digital. Soundstream revolutionized the art of recording by converting sound from analog to digital. This would offer Fleetwood Mac the opportunity to achieve nearly perfect sound quality that would never have tape hiss and always sound the same as the original tape.

"They said they could bring the gear down for a demonstration whenever we had time. We should get on this."

"Sure. We've got time," Lindsey responded. Then, he spun around in his chair. "Okay, let's get serious. What's everyone wearing for a costume? Carol and I went down to Western Costume and got some killer costumes to wear!"

"Fucking great, Lindsey. What are you going as?" Christine asked.

"I'm not telling," he smiled mischievously.

"I've got mine figured out. Easy," said Stevie.

Mick and John just looked at each other quizzically.

"No way; you'll have to pick me out at the party. You guys have probably waited too long if you haven't got a costume yet, but it's okay," Christine winked at us. "I talked to Wongie, and she already called Western Costume and reserved outfits for everybody. So, everyone call down and tell them your size and what costume you want. Or better yet, go down there now and pick it out."

Richard and I thought this was an excellent idea, so we decided to go directly down there ourselves. Western Costume Co. was the professional costume house where the movie studios go when they don't have the wardrobes they need for a movie. Located in the heart of Hollywood near Paramount, Western sewed Dorothy's ruby red sequined slippers and clothed all of *Gone with the Wind*. So, if you wanted the dress that Elizabeth Taylor wore in *Cleopatra*, you went to Western.

On the way there, I asked Dash what costume he wanted, and he said, "Not sure, Cutlass; maybe a race car driver like what Steve McQueen wore in *Le Mans* or a prison outfit like in *Papillon*.

HERE COMES THE NIGHTTIME

"Cool; you like McQueen?" I asked.

"Yeah. I'm about his height and I'm pretty badass!" he said, laughing.

"Well, I'm sure if music hadn't found you, you'd probably be in jail or race car driver, or making a getaway."

"No argument there, buddy!"

We got to the enormous ten-story building, and it was definitely a big deal. The security was heavy and we almost expected to see movie stars walking around. They told us to put out our cigarettes in what appeared to be a very well-used ashtray. They even appointed a special clothing person to escort us around.

Our assistants took us to our dressing rooms—mine was nearby, and Richard disappeared among the endless stacks and racks of clothing. I was offered a glass of Champagne while they took my basic measurements. My mind was racing, trying to think of the perfect costume.

"How about one of the Beatles? Colonel Sanders? The Wright Brothers!"

My assistant winced.

"I'm sorry, sir. You're are coming in at the very last minute, and most of the best stuff has been reserved for weeks, but we did reserve a lot of nice uniforms. Perhaps you'd like something from one of our armed services branches? German, French, Japanese army? Something from the last century? Napoleonic Wars? Civil War?"

He looked at his watch. I realized that smoking Richard's joint on the way over probably wasn't the best idea when decisions had to be made in a hurry. I gulped down my Champagne and impulsively blurted out, "How about an air force pilot, like my dad was? That will make him proud, to see me in a uniform, kind of." After being fitted, I met up with Dashut and we decided to keep our costumes secret until the party.

GET TUSKED

▼

Through all the long months of Tusk, the band and the crew needed an event or happening to add some R & R to our intense schedule. The timing of Halloween was perfect. Lindsey and Carol were hosting a full rock-and-roll star extravaganza at their beautiful mansion in Hancock Park. Their preparation for this one-of-kind celebration was high, and included elaborate costume schemes that included special treatment at Western Costume for the entire band and us. As Halloween drew closer, the conversations and focus in Studio D switched from music to trying to guess who was dressing as what.

Like Ken and Richard, I also ran over to Western Costume to take advantage of this great Hollywood institution and look for my character. By the time I made it there, most of the interesting costumes were assigned, including the pirate costumes I'd loved as a child. After searching through what seemed like a surreal "Alice in Wonderland" trip of rooms full of Hollywood movie memorabilia, I found what I believed fit my innocent, long-haired personality: Little Lord Fauntleroy. The costume was based on the novel by the English-American writer Frances Hodgson Burnett. The Fauntleroy suit had quite an impact on young boys' fashion in the late nineteenth and early twentieth century and the Freddie Bartholomew movie adaption of the book had been a worldwide hit. Kris suggested the final touch: a big, round, red-and-white lollipop.

The thought of the party really fired up my imagination, since it was going to be my first big-time celebrity event where I was not an outsider. The solemn and affluent Hancock Park neighborhood was the ideal backdrop for a rock star Halloween party, with its big mansions of reproduced English country manors, neo-Gothic French chateaux, and art deco originals. Most

HERE COMES THE NIGHTTIME

of the original residents were rich LA families that had coexisted with movie stars with hardly any conflicts until the beloved Nat King Cole famously integrated it in the late '40s, which resulted in tragic racial hostility.

I arrived at Lindsey's front door with Kris, who was dressed as a high fashion alien model, and Screamin' Jay Hawkins's "I Put a Spell on You" welcomed us. Lindsey, in his spare time, was a master mixtape maker, so the whole night we were treated to a sensational Halloween seasonal mix together with some post-punk and New Wave that for most of this crowd was completely new, in spite of their music industry affiliation. The Cramps, the Ramones, The Rocky Horror Picture Show, assorted garage and surf rock, spooky horror and gore sounds from Hammer movie soundtracks, Bernard Herrmann scores from Hitchcock films, and classics like the "Twilight Zone Theme" roared out of the speakers all night.

Lindsey's house was seemingly designed for an occasion like this. It had a grand entryway that led into a huge, high-ceilinged hall, rimmed by a spiraling royal marble staircase. Upon arrival, I did as my father always instructed and headed straight to the bar. Fortunately, the bar was close by and had a couple of experienced barmen shaking and blending very cool tiki drinks, including one of Fleetwood Mac's favorites, the Scorpion. This Trader Vic's original cocktail was a mixture of rum, brandy, orange juice, lemon juice, orgeat syrup, and ice topped with a gardenia, so it had a very fast kick and made you feel happy and ready to party instantly. This state of mind and body in the band's studio jargon was called "Feelin' No Pain," the perfect party nirvana.

Kris and I agreed to meet up later in the night when it was dancing time, and to each wander alone to explore what surprises the crowd had for us. She knew many of the band members and team, so I wasn't abandoning her to the vultures. With a full tank of fun and laughter, off I went to venture *into the jungle of real and wannabe celebrities that mingled with industry and business managers.*

I picked up my costume a few days before Halloween, full of anticipation for my first major Hollywood celebrity party. Everyone would be there: rock stars, actresses, actors, producers, directors, athletes, and of course, everyone that made money off them—their attorneys, accountants, managers, spokespeople, and agents—who were always fun to watch getting buzzed and trying to keep up with all of us. At least that's how we thought about things then. Some parties felt like shameless attempts to see and be seen, but all the best ones were a blend of creative and interesting people just cutting loose.

Air force lieutenant Ken Caillat arrived at Lindsey's Hancock Park mansion fashionably late in his Blue Ferrari Dino. I had to park a block away because limos were packed in front, and the valets were busy helping all the good-looking people inside the mansion. Walking back from my parking spot I noticed all the homes looked like the wealthy part of town in San Jose, where I had grown up, built in grand fashion in the '30s, all two to three stories with hardwood, marble, and tile. Both the mayor and the chief of police lived down the street from Lindsey, but I doubted that there would be any trouble from them. LA was a town that was born to party.

Inside Lindsey's home was exactly what I had expected, a formal entryway, a spiral staircase, and microphone cables draped about. Through the darkness of the house, I found it funny that that guests were tripping over cables that Lindsey hadn't bothered to clean up. I could see that he had been taking advantage of the house's natural reverberant acoustics.

HERE COMES THE NIGHTTIME

On the landing of the staircase was possibly one of the most beautifully elegant women I had ever seen. Dressed in a skin-tight red gown, she was five foot ten with a model's body, perfect breasts, and long brown hair. Judy Wong came up to me and grabbed my arm.

"Hey, Judy, is that Stevie's friend?" I asked, giving Judy a half kiss.

"Well, hello, Captain Kenneth; you look very handsome tonight! Yes, that's Sara. Everyone's talking about her."

"She's stunning!" I mumbled, shaking my head.

I went over to Sara, pushed my way in past some people, and said, "Wow, hello, you look great! I'm Lieutenant Ken Caillat, at your service. I don't think we've been properly introduced. Are you with anyone tonight?" I always get chatty when I flirt.

She laughed and extended her hand, "Nice to meet you, Lieutenant. I'm Sara. I'm one of Stevie's friends. I've come by the studio before," she said, smiling.

"I have to tell you that you look ravishing in that dress!" I could see the throng of people waiting for me to finish talking to her, so I made one last-ditch effort, "Listen, Sara, I have to leave for the war tomorrow, so this may be my last chance to get to know you. Do you want to go outside where it's quieter?"

Just then, Stevie came out of one of the upstairs rooms, dressed as a white angel or a vampire in white face and said, "Come with me, Sara. Ken's a great guy, but you'll have plenty of time to get to know him later." As Sara was being pulled away, I said, "Come see us again!"

"Absolutely!" she said and kissed me on my cheek and disappeared into the mysterious bedroom with Stevie. I guessed that was Stevie's temporary party room, and then it dawned on me that she was dressed as Rhiannon, of course.

Since I was already upstairs, I decided to go exploring. I hadn't gotten far before I ran into Lindsey, Carol, Dashut, and Steve Ross. Steve was our freeloader friend, and funny as hell. He would meditate by day and party by night. He would do everything fun with us—such as boating, vacations, party, drug—without ever paying one penny. He was a very nice guy who would smoke your last joint, drink your last beer, steal your girlfriend, and somehow you didn't mind. At one point, Dashut bought a house and Steve convinced Dashut that he should, in fact, sleep in the master bedroom. Steve, Richard, Tom Moncrieff, and Lindsey even started an outrageous joke band called Codpiece. It made me wonder whether this was the kind of band Lindsey would have formed if Mick Fleetwood hadn't plucked him from obscurity.

We all were impressed at how good we all looked in costume. Carol was dressed as a sexy model, which she in fact was, and Lindsey was an Italian, pot-smoking priest.

"Callait! Welcome to my house! Happy Halloween!" Lindsey said, offering a hit off his joint. I cautiously obliged, knowing how powerful his stash was.

Mick and John came out of another bedroom, followed by someone I didn't recognize, who was suspiciously wiping her nose. I didn't recognize Christine at all. I had to do a double take. She was in blackface and dressed as Aunt Jemima, the famous grinning chef on pancake boxes. I just sighed. John one-upped her, dressed as an inebriated Nazi SS officer, his idea of pure evil. Mick was dressed more conservatively, as a sort of English gentleman vampire who joked that he sucked all the blood from those around him.

Watching and discovering who was within some of the costumes was so much fun that night. It wasn't so hard with most of them, but Christine totally surprised me with Aunt Jemima, fooling me until she went back to her usual cockney Brit accent. Completely outrageous! I thought. It's hard to imagine in today's selfie culture, when phone cameras weren't in everyone's hands, how wild these parties could get.

It was especially great to see Bob Welch again. We talked awhile, recalling his album sessions for "Sentimental Lady" where we had hit it off well. He had lived in Paris for many years and had an open mind to world culture. We wandered through the house, laughing at some of the creative Halloween costumes. It was hard for us to ignore this one guy who had built a large penis suit out of papier-mâché, with metal shavings for pubic hair. He just meandered through the hallways, bumping into everyone amid bursts of laughter. Today, I'm not sure whether that was Harvey Weinstein or not. One liners, charisma, and daring were key strategies to get noticed, whether it was to impress a lady, get a record produced, or make the deal of the month.

I had noticed that most of the band and our team had gone upstairs, where the best action of the night was taking place, apparently. Like everyone, I had admired Sara at the beginning of the evening, as she walked up with Robin and Stevie. I liked them all. They were fun girls to be around, and their costumes only made them more intriguing. The laughter and loud voices guided me to a room where Stevie was holding court, and as I walked in with as Little Lord Fauntleroy sending the room into an uproar.

"Ooooooh!!! Who's this cute boy that has offered me his candy cane to suck on?!"

"I want some of that candy, too!"

The previous weeks in Studio D befriending Stevie and her friends made me feel at ease and part of the entourage, so I joined in the fun. Stevie was telling some of her funny stories with such histrionics that she had us all cracking up in laughter. Her Rhiannon outfit, the Welsh witch that had inspired her hit song, gave her a spooky, sexy air.

By midnight, my version of Little Lord Fauntleroy had transformed into a full party rock-and-roll animal, exchanging sugar candy for nose candy that turned me into another of the talking heads that littered Lindsey's mansion. I had tons of fun with Stevie and the girls, but it was time to move and check where Kris was, and hopefully get in some dancing before the night was over. As I wandered through the second floor of the house, I saw some crazy love scenes, in closets, bathrooms, and dark corners, celebrating what was to be the last year of the '70s free joy ride, before Reagan's Moral Majority and conservative wave would hit the United States.

Close to the stairway I tripped over some of the cables and microphone stands that Lindsey had set up for his "lo-fi" recording adventure. Off the kitchen, in the maid's quarters, Gary Starr had set up a studio for him, full of expensive microphones, multitrack equipment, and processing gear. I couldn't help feeling envious of his home setup, since I mine was on a much smaller scale. I realized that Lindsey was following Brian Wilson's footsteps all along.

Finally, I found Kris talking and laughing with Steve Ross, of course—our Casanova freeloader friend and member of our Studio D entourage who, as we knew, wasted no time when a beautiful girl got in front of him. I took Kris by her waist and threw her onto the dance floor to do one of our favorite things, dancing the night away.

After we all said our hellos and laughed with one another, Lindsey took the opportunity to show me his bathroom to check out the acoustics.

It was large and completely tiled with glass everywhere, with just one macramé hanging as the lone decoration.

"Be careful you don't trip on all the cables," he said in his high voice. There were mic cables going everywhere.

"I hope nobody pisses on 'em," I joked.

He laughed, and shot back, "Nobody uses Studio B but me."

We alternated yelling out to listen to the natural reverb in the room. I could see how Lindsey could go crazy with sound toys like this available to him. We were two boys having fun.

"This is better than Capitol's echo chamber," I said, really impressed. The toilet had a guitar amp sitting on it and a couple of mics to capture the sound, along with guitar cables going everywhere as well. He had a mic set up in the shower and another in his cavernous walk-in closet. "So, where do you go if you *really* have to use the bathroom?" I asked.

He laughed. "If you haven't guessed, I'm working on tapes all the time here. Carol and I use the bedroom suite down the hall."

"In that case . . ." I thanked him and hurriedly headed in that direction. I closed the bathroom door and had to squeeze by some mic stands and a speaker cabinet to relieve myself. Apparently, Lindsey had been experimenting with the sound of his master bathroom, also. In one of the guest bedrooms I passed, I noticed his makeshift studio with a console and a large Ampex 1-inch tape machine from the Village and a bunch of smaller reel-to-reel machines. These were all Lindsey's playthings for making music his way. There were cardboard boxes with drumsticks inside and lots of electric and acoustic guitars. There was an upright piano, an electric piano, and some toy pianos, too, almost as if he was purposefully regressing back to childhood—hi-tech primitivism.

I went back to Lindsey, and Mick was giving both him and Richard a toot. "Caillat?" Mick gestured to me, but Steve Ross jumped in front of me from out of nowhere and said, "Sure, Mick, I don't mind if I do!"

"Thanks, I'm okay, Mick; I'm going to take it slow tonight. You never know, I might find my future wife here," I said raising my eyebrows. "Did you see Stevie's friend, Sara in the red dress? She's a ten."

Mick perked up, "No! Where?"

"First room at the top of the stairs," I answered.

"And Stevie's in there, too?" his brow furrowed.

"You're too late, Mick, I already did her in the closet," Ross bullshitted.

"Actually, I think Hernan is in there," Richard said. "He works fast."

"Hernan is in there with Stevie and Sara?" I asked surprised.

Mick dashed off down the hallway to aforementioned bedroom, twirling the end of his mustache like Snidely Whiplash with a lecherous smile on his face, "Lads, I'm off to find love!" I watched him go into the room, and that was the last time I saw him that evening.

I turned to Monsignor Buckingham, and as sincerely as possible said, "Thanks for showing me your . . . uh . . . studio. It looks like you're having a lot of fun working there." Lindsey thanked me and accepted my olive branch for what it was.

I went downstairs and stopped to watch the high-powered moneymakers and money takers dancing, when Gabrielle Arras came up to me in a sexy harem costume.

"Hello, soldier; would you like to go for a ride on my magic carpet?" she asked in her seductive Austrian accent.

"It depends on whether you rub the lamp . . ." I countered.

We talked for a little while and laughed at the dance moves of our attorneys, Mickey Shapiro and Steven Steinberg. Gabrielle was every bit as beautiful, blond, and tan as Barbara Eden. I'm not sure why we never hooked up. We came close a couple times, but we never seemed to be able to get alone or to not be interrupted, or maybe it was because she was a ball buster and only occasionally allowed herself to be soft and open. You had to be hard in this business—male or female—to get respect.

"I need a drink," I said, gesturing with my empty hand. "Can I get you something from the bar?"

"I'm good, thanks," she answered, raising her full cocktail.

The line at the bar was both sizable and notable. I was happy to see Ron Cey of the Dodgers chatting to Bob Welch, the band's old singer-guitarist, who was dressed as a Japanese Imperial Army soldier (complete with bald cap and Fu Manchu mustache) and John Courage, the band's hard-nosed road manager who was dressed as an RAF officer. I couldn't help but think how much of a shadow World War II still cast over us war babies, either that or they were late on their costume rentals, too. Next to them were Tom Moncrieff and Annie McLoone, two old friends of Lindsey and Stevie's, who were brilliant musicians in their own right, talking about how good the new horror movie *Halloween* was that had just come out. Also barricading the bar were some select folks from Fleetwood Mac's road crew and some of the techies from the Village, getting along famously, screaming and pointing at friends.

While standing in the line, I remember thinking everything seemed to feel perfect at this moment: people were having fun, people were dancing to great music, people were young, people liked each other.

Suddenly, someone tapped me on my shoulder, "May I have this dance, mister, or should I say, 'sir'?" said a very familiar voice standing behind me.

My heart leapt.

I whirled around just in time to see Cheryl, smiling up at me and wearing a Girl Scout uniform. It was fortunately too small for her, so she had to unbutton it some to stay in it. Her twenty-one-year-old body was yelling at me at the top of its lungs. I impulsively grabbed her and pulled her close to me. We hugged long and hard before our lips found each other and we kissed sweetly.

"Oh my god, I've missed you!" we said almost simultaneously, and she subtly brushed the front of my pants with the back of her hand and said, "Why don't you get us a drink and we can go someplace and talk?"

"Anything for my favorite cookie." I dutifully pushed through the line and got us two Manhattans.

Cheryl waved me over to a closed door that appeared to lead to another bedroom. We entered, but the room was basically a junk room filled with unpacked boxes.

"Why do we keep doing this to each other?" I asked.

"I don't know, but I wasn't going to let it slip away. I had to come see you."

I set the drinks down right as she leaned heavily into my body, kissing me. She was a great kisser. I could feel the boxes behind me giving away as her body leaned harder on mine. There was no hiding it; she could feel what was between us. She unzipped my pants to give me some freedom.

"I missed you, both of you," she grinned, her nose crinkled up cutely. I could see her freckles in the dim light coming from under the door. She slid down further and began to kiss me. Everything started to spin. I quickly realized she was in charge and we were doing it her way this time. I just went with the flow.

HERE COMES THE NIGHTTIME

▼

The laughter and music were getting louder and louder as we straightened up our clothes and went back out to the party. Standing in the backyard, smoking, I promised I would call her now that we had a little time off. "Or you can come live with me?" I offered somewhat jokingly.

She had already lived with me while making *Rumours*, and she was understandably cautious about moving back for another album. Cheryl and I mingled together like old times, and eventually we kissed and hugged good-bye. I told her I didn't want to be alone anymore; that it was getting too weird going from stranger to stranger. It was easier when it was just us. She nodded, but said nothing.

It turned out that my dalliance wasn't the only thing that happened that night. Mick became completely infatuated with Sara, and he did so much coke that when Sara left in the limousine, Mick ran nearly quarter-mile behind it, trying to get her attention so she would stop the car. He was all in with Sara. He was convinced she was *the* one. It didn't matter that they were both married; this was the '70s, and these kinds of things tended to happen. They were inseparable for several days after the party. Richard came in one day and told us he and Steve Ross had gone over to pick up Mick and found him in bed with Sara before they both fell on the floor laughing. As history would have it, Sara did indeed become Mrs. Mick Fleetwood after a few bumps in the road.

Later that same night, I found myself heading home alone down a moonlit coast, thinking about Cheryl. My little Dino was so low to the ground, it felt as if I was driving a very expensive go-cart; the 300-horsepower, V8 engine that sat right behind my shoulders purred like a baby tiger. I gently nudged the accelerator and was pushed firmly back into my seat. I put my head back on my headrest and let the music of my favorite station clear my mind, enjoying the rare blackness of an empty highway.

10

LIFE ON THE LEDGE

> I mean, you reach a stage when you're just sick of listening to other people's records cos they're not doing it properly, so you set out to do it yourself. You make your own entertainment, and that's the way we are now: We make records for ourselves, not for audiences. You can't be condescending about it. I don't agree with bands who make records to please audiences, that's bad.
>
> —John Lydon, *Melody Maker*, 10/28/78

Every day you were naked and on the front lines, facing a withering amount of criticism in the face of uncertainty. You took what you knew and tried to make up the rest as you went along. On any given day, it was hard to know who was your friend and who was your enemy. Everything was a handshake deal based on your last success. There was no such thing as security in this business. Any peace of mind we had went out the door when our star producer's instincts told him he would be a sellout if he made *Rumours 2*. Lindsey instead embarked on what the *New York Times* recently described as "a deliberate act of crazy defiance."

In the immediate context of the time, this insecurity made sense.

The world of pop music was expanding fast. Famously, disco was the hottest sound in LA. The Bee Gees, Andy Gibb, Donna Summer, the Commodores, and too many one-hit wonders to name, were cashing in on the craze; even the Rolling Stones and Kiss had massive hits with "Miss You" and "I Was Made for Lovin' You," respectively. The general rule of the Top 10 in those days was that, if you couldn't dance to it or hum it instantly, it was a flop. This was a very intimidating standard to maintain.

Then, you had the liberating countercultural world of punk and post-punk—a so-called New Wave of music taking a stance that was diametrically opposed to disco, prog, and soft ballads with its aggression, jerky multicultural rhythms, and synthscapes. These were bands made up of art students, intellectuals, dropouts, and other self-styled bohemians. The Clash, the Talking Heads, Wire, Joy Division, the Cars, and Blondie all spoke to Lindsey, and he regularly made trips to Tower Records grab their records or anybody else he'd heard about. These bands were hip. These bands were smart. These bands were avant-garde. These bands made a statement.

Lindsey's first goal was to change the sound of his guitar. He was looking for new types of distortion, and plenty of it, along with different tones, too. Sounds you'd never heard on *Rumours*. In many instances, he didn't want Mick and John's expertise to make his unique tracks too "slick." In short, he didn't want the "Fleetwood Mac sound." Lindsey rationalized his new working method—recording at home on his own and in Studio D with the band—thusly: "[It] got me to more esoteric places than I could go in a group situation. Then I'd take the songs back to the studio, and having the band build on it was the basic premise for much of *Tusk*."

LIFE ON THE LEDGE

Christine described recording his songs perhaps more diplomatically with the depressing euphemism: a "non-communal rotation system." Stevie, as usual, was blunter: "He announced it so viscerally, so demandingly, that I think he scared all of us. We were like, 'What the fuck?'"

As I look back on those days now, I have so many emotions. Nearly four decades later, I still have dreams about being in the studio with the band at least once a month, and more times than not, there is an unpleasant tone to them. I am not alone in this feeling, as others have expressed having the same experiences. For me, a large part of it had to do with the wrenching trials of making *Tusk*.

I realize now that Lindsey never really articulated his feelings or his master plan to me or anyone. I really don't think he was fully aware of them himself at the time—it was all gut instinct. It wasn't as if we sat around talking about how *Rumours* was the artistic summation of *Buckingham Nicks* and *Fleetwood Mac* and that we all had to change everything going forward. We didn't think like that in the moment. Stevie and Christine were content to let their songwriting evolve gradually. Lindsey was always tense and irritable and no longer the calm stoner I had just spent a year with while making *Rumours*. It occurred to me how shrewd it was of Mick to ship everyone off to Sausalito for the last album to maintain the esprit de corps and keep everyone in the same room working together—to compromise.

I believe that if Lindsey had been a better communicator, he could have gathered us around and explained his crisis of confidence, that he didn't think we could or would follow him where he wanted to go, or that he really didn't need or want any of our input. Then, we could have come to a more creative compromise without any of the fallout. In the past, Fleetwood Mac was more of a democracy, but in the course of a few months, it had become a dictatorship that would fracture the band to this day. This is why, for better or worse, *Tusk* sounded nothing like what anyone else was doing.

Lindsey's self-appointment as ruler of the Fleetwood Mac empire cast a pall on most of our working days. At this point, I had a pretty good sense of Ken's temperament and humor, and his face showed some early signs of tension and worry. We probably didn't read the misadventure of the first day back in June with enough attention, given the eagerness we all had to get started. Lindsey's first attempt at having to deal with his band, and at the same time, satisfy his sonic vision, obviously had been rocky, something that for all of us had augured a dark road ahead. Since I was the only new member of the gang, and still had a fresh and somehow naive outlook on all these events, I took away the thought that the first day's occurrences signaled something interesting and new.

I realized that Lindsey's direction and approach for his songs had strong roots in rockabilly and the whiter country side of rock and roll. There were no traces of the bluesy roots on "The Ledge" that had so characterized Fleetwood Mac's sound from the beginning, and even in those days, was always present in Christine's songs. The way Mick and John constructed the rhythm section for most songs featured syncopation, shuffles, and blue notes. All of that was completely stripped away from Lindsey's new songs that were coming in as demos.

Lindsey's first attempt at recording "The Ledge" was a struggle because his inner vision of how this song should sound made no room for others. All through that session, he was giving directions to John and Mick, whose blues imprint was all over their playing, deeply imbedded on every note, and impossible to erase. Lindsey's demented Duane Eddy guitars and the start/

stop structure of the song was something completely new to these British boys, who finally ceased to resist. There were no traces of Peter Green's Mississippi Delta–inspired riffs on "The Ledge." Instead, the insistent two-and-four beat proto-rock of Eddie Cochran and Gene Vincent was the order of the day. The fact that Lindsey wanted no cymbals, hi-hat, or toms from Mick and no walking bass notes beyond the basic quarter notes from John, was a clear signal of his new music beliefs.

Another goal that Lindsey had from the beginning was the elimination of artificial reverb; only natural ambience was allowed. The use of reverb obtained from echo chambers or EMT plates was a major part of a recording engineer's handbook, allowing us to give depth, roundness, and silkier sound to the tracks. Indeed, it had been the very essence of hi-fi for the past thirty years. So, to give up on it and only rely on the room's ambience was quite a challenge for Ken and the rest of the team. First, it demanded that we position the source instrument or voice at the right acoustic space, balance dry sound with ambience, and then accommodate it in relationship to the other tracks. On "The Ledge," and many other of Lindsey's songs, there was also the fact that his guitars, drums, percussion, vocals, and other instruments were treated with extreme settings to have a sharper edge or a darker tone, especially distortion, which made our task even harder.

Ken's quest for clarity and crisp high end was sliding through his fingers, and once again presented us with challenges beyond the norm. Only Mick's snare survived from that first session as "The Ledge" was taken over by Lindsey, who recorded most of the parts at home. He packed this simple little song with a million details, including speeded-up and slowed-down electric guitar tracks, some of which were tuned down half an octave, and then warped and twisted through the preamps of our recording console to give them that rubbery sound.

GET TUSKED

The vocal passes were treated the same way and got wilder and wilder as Lindsey layered multiple spliced overdubs of the song's tag, "Someone oughta tell ya what it's really all about!" During mixing, we were able to do some cool variations from the norm, such as panning the muted kick drum extreme left and the high-pitched snare extreme right, going back to the early days of stereo, and playing with the dryness of the chorus of Lindsey voices as the stop section of the song jolted the listener and shot toward the fade.

Today, I realize that what Lindsey was doing with his music was pioneering, laying the groundwork for what would later be called psychobilly, a kind of gritty honky-tonk that mixes elements of rockabilly and punk done with frantic pulses and loud dynamics. Lindsey's foray into old garage rock and rockabilly and full embrace of home recording at breakneck tempos would also inform the subgenres of "lo-fi" and cowpunk for the next two decades. The first true psychobilly album arrived six months after Tusk *with the Cramps'* Songs the Lord Taught Us, *produced by another power pop artist turned lo-fi garage maverick, Alex Chilton.*

Lord Buckingham intentionally was going to show himself as the king, putting us all under him, both band and team, as his subjects. At Lindsey's disposal were one of the most seasoned and proven rhythm sections in all of rock and roll's history, Mick Fleetwood and John McVie, who together with Christine McVie's exquisite keyboard chops and feel, provided one of the best backing bands a songwriter could wish for. Put this band in the most modern and innovative studio manned by the Grammy-winning duo of Ken Caillat and Richard Dashut, and you had the perfect setup for a musical and sonic dream team. If this wasn't enough, Lindsey had the brightest rising star in the rock universe, his ex-girlfriend Stevie Nicks, to sing with. But his mind was somewhere else, not on the polished hi-fi jewels of Steely Dan, the Alan Parsons Project, or Pink Floyd but, rather, on the raw, rudimentary sounds of DIY, or Do It Yourself, and do it himself, he did.

For the punk and hard-core movement that was maturing during those days, this manifesto referred to the ethic of self-sufficiency through doing your own recording without the sophisticated aid of experts or technology. It preached searching outside the box, and that was exactly what Lindsey was hacking into. Lindsey got his own way with his improvised home studio, and within it, he was allowed to beat Kleenex boxes relentlessly, search for weird guitar tones, do some primal screaming on the floor of his bathroom, play toys and funny instruments, and have no one to answer to or negotiate musical parts with or debate sound quality.

What you really hear when you listen to "The Ledge" is an introverted guy exorcising demons and having fun playing music by himself. Lindsey was frustrated with being in a band and completely at odds with the type of Fleetwood Mac music he had helped create, and he was addicted to the intimacy and immediacy of home recording. It was a blessing and curse for him that he could do it all, which didn't leave any room in his new songs for the others. He was now the leader of a band he didn't want to be in, named after the band members he didn't want to use. To put it bluntly, Lindsey wanted a divorce.

The '70s were coming to an end. Kramer vs. Kramer *won Best Picture in 1979 and divorce was gaining cultural acceptance and cachet. Bands were marriages, and marriages were ending at an astounding rate. Most bands were clueless about how to proceed making music into the '80s. Some entertainers pulled it off, but the vast majority released embarrassing albums that all but ended their career. With rare exceptions, restlessness in searching for new highs in sound and composition have nurtured the creative ecosystem of rock and pop music. Time and time again, when a specific music scene or* genre gets stale and repetitive, a visionary artist or band takes the baton and leads everyone to new sonic grounds.

This was the case with Lindsey's revolution. He was trying to take one of the most traditional British bands forward. He was brave to take left turns when the record company, fans, and the rest of the band were pinning their hopes on more of the same. He had made the decision not to rest on his laurels and was defiant to the band and world. The heavy sound deconstruction that Lindsey was initiating on his songs was groundbreaking for me. As much as I loved Mick and John's trademark pulsating and hypnotic rhythm section work, this raucous sound had something about it that, as the album continued, I understood was not only a rebellious outburst of sound, but a true cry to cleanse inner emotional forces unknown to us at the time. It was a cry for recognition, not only as the polished music maker for Fleetwood Mac, but also as a rebel in the biggest band of the late '70s.

But the question remained: Would Lindsey's rule going to allow for outside sound and musical input from Ken, Richard, and me, and from his fellow band members as well? In a sense, he had demoted them and us. I knew Ken well enough to know that he was a shrewd recording engineer with a hard work ethic and a worshiper—like most of us were—of sonically polished music. Our mission was both to cater to the artists, but also to make the music charm people's hearts and minds. So, what do you do when the artists in question are experiencing an internal schism? Having to settle for mediocre sound quality one day and reaching for perfection the next was not part of Ken's philosophy. I suspected that his initial acceptance of Lindsey's way was a strategy to win him over, but as time went on, Lindsey convinced himself that Ken couldn't adapt and was holding him back. The Buckingham rule didn't brook dissent.

Tusk was definitely going to be a trendsetter in terms of the studio *dynamics within the band and the rest of us. Beyond the first power struggle between Ken and Lindsey, and the subsequent challenges that this situation rendered, the key to survival was that our studio team had to stand together. I knew right away that for this to happen, the ace team of Ken and Richard had to stand together and maintain the old partnership forged through* Rumours. *But this alliance was not as strong as it should have been, as evidenced by Richard's not taking a stand. This was a warning that maybe their fraternity had eroded somehow, and the fact that the band members were going through their own individual storms.*

Richard's role from my perspective during the remix sessions on the Rumours *singles, and now during the days of* Tusk, *was beyond an extra set of ears to all creative decision making, but also to keep things rolling, either through clever schemes involving sound techniques or well-placed stories and humor. This is not to downplay the importance of his role, which today we define as emotional intelligence and the positive psychology required in a confined space to prevent the band from going at others' throats. He rarely handled the console or the outboard gear directly, nor did he operate the tape machine, which is where a lot of the action is when overdubbing instruments or vocals. He often played the role of the jester in the Fleetwood Mac court that had different ruling characters. When the heat was on, he threw water on it with great humor and charisma. He listened to complaints, held hands, nurtured the band, and massaged egos when the job required it. Coming from their live sound engineer and close friend, Richard's opinion of their performances was trusted by the band above all others'.*

Ken's role included handling the technical and creative recording processes, through thick and thin, from the basic microphone setups and positioning instruments in the various rooms, to starting conversations with Richard and the band as how to best tackle each song's sound and musical intention. Because his hand was on the rudder to steer the ship back on course, his job put him on rough seas with gale force winds. For Lindsey's part, his grip on how his songs should sound would not slacken. This was the daily confrontation that, through professionalism, friendship, or chemicals, we had to deal with to move forward.

My main role was making sure all the recording tools and equipment were ready to go at any time, and handling the logging of the multiple reels of tape that started to accumulate as songs evolved with alternate takes and versions vying for attention. My influence on Tusk grew as my input started to be well received by Ken, Richard, and the band, as sessions grew more intense emotionally and technically. I was also called upon to back up Richard when Lindsey pushed Ken out of some of his sessions, which was a very delicate time to come to work. Eventually, I would work alone with Stevie, helping her with her demos, and campaigning to get them recorded.

I knew then that my place on the team was beyond the technical role. I also had to watch Ken's back. The fact that Ken and I had established a good level of friendship and rapport through the sessions we had done together previously was an important component. As the new guy, I also had to bear some of the brunt.

For example, during one of the countless times we were experimenting with drum sounds, I had to go out to the studio to adjust microphone positions on the kit while Mick kept playing so Ken could listen for the perfect placement. Unsuspected by me, while this was happening, Richard and Mick had planned another of their practical jokes on me. Mick insisted many times that he had never heard of such strange miking techniques:

"Fernandez, you idiot, what are you doing with those microphones on my drums? That snare microphone is not the right one!"

In total confusion, doubting myself and Ken's instructions, I changed

LIFE ON THE LEDGE

microphones two or three times, from an AKG 451, to a Shure SM56, to a Neumann 84, and finally settling on a Sennheiser 441, all of which wouldn't satisfy Mick's demands.

Mick looked over his rack toms down at me and hissed in his most haughty tone, "Fernandez, we thought you were a professional recording engineer, not a correspondence course fellow. You're finished in the business!"

As I was about to burst into full despair, feeling quite insecure and dejected, through the corner of my eye, I looked into the control room and saw the band, along with Ken and Richard, laughing wildly.

They had played me.

They found this ritual humiliation hilarious. My tough British schooling at the Grange School helped me pull through this moment and many more like that during Tusk. *I remembered my old headmaster, George Lowe, and how he preached the importance of a stiff upper lip and how it had allowed him to play a crucial role in allowing Sir Edmund Hillary to reach the summit of Everest. From that day on, I knew I couldn't get emotional when they teased me. Instead, I'd return each jab with a better one-liner. This strategy for surviving helped me later be accepted as a member of the Penguins' Club.*

Everything old has a nagging habit of becoming new again, and so it was that the '70s were a boom time for nostalgia and reappraisal. Often, an artist's love for what came before is the driving force for something original. Brian Wilson was enamored with the vocal harmonies of the Four Freshmen, so he formed a surf band that sang harmony over complex arrangements. Waylon Jennings and Willie Nelson grew tired of the slick Countrypolitan sound of Nashville, so they moved to Texas and let their love of Hank Williams guide their outlaw country movement.

Early rock and roll was enjoying a comeback, too. It began when the low-budget *American Graffiti* and its hit-loaded '50s soundtrack struck a nerve with baby boomers and became one of the highest-grossing films of the decade. Shortly after, *Happy Days* premiered and remained in prime time for the next ten years. In the summer of 1978, *The Buddy Holly Story* continued the retro trend and almost won Gary Busey an Oscar. A month later, *Grease* was the smash hit of the summer that flooded the charts with '50s-themed hits for the rest of the year. Lindsey, by this point, had already produced and played on Walter Egan's "Magnet and Steel," which he gave a doo-wop arrangement that even featured a sock hop in the video. Lindsey's love for Buddy Holly would inspire his own straight-laced '50s-style pop confection with "Oh Diane" on the *Mirage* album a couple of years after *Tusk*. Before the Tusk tour, during prerelease promotional interviews, Lindsey elaborated on his love of stripped-down music when an Australian presenter from the show *Countdown* asked him whether he thought technology stripped away the raw, rock-and-roll feeling. This was his response:

> There's a lot of atmosphere around *Tusk* that does not particularly reflect this supposed state-of-the-art technology that is involved in the process of recording now. That's one thing that I personally feel very strongly about is that the process of recording has lost a great deal of its passion. Rock n' roll, as an art form, certainly the music of the '50s, a good deal of the atmosphere surrounding that music was the equipment it was recorded on, the limitations the equipment provided or held for some of the music. I think *Tusk*, as a work, does not

sound particularly sophisticated, and it was meant to sound that way.

Suffice it to say, after the cultural unrest and political turbulence of the '60s, white America wanted to reassure itself of who it was, and aside from early rock and roll, country music's "simple is better" approach acquired a new vogue as well. Suddenly, cowboy bars, line dancing, and western wear were fashionable and a visible part of the Los Angeles nightlife. Linda Ronstadt and her old backing band, the Eagles, took country rock from an underground sound to a Top 40 staple. With so many people playing country, Willie Nelson even took a risk and recorded *Stardust*, an album of pop standards from the American Songbook that went platinum.

Closer to home, in a strange fusion of cultures, Stevie, who had always wanted to be a country and western singer like her grandfather, was overjoyed that Waylon Jennings, the king of the cocaine cowboys, covered her LA druggie song "Gold Dust Woman" on his latest album. Lindsey, for his part, started wearing cowboy boots with his blue jeans and a cowboy hat onstage. He raved about seeing Elvis Costello & the Attractions, the darlings of the punk New Wave, playing a set of country standards at the Palomino Club in San Fernando Valley. Even John Travolta, the face of disco and '50s rock, sipped a Lone Star and mounted an electric bull in *Urban Cowboy*.

Thus, it wasn't with complete surprise that we greeted Lindsey's new song "That's Enough for Me (Out on the Road)," which was a true country rave up. At the base of it was his lightning-quick fingerpicking, a technique he had honed initially by playing guitar and banjo to Kingston Trio records as a kid during the short-lived folk boom of the

GET TUSKED

early '60s. He already had this music in his blood, and occasionally it would come out in songs, such as the banjo-picked "Say That You Love Me" or his Dobro playing on "The Chain." Lindsey referred to this song as "rockabilly on acid."

This ironic country tinge was one of the new secret weapons of Fleetwood Mac, used either for color or mystery. In between tracking a new song, the band would happily break into a country hoedown to let off steam with Lindsey's fingers flying like Chet Atkins's along to Christine's honky-tonk piano runs, while Mick and John played tight in the pocket like Austin's finest. Lindsey did a straight cover of the country chestnut "A Satisfied Mind" on his first solo album after *Tusk*, and the full band followed suit on Stevie's marvelous "That's Alright" on *Mirage*.

Initially, this was how the band tried to track "That's Enough for Me," like a true country ripper. Lindsey's chicken-pickin' tempo for this song was so fast that on one of the takes, Christine can be heard making a false start and saying, "Shit, that's fast," in disbelief before playing some fine saloon tack piano, glissandos and all. Then, Lindsey was off to the races on the guitar break, letting out an ecstatic, "Hoo-RAH!" that matched the mood. That was the sound of Lindsey having fun with his band, which is why "That's Enough for Me" found a second life as a live stomper on the *Tusk* tour.

"That's Enough for Me" has the fewest lyrics of any Fleetwood Mac song, practically a haiku of one short verse and a wordless chorus. Lindsey was always an expressive singer, but never the most revealing, emotional and at the same time, distant. The song itself barrels along so fast that it doesn't even reach the two-minute mark, a sliver of a bluegrass song that's nothing but pure speed and cocaine excitement. A few years later, Lindsey's fondness for this song and his new sound

LIFE ON THE LEDGE

would find a wider audience with his infectious '50s-by-way-of-the-'80s country mashup "Holiday Road" from the *National Lampoon's Vacation* soundtrack.

During November, tensions between Ken and Lindsey had grown further, as he kept a strong grip on how he wanted his songs to shape up and sound. After some weeks of his seclusion, Lindsey came back to check some of his tracks at Village, and complete some overdubs. He requested that Richard and me to be the only ones present. He also brought us a new version of "Out on the Road" that he had renamed as "That's Enough for Me," recorded on the MCI 16-track at his home studio. We proceeded to spool it on one of the tape machines. This situation was weird for me. Although it was a great privilege to be recording Lindsey, my loyalty was with Ken. Still I couldn't voice my concerns to Lindsey that he was in error. I felt as if I had a front row seat to the Camp David Accords.

"That's Enough for Me (Out on the Road)" had gone through many transformations and versions by the time Lindsey brought it back in, including slowing it down to 15 ips to make sound like a country song on Quaaludes. Like "The Ledge," it had a breakneck speed, close to 248 bpm, with twangy guitars and intense vocal lines. Many music critics rightly refer to rockabilly as early punk music, with roots in jump blues, western swing, and boogie-woogie. Like punk after it, rockabilly depended on simple I, IV, V chord progressions, fast tempos, and simple in-your-face lyrics.

Lindsey was trying to trim all the extra ornaments and build up from the bare bones for this new phase in his career. Whether in his home studio or at the Village, he definitely resorted to the early recording tricks and characteristics of the limited technology and equipment that such studios as Sun Records in Memphis had available in the '50s. During Tusk, Lindsey always had the *Elvis Presley* Sun Sessions *record his brother gave him around the control room. The licks that he plays on "That's Enough for Me" are straight Scottie Moore and the distortion is courtesy of Pat Hare, who played with Little Junior and the Blue Flames.*

Lindsey had already added a couple tracks of electric guitars through a Fuzz Face at normal speed, a new electric bass, new snare and kick overdubs, and a track of lead vocal layered on top of the kick and snare from Mick and a bass from John. The overdubs continued for "That's Enough for Me" for weeks. Ken was back at the console in Studio D after coming to an understanding with Lindsey that led to many of his songs' attaining higher sonic standard. One of Ken's strengths was assembling a fast and rough mix as close as possible to what the final mix would sound like. This was important because if some of the key components of the song are not heard, or the reference mix is too different, it might mislead an artist in his or her decision making.

Listening to playbacks was just as important, if not more so, than the actual tracking of a song. It had become an institutionalized practice with Lindsey that at the beginning of a listening session some thai sticks of premium weed had to be burned. Since it was just going to be Lindsey, Richard, Ken, and me again, I wanted to make sure all the creative juices were flowing with no bad vibes, so what better way to free our imaginations than a little help from the delicacies of the Orient? I got hold of some pure opium from a friend who had just escaped the overthrow of the shah in Iran.

Big O, as it was known, was used for ritual purposes for thousands of years, before encouraging inspiration from the muses of such poets as John Keats, Samuel Taylor Coleridge, and Charles Baudelaire. This highly addictive brown tar paste, when smoked, reduces anxiety and gives a

LIFE ON THE LEDGE

total feel-good vibe that was perfect to tackle some of Lindsey's songs with a totally open mind-set. I made sure we wouldn't risk going beyond the point of no return, and the results were amazing. The studio environment became intimate and conducive to getting good work done on Fleetwood Smack's "That's Enough for Me."

So, after a few additional passes with what sounded good to us, he decided that we would reinforce the rhythm first with more snares and kicks. This we did by overdubbing drums and maximizing the room ambience through a ribbon Beyer M360 for the faraway signal, as well as a M160 for a tighter tonal quality.

The overdubbing work continued with Lindsey playing an acoustic bass accompanied by low-speed acoustics and electric guitars, and one of my favorite string instruments, a steel resonator guitar, or Dobro. It, too, was recorded at low speed and then sped up to achieve that fast, high, and urgent strummed and fingerpicked frenzy of sound. Some of the distinctive fuzz guitars on the song were recorded through a Pignose mini guitar amplifier placed on the empty toilet of one of the stylish bathrooms of Studio D. The Pignose 7-100 amplifier was a battery-powered, 5-watt portable guitar amplifier with one 5-inch speaker that included a rubber volume knobs shaped like the end of a pig's nose. Sometimes, cheaper is better.

Finally, Lindsey's helium lead vocal was triple tracked—a Tusk *trademark—and in the choruses augmented even more. Some of the passes were recorded at lower or higher tape speed to obtain different timbres. We also recorded Stevie and Christine voices complementing Lindsey's, but in the final mix, they were barely audible as an effect. One of the curiosities of this song is a track labeled "Porcelain God" that originally had been the toilet flushing the water out. If you listen closely, you too might hear the Porcelain God giving his blessing to the track.*

11

DROWNING IN THE SEA OF LOVE

> As simple and pretty as the song was, it turned into
> a magical, rhythmic, tribal thing.
>
> —STEVIE NICKS

We were thankful that Hernan was making some behind-the-scenes headway with Stevie, although truth be told, none of us were really aware that Ernie was hanging out with her. He managed to get "Sara" over the finish line with some degree of anonymity by getting the skeleton of the song built. Stealthily, he had been making eye contact with Stevie, the both of them occupying the back of the room, Stevie crocheting and writing on the sofa and Hernan, dutifully taking notes, labeling tape boxes, and operating the 24-track machine.

Hernan had been asked whether he could come in over the weekend and help Stevie record a few demos with Tom Moncrieff, her former bass player in Buckingham Nicks, and his girlfriend, singer Annie McLoone. I had a similar experience with Stevie several years earlier, recording her song "Smile at You" that we couldn't get past Lindsey because she used Tom instead, who played a smoking guitar solo. It would later find a home on the band's *Say You Will* album decades later, which couldn't compare to the original. So, big kudos go to Hernan for getting "Sara" heard.

My conversations with Stevie continued as we found time during the long sessions. She intimated to me her trials and tribulations. Our extended time in Studio D only got longer, and by then we had no set schedule, even through the weekends. Time to rest was a matter of when the majority of the band and recording team just couldn't go on, in spite of artificial stimulants. Encounters with Stevie were a balm in such marathons, especially as tensions grew and exhaustion took its toll. In my case, the day's journey was longer than everyone else's. My responsibilities were extended to opening the studio as well as closing it, to say nothing of the daily engineering duties on the album.

Stevie confided her hidden romance with Mick, which by then had turned into a painful breakup. She also had opened up about how the band had been roughing her up because of her high exposure, which had made her the darling of the press. I had noticed through the weeks after her return from the tour that whenever she was in the studio, she knocked herself out with a cocktail of different stimulants and downers, pot, cocaine, coffee spiced with cognac and Grand Marnier, which rendered her less than combat ready, with the obvious consequence that her chance of fighting for her songs to be included on Tusk *were diminished.*

The band thought that she was a prima donna, and over time, I realized that these conflicts had direct ties to the ongoing feuds she carried on with Lindsey and Mick due to their breakups. Christine and John were out of the ring, but were still confidants and sparring partners. The common ground Stevie and found to nurture our conversations was always music that we both liked, inside jokes on the band and team, as well as her always funny stories that she delivered in a delirious stand-up comedian mode, still full of the beauty, romance, love, and mysticism that she's known for and were important in her songs. She brought cassettes to the studio with songs that she had been writing in those days that I listened to patiently, both commenting on and contributing ideas about how to get them ready for presentation to the band.

A couple of times, she invited me to visit her house after the sessions when we managed to get out at a reasonable time, giving me a chance to experience what the life of one of the hottest female rock star singers was like. To my surprise, it wasn't a pompous state of affairs, with no butlers or bodyguards around, only a few friends that I had met at the studio, and what eventually I realized was her entourage of personal assistants. Stevie showed me some more songs that revealed that her song chest was quite large and there was no shortage of candidates to be part of Tusk. One song in particular stayed in my mind: "Sara." Its melody and lyrics kept coming back to me. She told me that it came to her while clearing her mind doing ballet with a Russian teacher in her special mirrored room while listening to Jean-Michel Jarre's great albums Oxygène and Équinoxe.

By December, I kept up my positive psychology with Stevie, reinforcing the message that she could not afford to let herself down and act victimized, since she had so much to give and express artistically. I told her she wouldn't be happy if she gave in. I helped her get back on her feet. She recovered her usual happy and free-spirited self, was reenergized to hit the studio, and ready to sing, putting forth songs to be part of the gang again.

Tom Moncrieff was a songwriter, producer, and close friend who had been part of the touring band that Lindsey and Stevie put together to support their Buckingham Nicks album. The two of them had been doing home demos that sometimes were just tapes on boom boxes. Basically, the method was simply to record a voice and acoustic guitar or piano pass onto one of the cassettes, which later would be played through the speakers, giving Stevie a chance to add an additional pass of vocal harmonies as it got recorded on the second cassette deck.

After the Thanksgiving break and into the first week of December, the weather had been rather cool, so being indoors in Studio D felt good, allowing us to really focus on the vocal work with the girls. Not missing the sunny SoCal beach that we had most of the year, the band minus Lindsey finished vocal overdubs on "Brown Eyes," "Honey Hi," "Never Forget," "Storms," and "Sisters of the Moon." Of course, the studio ambience with them present was quite different.

By early December, Stevie was recording her lead vocals on "Sisters of the Moon," leaving them unfinished, hoping we could get better takes later. During one of the breaks, she invited me to come in the following Saturday while the band was resting for a couple of days to record a few of her songs in Studio D. The idea was to take full advantage of all the wonderful equipment and rooms in the facility to get some good demos going that could finally make it onto the album, especially the song "Sara." I was delighted. I could cut new songs for Stevie and engineer probable hits for Tusk. Tom Moncrieff would join us as her musical director, since he had been part of an important part of the writing and structuring process in the past, taking on the role that Lindsey usually held.

As I listen to "Sara" today, chills run down my spine, recalling what a trip it was to be a part of it. Stevie's invitation to help her record "Sara" and some other songs couldn't have come at a better time. We had been making Tusk laboriously for more than four months, with me handling various recording duties that went from the most basic to some of the complex tasks involved. So, going into Studio D with a looser and freer mission was just fabulous, especially under Stevie's initiative, which implied good energy and vibes, plenty of laughs, and no tensions whatsoever.

Saturday, December 9 started out very well. I felt rested, as the night before, the band had been reasonable and cut off work by ten p.m. I walked into the kitchen area of Studio D that morning, made some coffee, and turned on the morning news: the Pioneer satellite was probing Venus. Cutting through to the live room, I noticed Stevie's rented tack piano was in place, tuned, and ready to go. I moved it carefully to the middle of the main live room, and placed it sideways so that I could see Stevie's face while she played and sang.

I inserted two AKG 451 microphones close to the high and midsection of the harp of the upright piano, and angled her favorite Sennheiser 441 as her vocal mic. Tom Moncrieff showed up early so we both had time to set up his Fender Precision Bass through a Fat Box close to the piano. He had also a Roland TR-77 analog drum machine that was going to provide us with not only a beat, but also a more elaborate drum pattern. The TR-77 is now a vintage collector's item because it had a warm sound, a bassy kick, and nice percussion sounds that provided cool Latin rhythms. We ran the beat box through the console by way of a Direct Box so we could record it and feed it into everyone's headphones for reference. This was important because if "Sara" was approved by the band for Tusk, the pulse reference was important for what could happen later with the overdubs.

Accompanying Tom was the singer Annie McLoone, who I had met while working on Walter Egan's Not Shy album a year earlier, produced by Lindsey, Stevie, and Richard Dashut. Annie had befriended Stevie while they both sang backgrounds for Walter, even appearing together in the video for his '50s homage, "The Blonde in the Blue T-Bird." Annie also had a wonderful raspy voice like Stevie's and barroom sense of humor that left no one sad. I made sure to position her mic so she and Stevie could look at each other while they sang.

As was Stevie's tradition, she showed up fashionably late with her entourage of friends. She was in great spirits, making jokes and telling stories to us all while lighting some incense and hanging some of her colorful silk scarves. The good vibes were spread throughout Studio D, in which it was in hard need. Stevie, Tom, and I conferenced on what she wanted out of this session, hopefully recording more than a couple of songs, and if we had some extra time, maybe some harmonies and acoustic guitar.

Stevie had many pages of lyrics for "Sara" that she was hoping to get into the song, and a simple chord progression in the key of F with a nice groove in its repeating syncopated pattern. "Sara" was quite different in its style and basic arrangement than Stevie's previous songs, and it was definitely a departure from the country and folk-rock that had characterized her music until then. I felt it had a blend of jazzy feel to it, which together with Stevie's storytelling and sultry voice was really engaging and enigmatic. This song, I knew, was special.

I had a bit of stage fright at the beginning of the session, given the intimacy and importance of the moment that was unwinding, but Stevie's warm, nonchalant persona brought down all the walls, and after a couple of rundowns to get the proper headphone balance, we were set to record. Tom adjusted the tempo of the Roland beat box to a slightly higher bpm to give the song more swing, while Stevie went through some variations on the first incomplete takes, some of which lasted twenty minutes. Stevie was notorious for having difficulty in cutting sections of her songs. It took all of us to finally hone the lyrics and chord changes for a master take that still lasted sixteen minutes!

As we were cutting the song, I felt that "Sara" was already her best song on the album so far, and perhaps her best. Stevie was exultant when she came in with Tom and Annie to hear the master take, asking to hear it again and again, as she tried out some harmonies in the control room, something she always did that resulted in lush background vocal overdubs later. Tom proposed we add a strummed acoustic guitar and a pass of some minimal vocal harmonies by Annie and Stevie.

That evening, we had some extra time, so we cut a couple of new songs that included "How Still My Love," "Outside the Rain," and "Blue Water." As we were wrapping that evening, my intuition was telling me that I had to go all out for "Sara" to be included on the album, as its potential was enormous. As I was saying goodbye to Stevie with a big hug, I told her that "Sara" had to be on the album, and that I would make it my mission to get the band into it.

She looked at me with a sweet smile that said a thousand words, and said, "Well, Hernan, you do it. Go break down my band's wall and fight for it. You have my full blessing!"

I knew then that a special connection had been established with Stevie, but I never suspected how it would turn my life around completely in the following months. I stayed behind after everyone left and cut a reference mix to keep handy when the occasion arose.

By Monday we were all reconvened at Studio D, including Ken and Richard, who I excitedly told of the weekend recording adventure with Stevie and the gang, while not giving them too many details so the mission wouldn't get spoiled before it was time. Lindsey was back to his role as the musical director of Tusk, calling the shots for some of the work we had lined to accomplish before the Christmas break. He was hot to continue working on "That's Enough for Me," and so we did for the rest of the day.

As nighttime came and most of the band and crew left, Mick looked at me with that Rasputin expression that meant transcending time was coming up. He knew that I couldn't refuse, offering me a full mug of beer while thinking of what off-the-wall instrument would fire his imagination to start the after-hours fun. After all our previous transcensions, I knew that it was the perfect moment to grab his attention and try to sell the idea of playing drums on "Sara."

"Hey, Mick! Take a listen to this song that we recorded with Stevie during the weekend. It's called . . . 'Sara.'"

"Sara?" he said suspiciously, with a wink of his eye.

"Yeah, 'Sara,' and its very cool!"

I had the mix ready to roll with the speakers at a good volume. I hit Play with no hesitation. As "Sara" played through its long sixteen minutes, I searched his face, looking for signs of approval or dislike. After the first few minutes, his face was lighting up while his fingers tapped the edge of the console. This was definitely a good sign.

He asked me to turn down the volume and said, "Mmm . . . I like it." He may have only meant the music, but the Sara connection wasn't lost on him after the Halloween party.

"Well, Mick, I would like to ask that this time, maybe instead of transcending, you take a pass at 'Sara' with your drums. I strongly believe it would make a fine contribution to the album."

"All right, Hernandez; let's do it!"

Mick's drum kit was always set up in the live room to the right of the control room window under the moving louvered ceiling, so it only took me a few minutes to position our basic microphone configuration, a Beyer 88 on the kick, an AKG 451 on the snare, a Neumann 84 on the hi-hat, and a pair of AKG 414s as overheads. As I rolled the song for him, he had the brilliant idea of playing the snare with brushes. Mick's an amazing groove drummer, so he got the flow right away, and in a couple of takes nailed the drum part that gave "Sara" such a distinct sound and feel. The song gained in energy and flow immediately from Mick's contribution. "Sara" its first layer of rhythmic arrangement. I thanked Mick for his support and trust, and then we turned our attention to transcending into the wee hours. I thought it ironic that Mick, left to his own devices, still chose a "less is more" approach.

My next move was to get John to play some bass on "Sara," something that I felt quite confident about for several reasons. First, his best mate Mick had already added drums. Next, Tom had already patterned his bassline on John's style, so going off it would be easy. And lastly, I always had John to myself in the mornings and I knew he disliked that his participation had diminished considerably since Lindsey's decision to be a one-man band. Before baiting the hook for John, I decided to give "Sara" a good trim so that we could get a working version for what the future would bring.

The next day, I got to the studio early enough to undertake some major audio surgery. Editing multitrack tape is a delicate operation that when done right can be an amazing creative tool, but on the other hand, since it's done directly to the master, it has to be flawless, which is nerve-racking because if you make a mistake, you've damaged the tape permanently. I managed to trim a few minutes so I had a new version that ran close to thirteen minutes and would be ready for John's contribution. John dutifully arrived first and I gave him a brief intro to what he was going to hear. When he heard the rough mix with Mick's drums, I saw how his face lit up. His eyes were closed and he was moving his head and arms like Joe Cocker at Woodstock, giving me hope that he was up to it. One of the reasons this primary mix with Mick on the drums is so compelling is because Stevie's voice is amazingly strong, clear, and full of feeling. The final version of "Sara," much like on "Dreams," actually used most of this demo vocal recorded live while she played piano. We tried to improve on the original, but we always went back to it.

After this long audition, John opened his eyes, and with his quiet, gentle lilt, said, "Hernan, I like this song from Stevie . . . it would make a wonderful contribution to the album . . . I like its bluesy shuffle feel . . .

And . . . , I thought.

"Let's do it."

Fucking great! *I screamed inside my head.* I asked John what his choice of bass was, and he decided on his Höfner 500/1 violin bass to get that retro midpresence. It took him a couple of passes to nail the track, but he played with so much feeling, maybe, I thought, as a way to get even with the raw deal he got from Lindsey. The passing notes John played gave the heart beat a flow that saturated every measure, practically dueting with Stevie's vocal melody. I was liking this song more and more. John and I celebrated with vodka tonics, John style, which is to say, doubles.

So, it was time to sell "Sara" to the big bosses. I was confident that they would love it and see its hit potential, something that Tusk *was in high need of at this point.* As I hit Play on the multitrack, Richard closed its eyes, as was his usual playback mode, and Ken, ever the instinctive mixer, grabbed some of the faders and tweaked the equalizer on the kick drum to get a mix that he liked, while nodding his head to the beat. It didn't take long.

They were in.

They congratulated me on the work I'd done, but at the same time simultaneously said, "Hey, Airnan, you know that the odyssey doesn't finish here. We've got Lindsey to deal with. Do you want to break it to him and get him on board?"

"Of course. I'm only more convinced now that 'Sara' has to be on the album," I said, without batting an eye.

"Have fun with that," Ken said sarcastically and smiled.

"You know what, Hernan? I'll help you get Lindsey in. We'll wait until he's lighting up," Richard volunteered.

An hour later, as Lindsey was busy at his joint-rolling ceremony, both Richard and I discreetly invited him to listen to this new Stevie song, explaining to him part of the genesis of it and how we'd gotten it to its current thirteen-minute state with Mick, John, Tom, Annie, and Stevie's wonderful live vocal accompanied by her tack piano. Lindsey was intrigued. I don't think he was used to being presented a demo as far along as "Sara" was, and this is where the similarities between Tom Moncrieff and Lindsey became apparent to me.

Lindsey listened earnestly on our big JBL monitor sound system at full volume. A mix of anxiety and confidence ran through my mind, with every minute of music lasting forever. This song was different, an epic. Its poetry was such a distinct change from the tight-lipped lyrics of Lindsey's songs, and its willful ambiguity a far cry from Christine's simpler love nest hymns. As the last note faded, Lindsey turned his face slowly toward Ken, Richard, and me with a meaningful silence before saying matter-of-factly:

"I like it. It's a good song. Let's get to work."

I was so relieved, I could have cried.

Lindsey was hip to it, and that meant that he was going to put his best creative energy into taking "Sara" to its full potential. If anyone was an aficionado of Stevie's writing, it was Lindsey, and he knew exactly what had to be done with all his musical arrangement and production arsenal. The first thing, of course, would have to be cuts.

We sat down to give "Sara" another series of cuts in the 2-inch master, to bring it from thirteen minutes to a reasonable length for a pop album. Our biggest challenge was to keep the core of Stevie's lyrics without butchering its powerful poetical meaning and flow, and at the same time win her approval. To prevent errors, we transcribed the lyrics and edited the text on paper first, and also decided on the general musical structure, or road map, of the song, visualizing which verses, choruses, and bridges were going to be cut. Throughout, I was reminded of Paul McCartney's cutting and shaping John Lennon's long dream poem of Liverpool into the song, "In My Life."

After banging our heads around for a while, we went for the editing blade and started to mark the master with the special white wax pencil, making sure the cuts were done precisely on the beat. Making the crucial tape edits was usually Ken's job, and why Richard nicknamed him "Cutlass." That usually meant beat 1 of the measure with a strong kick hit. To accomplish this, we had to rock the tape moving the reel spools at low speed to hear and mark the exact space previous to the kick drum. Finally, we had a brand-new version of "Sara" that was approximately half the length, to receive the most elaborate set of musical overdubs in Fleetwood Mac's history. Many are so subtle it takes many listens and the use of professional headphones to hear all the layers.

The first round of overdubs started with Christine's doubling of the tack piano, which was no easy task, since Stevie's original track was quite loose, not too tight on the beat, and had a sharp decay. Another problem that we encountered was the fact that the tack piano's tuning had shifted a bit, and there was no time to call for a piano tuner. But all during Tusk, an apparent problem become an opportunity to create some musical magic. In this case, we panned Stevie's piano left and Christine's piano right, conjuring a beautiful, psychedelic calliope effect. Completing the basic instrument structuring of the song, Lindsey played a couple of tracks of acoustic guitars that between muted fingerpicking and strumming foreshadow what Mick will do with brushes later, opening up the song to the bass and drums, and the full syncopation of both pianos.

Something unknown to us got hold of Lindsey when it came to "Sara." He unfolded his best musical artistry with our constant assistance to devise layer after layer of ultraprocessed, highly involved, electric guitar tracks. This is where Lindsey's love for Ken is based: Ken's magic with guitar sounds. He used the same tricks he used on "Silver Springs" during Rumours. The electric guitar tracks were played clean on his Fender Stratocaster in the control room through a volume pedal with feeds to multiple devices, starting with a direct injection to the Neve console through Ken's Fat Box. Another line went to his new Mesa/Boogie amp for its famous warm sustain and growl, while we had a third Sony ECM50 lavaliere microphone taped under the strings between the pickups to capture the subtle string work. This sound source was probably what gave the total sound of the guitars its special character, which we then filtered, equalized, and compressed heavily before sending it to a Leslie rotating speaker placed inside our live echo chamber that we damped a bit with sound blankets. The swelling effect of the volume pedal can be heard through the song, especially close to the end, adding underlying musical drama that complements and enacts Stevie's torn singing. This is how hits are made.

To top it all off, Stevie, Lindsey, and Christine again joined together to add lavish, multilayered background vocals to give "Sara" its special unearthly character, holding off on singing the song's name as long as possible like a dream deferred, felt but not seen, like Catherine's ghost in Wuthering Heights. "Sara" was many things at once: forbidding, alluring, erotic, sorrowful, hopeful, reassuring, and triumphant. This was the power of Stevie's romantic poetry at its best, when she could channel Wordsworth with *a phrase that would hang in your mind forever. I didn't bother to try and decipher the meaning of every line. I'll leave that to the fans. What mattered to me was the overall feeling that comes over me every time I hear it. That has never changed.*

"Hernan, can you load up 'Sara?' Let's take a listen this rainy morning."

It is remarkable, I thought, as I lifted each faders one by one to hear the sounds we recorded for "Sara." I started with the foundation: kick, snare, hi-hat, toms, and overhead drum mics. As I pushed the faders up, I left them in the proper balance with each other, adjusting the panning position in the stereo speakers, center, center, right, left, right, left right, putting it all together.

I brought up the two acoustic guitars hard left and right. Then, I added the two rhythm guitars playing full chords and positioned them hard left and right. Then, Chris's piano in stereo that had been bounced to mono to conserve tracks I placed right center. What was remarkable to me was that, individually, none of these tracks sounded "Grammy-like," just ordinary-sounding instruments, but when I let them all play together, they formed the most beautiful symphony of sounds, a sonic treasure, literally the reason I got into this business in the first place.

Each instrument filled a spot in the sonic landscape with just the right amount of bass or treble to fulfill its intended mission. I nudged the volume of the enormous 15-inch speakers up just a tad, pushing the machine harder until the sweet music filled the room completely and gracefully. Hernan and I looked at each other and nodded with self-satisfaction at our work.

"I think we've got a hit record on our hands, Caillat!" Ernie said, patting me on my back.

DROWNING IN THE SEA OF LOVE

Ray and the rest of the band's roadies even came into the control room from the lounge and exclaimed, "Holy crap, you guys, it's sounding fucking great in here!"

"Yes, it does," I said.

Dashut entered the room in his Greek fisherman's cap, his Ferrari T-shirt, and his *Mork & Mindy* rainbow suspenders—a very distinct look.

"Morning, Richard! Come here. We were just listening to 'Sara.' Listen to this." I hit Play on the Studer.

He reached by me and somehow turned up the speakers even more as he took the joint out of Ray's mouth and took a long drag on it, shaking it as he finished, as if we were breaking the speed of sound.

"Sounds great! Doesn't it?" I yelled.

"What?" he yelled back over the speakers that were easily hitting 110 decibels.

Whenever we begin working on the insides of a song, we open the possibility that we might want to stop and improve or change something. Sure enough, when Lindsey arrived, we repeated our daily entrance routine:

"Morning, Lindsey. Listen to this."

(He takes a hit of pot.)

"Turn it up! It sounds Fucking Great!"

"What?"

The console was always the center of things where we massaged our creations, like sitting in the cockpit of the *Millennium Falcon*, surrounded by banks and rows of lights and switches. At the rear of the room were couches and chairs where Stevie and her entourage and visitors would usually sit next to a floppy-eared bunny doll that someone had sent as a gift. Mick would stand behind the board, staring down at us, and John would usually float listlessly somewhere in the middle of the room, while Lindsey, Richard, and I would paint sound pictures with our $400,000 console. Hernan would move between the console and the tape machine and tape logs, twelve hours a day, every day. This was the world that "Sara" and countless other great songs were born into.

It was on one of these days that Stevie, already a superstar, prepared herself to create a performance that would stand the test of time. The formula this time was not enough sleep, two or three hits of pot, a few sips of Courvoisier, a little hot tea with lemon and honey, and a couple of carefully timed hits of coke, all administered at precisely the right time so as liberate her soul and inhibitions to create the performance of a lifetime. As we queued up the song, Stevie proclaimed playfully like Scarlett O'Hara into the microphone, "I wanna be a star . . . I don't want to be a cleaning lady!" and then proceeded to blow us away with three full takes. When Stevie reached to the top of her mezzo-soprano range for the climactic line, "Sara / You're the poet in my heart," somehow, I felt sure, she would never have to clean another house again.

12

REAL SAVAGE LIKE

> I hate turning on the radio and being able to guess what an entire song is going to sound like in the first five seconds.
>
> —Lindsey Buckingham

For the next two weeks of December, we worked on as many songs as we could, trying to cram in as much as we could before the next holiday break. Mick added a tambourine to "Never Forget," Christine redid her vocal for "Over & Over," Stevie did the same on "Storms," and Lindsey returned to for more overdubs on "Out on the Road," a breakneck hillbilly stomper that would eventually morph into "That's Enough for Me." After these sessions, everyone had different plans for Christmas and different distances to travel to get where they needed to go. Hernan was one of the first to leave, since he was going back to Chile.

The rains that winter season were extraordinarily harsh, with 12 inches of rain in Los Angeles scattered over three months, forcing their way into our sunny days. One day, Richard came into the studio and told us the Tale of the Tub. He awoke that morning and found his hot tub had floated out of its hole, breaking away from the concrete and all the pipes that held it in place. We didn't believe it. He then produced a Polaroid image of it that showed the entire wood-paneled hot tub out of the ground and tilting at a 45-degree angle. Naturally, his description of the event was unforgettable. The face he made, with his eyes bulging out of his head in amazement when he saw his new hot tub floating away, was funnier than his tale of woe. When Richard tells a story, he starts laughing, and the funnier it gets, the more he laughs until he's crying on the floor with laughter, which is very contagious.

Christmas provided everyone with a sorely needed time away from each other and more quality time with their loved ones. I was able to take Cheryl out a few times to some holiday parties. On the way home from one of them, we stopped into a liquor store to pick up an aperitif for an evening of continued pleasure when I noticed a silver coke spoon attached to a Christmas card sitting on the store counter. The card had all the usual colors and decorations with the caption: "Don't Let the Snow Fall off Your Shovel This Christmas!" I showed it to Cheryl, and she smiled and laughed, saying, "We should send one to each of our friends!" There were about fifteen left in the display and we bought them all. We addressed one to each of our recreationally inclined friends, but we decided to address them all anonymously, and sent them all out about two weeks before Christmas. One by one each of our friends asked us whether we sent them a naughty drug toy, and each time, I denied sending the cards. In fact, I started complimenting whoever did because it was such a nice spoon.

The band wasn't officially back to work after Christmas, with Christine and Stevie deciding to extend their break into mid-January. This left us with an opportunity to get Lindsey back in the studio alone to work on his home recordings. Richard made the point that since it was going to just be us guys, we might want to bring in some "outside entertainment." I said we should get Sweet Sweet Connie in to break up the routine.

Connie Hamzy was the infamous groupie who was namechecked in Grand Funk Railroad's hit song "We're an American Band." She got her thrills by being many bands' intimate girlfriend. She supported herself as a substitute teacher when not on the road. I had met Connie when Fleetwood Mac passed through Little Rock. She was by turns equally gorgeous and aggressive. She took me out to the lawn of the auditorium next to the parking lot and offered a sample of her talent. I kept her number. One of our roadies dutifully called Connie on the spot and came back into the studio and said, "Guys, Connie will be here next week. We just have to pay for her flight and hotel!" This idea passed unanimously. We could just imagine Lindsey's face when she came on to him. He was an introvert, and she very much was not. We were in hysterics about it for days.

I arrived for Lindsey's first session back and pushed through the big double doors into the control room, to see Richard kneeling at Mick's feet, groveling for cocaine. This was always a very amusing game they played and everyone just hung around watching the show:

"Please, sir, may I have a toot? Just one, sir, so I can maintain my strength and energy and continue to do your bidding?" Richard begged. You could see in Mick's face that he was thoroughly enjoying the game as he stood above everyone.

"All right, minion, you may have some of my special powder, but only so you can continue to do my bidding," Mick said snidely.

Mick extended his index finger and thumb as straight as they could be and deliberately moved them slowly into the top pocket of his jeans and pulled out a small glass vial containing some very fluffy, slightly brown-colored powder.

"Oh my god, is that pharmaceutical cocaine I see?" I exclaimed.

"Why, yes, it is, Caillat, but you have to wait your *turn*," Mick said to me and immediately turned to Dashut. "Now, beg, minion, beg!"

Dashut grabbed a pencil off the table and, pretending it was a knife, sprang up, holding it at Mick's throat, "Now, sir, I protest! I won't beg any further! I will take what I want! Now, stand and deliver your bounty to me!"

Mick's body stiffened as if his life was in mortal peril. He whispered, "All right, man; keep a cool head. There's no reason that anyone should die today . . . take my tootiledge, but spare my life!" he pleaded. Richard took possession of the small vial and said, "Now, off with you before I change my mind!"

Mick turned and skulked away and they both broke up in hysterics, as did the rest of the room.

"Caillat, I believe you're next," Mick offered, with a raised eyebrow.

I stepped forward and received a small spoonful for each nostril. Pharmaceutical cocaine was just what it sounds like, pure and uncut, but surprisingly more mellow then the standard street variety. It's maybe equal to a half a cup of coffee. Back then, cocaine was something that everyone shared. Even the consoles had little places where you could chop it up. Refreshed, I turned to the room with as much authority as I could muster after such shenanigans, "Let's get down to it."

For Lindsey's session, we decided to start work on "Not That Funny." It was another of Lindsey's punk rock songs, and like "The Ledge," the song prominently featured a guitar and bass that we "detuned" for a lower sound that is further lowered further by hard bends during performance. To add some texture to the sludgy rhythm track, we used a Chamberlin M1 keyboard. The Chamberlin was the precursor to the more famous Mellotron, which was a polyphonic keyboard that played tape loops of other instruments, so you could have a whole band at your fingertips. They were notoriously unreliable and needed constant maintenance. They were soon replaced by the emergence of digital synths, but they were very cool and got sounds that digital just couldn't replicate.

For "Not That Funny," we chose the Cello setting on the Chamberlin, which Lindsey played and grunted along to, even screaming, "You son of a bitch! You bitch!" into the background vocal to accentuate the track's rawness. We then added Lindsey's phased, varispeed, tinkling Stratocasters over the top of the mix, along with another electric, and an acoustic guitar for a mariachi flavor. All the guitars were sent through the tape recorder and then to the console for compression and a squashier sound. We then sped up the lead guitar tracks for a bee swarm effect, the results of which sounded like a Bach fugue in a punk song—postmodern guitar soloing at its finest. With its three chords and two basic parts, "Not That Funny" was a song made possible by the studio to create hi-fi- sounding "lo-fi."

Our second week of bachelor party recording sessions began with more playbacks of experiments. Both Lindsey's Les Paul and John's bass were tuned down in an attempt to make them sound like electric tubas playing through broken speakers, which we then layered over Lindsey's demo track from home. I had gotten word that Sweet Connie had arrived at LAX and was being chauffeured straight to the studio. I pushed up the two distorted electric guitars loud in the mix and turned it up in the control room. Lindsey was slumped in a tall-back chair, eyes closed, listening to the playback I had set up. Suddenly, Sweet Connie came through the back door into the control room, and Richard and I whispered to her, "That's Lindsey in the chair; go get him!"

She then leaned over his chair from behind him and ran her hands down under his shirt, running her fingers through his chest hair. His eyes shot open and he stiffened like an electrocuted robot. She continued moving her hands deep down into his pants as she came around from the back of his chair and sat in his lap while kissing his neck. Then she stood up and took the clearly stunned Lindsey by his hand and led him out of the control room and into the roadies' workroom just past the left isolation booth. She had asked us for a bowl of ice cubes, which she took into the small room with her. Apparently, they were her special gift when performing. Lindsey came back half an hour later, weak legged, with a permanent smile on his face. Lindsey didn't want to talk about his time with Connie, realizing that it was probably best to keep it to himself.

My trip to Chile for Christmas lasted for a couple of weeks, and it was a good occasion to visit family and enjoy the summer weather of the southern hemisphere. This was my first trip back after five years in Los Angeles, so it was quite emotional to see my mother, father, my brother Felipe, and my three surviving grandparents, who were my emotional support when my parents divorced. My sister, Carolina, had left in 1976 to join me in California.

Chile was suffering the horrors of a cruel military dictatorship led by General Pinochet that everyone hoped would last no more than a couple of years. I discovered that a good friend of mine, Carlos Guerrero, had been arrested by Pinochet's secret police, the DINA (National Intelligence Directorate), and disappeared. Carlos had been my hippie, countercultural buddy. As teenagers, we had planned to run away from home together and take a ship to California so that we could join the fight against Reagan's riot police at People's Park in Berkeley who were shooting antiwar protestors with shotguns. We never fulfilled our plans together, but he continued along his path, joining the FER (Revolutionary Students Front) the student's branch of the MIR (Movement of the Revolutionary Left), which was the principal revolutionary movement in Chile, similar to the Weather Underground Organization and the Black Panthers.

After the military coup in September 11, 1973, he went underground and a fought against the dictatorship, hiding for some time before one of his companions was tortured into confessing his hideaway. The death squad soon arrived. Carlos was shot escaping and captured later. He was taken to the infamous Villa Grimaldi torture center and never seen again. Only recently, after investigations and testimonies, it has come out that soldiers had taken Carlos and thrown him into the ocean from a helicopter.

I was saddened and enraged by the news, empathizing with the suffering of all the innocent people that had been imprisoned, which couldn't have been more different from my privileged life in California. All of my years working in the music industry had given me a broader experience of the world. The wonderful moments I spent with my family were tempered by sadness, shock, and the fear that Chileans were living under the dictatorship of General Pinochet, who had no intention of restoring Chile's long-standing democracy. The situation was worsened by a territorial dispute between Chile and Argentina that threatened to bring both countries close to war.

I felt very fortunate that I was able to return and work in the United States and enjoy the freedom that allowed me to live my life and grow professionally. I missed Kris and her daughter, Katy, and was very concerned about my departure. Upon arrival in LA, the customs officer checked my belongings and found two beautiful sperm whale teeth that were a gift from my father from his days managing a whaling operation. Officiously, the agent confiscated them and was going to take them away, but I begged for their return, telling him that they were a sentimental family possession. I wanted them as good luck charms for the studio. Thankfully the agent relented, and I walked toward my gate, singing Arlo Guthrie's "Coming into Los Angeles.

Back in the studio, Carla Fredrick had replaced me in the Tusk *sessions, surviving the Mac humor and doing a good job at it. Carla was a wonderful friend who had been my assistant during the disco days. I missed the Sweet Sweet Connie session while I was in Chile, but Richard reliably gave a theatrical account of it. January 1979 was boys' time, as the girls had taken a longer Christmas recess. Mick, John, Lindsey, Richard, Ken, the roadies, and I continued the* Tusk *saga that by then had entered its sixth full month. Music-wise, we listened to Dire Straits's debut album that included its hit single "Sultans of Swing" that we all liked because of its rootsy groove, great guitars, and the similarity of Mark Knopfler's spoken-sung voice to Bob Dylan's. Lindsey also brought some of the albums he was listening at the time, including the Stranglers, the Jam, and the Clash's first and second albums. The Clash were kicking off its first American tour with Bo Diddley as the opener for the cheekily titled Pearl Harbor Tour in February, and Lindsey couldn't wait to see the band onstage at the Santa Monica Civic Auditorium.*

At this point, Lindsey had come back in full to Studio D, only using his home studio to experiment with ideas and sounds that he could bring to us and try out in full with our huge arsenal of equipment and the various acoustics of the different rooms. He had also teamed up with Ken again, realizing that it was much better to partner with him and us, given the successful results we were getting.

"Not That Funny" was one of the conjoined twins born out of Lindsey's original song "Needles and Pins" recorded at the beginning of Tusk in June 1978—the other being "I Know I'm Not Wrong." These were a batch of song ideas that Lindsey wrote born out of rage and frustration which share the same "Don't blame me" chorus and "Here comes the nighttime" bridge. They speak of a manipulative and ambiguous relationship, and the loud punk and psychobilly explorations served perfectly to convey this desperate message to the world. The lyrics of all of Lindsey's songs reveal bits and pieces of his struggles, either internal or external, which were aimed at Stevie or Carol's drug use or the band or his own insecurities. I felt that was the reason he took so long in writing them and deciding what stayed and what had to be left out.

"Not That Funny" has a fast beat of 135 bpm propelled by a stack of snares and kick drums doubled by another set of electric guitars recorded at high speed to make them sound lower pitched and thicker when slowed down to 30 ips. Lindsey chose to work on this track by himself, so it has a rock-solid bass track, and like most of his songs where he plays drums, there was no hi-hat to play eighth notes. Instead Lindsey relied on a great trick that appears in many of his musical productions, including his later solo albums. One particular example is on his production of Bob Welch's "Sentimental Lady," where a set of fingerpicked acoustic guitars are recorded at lower speed to make them sound like a harpsichord or musical box, which produces an eighth- and sixteenth-note feel. He played sparingly in the verses, and then more heavily in the bridges and choruses, shifting the song's movement and feel.

Lindsey overdubbed tom fills that also added a double speed rush as the song went into its vamp, including finally cymbals and hi-hat only at the end, quite similar to the Beatles' "It's All Too Much" and "Tomorrow Never Knows." The overdubbed drums would be the foundation for a loom of crisscrossing electric guitar riffs and licks, some of them reversed, that he would progressively thread through his vocal melody. In the final vamp, he just let all of these tracks loose, creating a wild feeling that at moments resembles what we called the bee swarm. The lead vocal, of course, was also doubled and tripled on some sections, and occasionally Christine appeared, but her voice was indistinguishable from Lindsey's. Lindsey relied on Christine many times for help on vocals, mainly because of their great tonal blend, but I would also venture to say that because they had no big emotional hang-ups between them, there was no studio bickering and wasting of time.

Another secret weapon we had in Studio D was the Dokorder 8140 reel-to-reel tape recorder. All conversations and musical ideas that happened at any given time in the live room were picked up through a set of mini ambient microphones. It was nightmare to search through since there was no automation or digital coding, but it was very helpful to Lindsey when he was searching for new electric guitar tones. Ken and I remembered that the Beatles had used their tape recorders that had microphone preamps on Abbey Road to plug their guitars into and manipulate the sounds. By saturating its preamp, we sent the Dokorder's signal back into the Neve console, where we compressed and equalized it into the resulting sludgy, rubbery sound on "Not That Funny" and "The Ledge."

But not everything was fun and games during those days, as destiny had an unwanted event prepared for me. A few days after we started the basic track for "Not That Funny," Ken had asked me to do safety copies for some of the songs that already had master takes with some overdubbing, to ensure that in case of any tape dropouts or other mechanical problems, we were covered. It meant that the master tape was played back on one of the Studer A80 and patched directly and precisely into the other Studer, which was recording. This required total concentration on my part, particularly to ensure that the master take was not loaded onto the wrong machine and erased by mistake.

By January, our tape closet had accumulated close to seventy 2-inch tape boxes, each weighing 12 pounds each, so I started early that morning to have enough time to get the job done, and be ready for the evening session with Lindsey, who wanted to continue working on "Not That Funny." I had gotten through most of the transfers by noon and was getting ready to finish up with "Not That Funny." This is when the band's roadie Ray Lindsey came in with an offer: "Hey Airnan, time for well-deserved break. Take a good hit of this joint!"

The fool in me took a deep puff of sinsemilla and chugged a beer with intense pleasure, taking my mind out of the delicate mission I had been assigned. After joking around for a couple of minutes, I told Ray I had to get back to work. And as Murphy's law states, "Anything that can go wrong, will go wrong," I switched tapes incorrectly, and hit Record. It took my brain a split second to realize this huge error, and I slammed my hand on the Stop button as fast as I could, but I was a beat too late. I had erased exactly one beat of the song all through the multiple drum tracks.

I had to figure out a way to repair this blunder, fearing the worst when Lindsey would hear it. Ken and Richard arrived first and saw the horrified look on my face and asked what was up. I confessed my crime and they were completely empathetic and helped devise a quick fix. I remembered that I had done a rough mix the night before that had the missing second from the intro. I proposed we patch the missing audio from that mix and edit it at *the beginning of the song with a surgeon's precision, so when Lindsey would listen to the song, he wouldn't miss a beat.*

It all worked seamlessly and sounded perfect to us. And then Lindsey arrived. We held our collective breath while he began his cannabis ceremony, simultaneously rolling joints and soloing tracks to remind himself of the details. He rewound the tape and played it from the beginning. A second later he jumped out of his chair in disbelief and turned to us with fury in his eyes and screamed, "What's going on, guys?"

"Well, Lindsey . . . the very beginning of the take was erased by mistake as we were making safeties and we repaired it the best we could," answered Richard and Ken in unison, their voices humble in the hope of calming Lindsey, but fearing the worst.

Lindsey interrupted their plea, "I can't believe you guys tried to fool me! Who's responsible for this?!"

Instantly, I realized that Ken and Richard had done their best to support, but I could not put them at risk, so I spoke up in a trembling voice, "It was me, Lindsey. I'm sorry for the damage done."

Lindsey squinted and spat, "You're fired. Get out of here."

I could not believe what was happening, as I walked out of the control room in a haze, looking down miserably with tears in my eyes. A thousand images and thoughts went through my head. I felt totally broken. I hit the lounge and kept walking out to the reception are of the Village. I couldn't think of much more than to sit down numbly on the pillows that filled the floor there. Fifteen minutes passed, probably the longest and most anxious minutes I had lived up to then, just hunched in total despair when I heard Richard's voice: "Hey, buddy, don't feel bad. You're pardoned. Lindsey wants you back." I screamed in my mind, and thanked Richard with a big hug. Apparently, the others appealed to Lindsey on my behalf and softened him up.

Lindsey welcomed me as I entered the control room, "Hey, Ernie, I'm sorry for overreacting. You know we're under a lot of pressure. So, hey, I like your work and welcome back." I accepted the apology and everyone happily turned back to work. It felt so good to be back in Studio D with the band's support. This incident burned on my mind the deep responsibility involved in dealing with master takes, and the care required to preserve them. Other conflicts and disagreements during Tusk tested the balance of the ecosystem that allowed of us to survive and contribute well beyond our individual roles.

Later that evening, as we were taking a break from overdubs of "Not That Funny," we watched the horrible news on the TV in the lounge that a sixteen-year-old girl who lived in a house across the street from a public elementary school in San Diego had injured eight children and police officer and killed the principal and custodian in a mass shooting. When asked about her motive, she answered, "I don't like Mondays. This livens up the day," which would inspire the Boomtown Rats' song "I Don't Like Mondays." A few days later, we heard the news that former Sex Pistols' bassist Sid Vicious was found dead from an overdose, a day after being released on bail from Rikers Island prison in New York. Sadly, some things never change.

When Fleetwood Mac was on tour, the band didn't always get a sound check before the show. Despite its paramilitary operation, something unexpected and uncontrollable would come up, such as like its plane was late or there was heavy traffic or someone made a wrong turn on the way to the venue. When this happened, the Mac would always perform a cool warm-up piece that began with Mick playing a low, contagious jungle beat that Lindsey added a funky guitar riff to and which John

McVie straddled by accenting the riff and locking into the drums for a propulsive groove. Not to be left out, Christine would accompany the boys on her organ with sustained chords.

Richard doubled as the band's live sound mixer and he would get quick levels of all the peaks of the band's instruments at their loudest. Any early arrivals in the audience always loved this "improvised" sound check. We insiders knew this tune simply as the "Stage Riff," and it would sometimes be only a minute long, or occasionally, it might run on for five minutes and become a preshow jam session, depending on how much pent-up energy the band had, naturally or chemically induced.

Back in the studio, it was late January and we had our boys' week and enjoyed the antics and it felt as if the sessions were picking up steam again. It seemed as though we were finally starting to get on the same page. Now that it was starting to look like a double album's worth of material, Lindsey had been trying to consolidate all of his ideas into songs. One of his main contenders was the good ole "Stage Riff," which had all of his favorite ingredients: screaming loud guitar and a flexible groove arrangement that could sustain his weirdest ideas. Perhaps feeling the competition from Stevie's epic, "Sara," Lindsey felt the need to make a bigger statement. He believed that "Tusk" would be his "I Am the Walrus," and that he had the making of a fearsome five-minute hit. Maybe it wasn't as melodic as "Go Your Own Way," but "Tusk" would certainly be an opportunity for uniqueness.

We transferred Lindsey's 16-track home recordings to a clean piece of 24-track tape on the Studer. The demo we first heard had a drum loop in place and Lindsey's highly reverbed acoustic guitar playing the D minor riff with a few lead lines sprinkled in. For five minutes, he sang nonsense syllables in a high register with only "Why don't you ask him if he's going to stay / Why don't you ask him if he's going away" as the only discernible lyric and only one pass at the chorus section with no mention of the word *tusk*. Also present throughout was the child's ghost voice of his "Here comes the nighttime" lyric of "I Know I'm Not Wrong" from reusing the same tape. It wasn't much, but it was cool and had enough to work with, since the song was more a groove with ideas that would come and go as it went.

We started tracking bass, fuzzed out guitars, distorted vocals, and a bunch of other out-of-focus instruments, but one thing that emerged from the sessions was the chorus tag: "Tusk!! Tusk!! Tusk!!!" Lindsey started to notice that the adolescents in the room laughed every time he said *tusk*. To them *tusk* was a hard-on, and the song a phallic celebration. Lindsey began identifying with his audience, slurring comically "reaaaal savaaaage like" into the microphone and adding screaming orgasms and goofy pronunciations of the title. Shortly after, Mick brought in his tusk trophies mounted on either side of the console, which he would indeed use to joke around with it between his legs. There were rubber masks, hands, rats, insects, bloody cuts, and a codpiece laying around the control room. It wasn't as if anybody really talked about it, but things were getting decidedly weird. Here's how Stevie described it: "We'd completely redecorated Studio D. We had shrunken heads and leis and Polaroids and velvet pillows and saris and sitars and all kinds of wild and crazy instruments, and these tusks on the console, it was kind of like living on an African burial ground."

Lindsey's idea of turning what we all knew as "Stage Riff" into a wild and creative song finally became flesh when Mick and John got involved. Lindsey brought his home demos and we discussed how "Stage Riff" could grow into a full song for the, as yet, unnamed album. The key musical element that jumped out of the song was the tribal drum arrangement played with heavy use of rack and floor toms. The other distinctive element was Lindsey's guitar riff that inspired John's funky, syncopated bassline that curls like a snake around the beat and propels the song.

Lindsey's quest for experimentation had both him and us brainstorming through some cannabis smoke on how to really take this musical idea to a new dimension. Studio D was commonly viewed as an instrument to create wacky recording techniques that resulted in unusual sounding parts on many of his songs, so here was another opportunity to keep experimenting. Here was our challenge: We would build the whole song on top of this four-bar drum loop.

First, we started recording a pass of full drums in the live room with Mick doing his own tribal delivery. The drum sound that "Stage Riff" required called for a raw, live roomy setup, contrary to the polished sounds that Rumours had. The snare, toms, and kick were treated with some damping to take away some of their liveness and overtones. In addition to the usual close miking, we used a pair of Neumann 49s farther away to take advantage of the ambience. After careful listening, we selected a four-bar section that had a stable pulse, and proceeded to mark on the tape the beginning and end before splicing it and make the loop. Running a 2-inch tape at 30 inches per second, the four-bar loop measured 8.9 feet and played for 10.7 seconds.

In the days before copy and paste, loops were sections of magnetic tape used to create repetitive, rhythmic musical patterns or dense layers of sound when played on a tape recorder. The challenge was it required very careful splicing of the cutting points, followed by very precise joining of the loop point with special editing tape. And then there were the logistics of threading the 8.9-foot circular piece of tape around the room with microphone stands rigged with tape guides, keeping it taut so it would play continuously while recording the loop. One Studer multitrack would perform the playback of the loop and the other would receive the audio and record for a little over five minutes, giving us a foundation to build on.

The band had used this technique on "Dreams" to evoke a soporific effect, but now we would use it wake up listeners and get them riled up. "Tusk" would be a war chant. We started overdubbing the rest of the instruments and voices onto the loop that would turn "Stage Riff" into "Tusk," the wild concept that eventually christened the album's title. Lindsey, Mick, and John were so turned on with this Frankensteined "Stage Riff" that we set out to build the basic bass and electric guitar that same night, and "Tusk" was born.

After the spooky intro of treated stadium ambience fades in, the drum loop takes us into the first verse. Lindsey's acoustic is the first one heard, joined by Christine's occasional pump organ chords. John's funky bassline jumps in with Lindsey's fuzz guitar and little later, a VSO'd Alembic playing cleanly. To add complete wackiness to "Tusk," Mick thought of recording a wild and free-form drum solo at a faster pulse of 167 bpm, to be spliced somewhere in the song. After a few takes, we selected an eight-bar section that I spliced into the master 24-track after the first chorus. Mick even smacked some lamb chops from the kitchen with a spatula. During the mix, we pushed up the Dodger Stadium–treated ambient track and overdubbed percussions to give his solo an even zanier feel. The tempo didn't match and it didn't have a strong downbeat to come back to the next verse, so Mick overdubbed a reverse cymbal to cut back to the song.

After Mick's jazzy drumbreak-musique concrete section, the song starts building in a frenzied mood with thick fuzz electric guitars being pushed up

GET TUSKED

in the mix that gets more intense with Mick's overdubbed toms that double the riff's rhythmic pattern. When the chorus finally hits, it's an epic call-and-response. The full tribal uprising bursts out with, "Don't say that you love me, aaaahah eeee!!!" answered with a massive shout "TUSK!" followed by another, "Just say that you want me! Aaaahah eeee!!" "TUSK!" Before mixdown, Lindsey thought something was missing. He wanted it to feel like the Disney Jungle Cruise he had gone on as a kid. He asked the room, "Does it sound Zulu enough?" Unsatisfied, Lindsey, Richard, and I went out to the live room to overdub a sound collage of cursing, tribal and orgasmic screams, our best animal sounds, whips, bottles clinking, and my own Chilean profanity, "¡Puta la cagó!"

Later, when Mick and Lindsey chose "*Tusk*" as the album title over Stevie's heated objections, they went a step farther and hired Peter Beard, the world-renowned photographer, to create an African photo montage. One of the days Beard was shooting in the studio, he caught my dog Scooter biting at my pants leg in a shot where his canine teeth were clearly visible: TUSK!

Subsequently, my foot and Scooter's face made the cover of the album, replacing an image of Stevie dancing and twirling, which apparently Mick had tacitly promised her. I don't think Stevie ever forgave me for that decision. Shortly after the album came out, Scooter was hit by a car while chasing some tail. Stevie told me soon after she was glad my dog had died and that she had put a curse on him for stealing her cover. Stevie loves animals, but I think the combination of having "Silver Springs" left off *Rumours* and the band choosing a dog and a foot over a beautiful image of their star singer represented the final slap in the face. Her resolve to go solo stiffened considerably after that, for sure. In the years that followed, it has become the ultimate fan question: "Who's on the cover of Fleetwood Mac's *Tusk* album, and what does it all mean?" Well, now you know, and the only thing I can think of is that boys will be boys.

The weirdest idea for "Tusk" actually came from Mick late into the song's life. While vacationing in northern France, he heard a village band parading through the streets during a fertility festival, and found it poetic. Ever the showman, he proclaimed his grand vision to us that when Fleetwood Mac went back out on tour, we would invite the marching band in whatever city the Mac played in to come up onstage and play along with "Tusk." And that's exactly what happened. In every city, when it was time for the climatic end of the show, the local marching band would enter through the front door of the auditorium, march through the audience, and file up onstage, playing along with the hook from "Tusk." The fans would always lose their goddamned minds in the resulting frenzy. We wouldn't get around to recording the marching band until the summer, but in the meantime the album had taken yet another distinct left turn.

Pleasantly buzzed with good day's work under our belts, we decided to go out to dinner again at Central Park. Everyone took their own car. Bob and Carla sat us all at a big table. We ordered several bottles of Chris's favorite white Burgundy, Pouilly-Fuissé, and we were soon laughing and feeling no pain. The more we drank, the more rambunctious our party became until a full-scale food fight broke out with bread and appetizers being flung like missiles through the air. If you heard someone yell "TUSK!" you ducked your heard because something was probably flying your way. The battle soon escalated to the entire restaurant, clearing the place of most of the patrons except for the more thrill-seeking folks and the staff who recognized the band and wanted to join the party. No one had a camera that night, and there were no paparazzi, just young people having fun. The band lingered after dinner—what was left of it—and hung out with the owners and a small group of fans who couldn't believe what they had just seen. These were some of the good times.

13

DON'T WORRY BABY

> The Beach Boys showed the way, and not just to California. They
> may have sold the California Dream to a lot of people, but for me,
> it was Brian Wilson showing how far you might have to go
> in order to make your own musical dream come true.
>
> —Lindsey Buckingham

The day had arrived at the studio for our digital audio sound demonstration by Soundstream out of Salt Lake City. It was the winter of 1979, and we would be one of the first rock bands to try, and possibly use, this new, cleaner, crisper sound format that would never lose its sound quality. This was the machine that restored the early Enrico Caruso recordings and made the first digital recording ever with an album by the Santa Fe Opera. After nearly losing *Rumours* to wear and tear on our master tapes, I was keen to give this a try on our own soap opera. Frank Wolf, our Village tech nerd and in-house jokester, brought in the Soundstream guy.

We soon found out that this little guy had to be there to babysit the sensitive digital equipment with its trays of custom-made circuit boards every day we used it. My red flags went up immediately. You see, Fleetwood Mac was a very close-knit family, albeit highly dysfunctional, and this newcomer would have to run the gauntlet to be accepted into the day-to-day studio life, or be a drug dealer. The band referred to this as "the Bubble," and life inside it could be rough. The kid's name was Rich Feldman. He looked like a teenager with a beard, but with a great smile that told you he liked to laugh.

"Boy, I don't envy your job!" I said. "Do you always have to babysit this equipment?"

"Yes, the company only recently was able to miniaturize the computer system into a portable rig, and it has to be monitored constantly," he replied confidently.

"Where do you want all this equipment to go?" Frank asked.

"I don't know. Somewhere out of the way? How's Chicago sound?"

"We'll put it into the machine room. If we do something long term, we can figure something else out," said Frank, looking it over warily.

Rich told me they had done some great orchestral live recordings. I said I wasn't interested in hearing something that we didn't work on since we didn't usually do one-take live performances in the studio.

"Can you record us now digitally and so we could compare it to the analog recording, and then A/B them side by side?"

"Sure," Rich said. "Do you want to play something live and I'll record you?"

"Well, let me make sure we understand how this works: your machine is only a stereo recorder, not a multitrack recorder?" I asked

"That's correct" Rich said.

"Then the only way we can use your system is to do our stereo mixes to it."

"Correct again."

"Okay then; let's throw on Chris's song, 'Honey Hi,' and I'll try making a rough mix of it and recording it to our half-inch analog tape machine and simultaneously to your rig. Then, we'll play both versions back at the same time and see whether we can tell the difference," I proposed.

So, that's what we did. We recorded the same mix of "Honey Hi" to both recorders, then played them back through two identical, unmarked faders. I let the band switch between the two mixes. Lindsey was especially guarded, but in the end we all agreed we liked the cleanness and openness of the digital recording, especially because it was exactly the way we intended it to be. Music recorded to tape is slightly modified in the recording process, whereas digital recording takes samples and translates them into on or off, or 1s and 0s, thereby making the information or music easier to manipulate without coloring the sound the way the transformer in our Neve console did.

Although today, there is a resurgence of analog playback, we weren't looking for that. We were looking for a piece of gear that wouldn't change our precious recordings. If I could go back in time, I would probably change my decision in favor of the organic analog sounds. At the time, though, we were shocked at how much analog tape recording changed our sounds, when looking at it clinically.

The first major label pop album that was released using digital was Ry Cooder's '50s throwback album *Bop Till You Drop*, which came out in the summer of 1979. Cooder used Soundstream's competitor, 3M's first digital 32-track recording machine out of Minneapolis, nicknamed "Herbie." Alas, if *Tusk* wasn't such a monster to record, it would have been the first. Music had now entered the digital age and CDs were just around the corner.

GET TUSKED

▼

After the demonstration, Ray came to me at the console and said, "Diane is in the lounge and wants to talk to you for a minute. She doesn't look very happy. What did you do, you jerk?"

"What?" I said. "Nothing yet!"

I handed the controls to Richard and went back to see her. Diane was standing and talking to the studio crew. "Okay, guys—back off; let me get in and talk to her," I threatened.

Diane looked beautiful and was wearing her "Itty Bitty Titty Committee" T-shirt, which made me laugh. We took a walk outside the studio and I asked, "Hey, so what's up?"

"I wanted to say good-bye," she said.

"What?"

"I got fired."

"Why?!"

"The studio manager doesn't like me," she said.

"She's probably jealous of you! I'll go talk to Geordie, and he'll unfire you!"

"No, don't. It's okay. I want to go back to modeling again, anyway. I don't like sitting behind a desk," she said and gave me a hug.

Being no dope, I threw my arms around her and pulled her close. She didn't let go, so I just kept holding and rocking her for what seemed like a very long time until I felt something coming between us and I pulled away. She looked into my eyes and said, "Don't be a stranger, okay? I moved in with my Aunt Penny. Here's my number."

She headed to the parking lot and got into Carmen, her little VW Bug. I went back into the studio and knew I would be calling her very soon.

DON'T WORRY BABY

▼

By the beginning of February, the spirit of the band was high, after making progress on a number of songs despite a near breakup when Lindsey had proclaimed he was going his own way a few months back. His home recording and the lonely sessions at the Village were behind us, and collaboration was once again in place.

Stevie was also feeling better now that "Sara" was firmly in place on the album, and she was more of a presence in Studio D, not only for her songs, but also for spirit and camaraderie, offering whatever was needed of her. John was probably the one that was still feeling some frustration with his exile from Lindsey's songs. After all, John was the father of British electric blues bass from his pioneering work with John Mayall & the Bluesbreakers where it all started, playing behind the guitar gods Eric Clapton, Peter Green, and Mick Taylor that changed rock and roll forever. John didn't relish being put out to pasture in his own band.

The band decided to work on another song from Christine that she had waited to track, the beautiful ballad "Never Make Me Cry." I couldn't help feeling thankful for Christine's solidarity with me when Lindsey fired me, and this song always reminds me of it. She had waited for a long time to record "Never Make Me Cry," so when the day came, we were ready for one of those magic "Songbird" moments. Ken and Richard had planned the session carefully, miking the room just so and placing the Yamaha grand piano in the middle of the room at an angle, so we could see Christine's face while she played and sang.

Lindsey decided to sit by Christine to play a soft strum to create some interplay and dynamics between the two. Getting the exact tempo took a few runs, while we moved the metronome up and down to finally settle on

77 bpm. Christine had this song very well into her system. She had written it on Dennis's boat, and it was a love letter to him. Like a stoic sea wife, she tells him that she won't cut his wings, and how grateful she is for his love. Christine sang and played the song on her grand piano many times and had worked up an excellent accompaniment that had an ear-catching introduction and a great hook of ascending piano chords that mirrored the climax of the chorus and its gorgeous melody. All of the musical and emotional nuances were together and in place.

While Christine ran the song down a few times, singing and playing piano, we decided that her vocal deserved to be tracked later to maximize her full range. Thus, it was only piano and Lindsey's guitar that we needed to get as a master take after only three takes. We doubled Lindsey's original strums, and as always, John added his bass, with total finesse and feeling. Lindsey invited Mick to try some percussion ideas that included a tympani and claves, and Christine to add some luscious Hammond organ swells and some Chamberlin Cello and Flute in the bridge, all of which can be heard on alternative takes of "Never Make Me Cry."

Over the next few months, Lindsey's gave "Never Make Me Cry" a complete overhaul, denuding it from a very forceful piano-heavy ballad and into an airy, slow, and heartfelt plea that emanates from the ocean floor. Lindsey erased Christine's piano arrangement completely and made it "sparse" with a suite of nine electric guitar tracks, mostly on his Stratocaster, some clean and some with growl. We injected his Stratocaster through Ken's invaluable Fat Box, which we used to boost the output of the guitar, and into the console with another line going to a Fender Twin amplifier in Stevie's Hawaiian iso room, to capture its warm, tube sound.

The instrumental layering commenced with strummed tracks providing the basic cadence of the song, while Christine's vocal was buoyed by fingerpicked tremolos and volume swells. Ken, Richard, and I used all the techniques in our bag of tricks to give each guitar sound a different character, creating a unique palette of subtle timbre colors, doused in reverb to conjure the blue, sun-shimmering seabed. The dramatic bridge that Christine originally wrote with a big lead-up into the third verse was now transformed into the softest of interludes with a minimal, repeating nylon-string guitar lick, and Mick's ominous timpani was now a breeze of light cymbals.

"Never Make Me Cry" is an ideal example of how brave creative decisions are made in the studio. What was initially a traditional piano ballad in the same mold as "Songbird," adequate by every possible standard, was taken by Lindsey and metamorphosed into something completely new, and yet the same. "Never Make Me Cry" is still a fantastic song, but by using a less-is-more approach and subtracting the big accompaniment, the most essential element, Christine's superb melody and performance, is left naked, expressing deep devotion and evoking the gentle rocking of the boat in which she wrote it.

To record the perfect lead vocal from Christine, we had to wait until July to take advantage of the warm weather on her voice, meaning a clearer throat to capture her full vocal quality. During the winter, many times it becomes hard to get the best out of a vocalist due to colds and nasal congestion, to say nothing of cigarettes, which permanently damage every singer's instrument. We ran the song from top to bottom, with no punch-ins or cuts to get full takes of the emotion that the song inspires. Christine was always an easy singer to record because she never screamed her vocals, relying on pinpoint delivery to convey emotion. We got a set of five wonderful tracks brimming with happiness because, for Christine's birthday, Dennis had thrown her an amazing party that included a big heart-shaped rose garden placed just below a gazebo where a string quartet *played "You Are So Beautiful" sung by Dennis, with the birthday girl in tears and fully in love.*

Christine's other new song tracked that same week in early February was "Think About Me," a refreshing throwback to the "old school" of Fleetwood Mac's cutting live in the studio soup to nuts, just as we did with Stevie's "I Don't Want to Know." It felt good to go into the studio and have everyone play together like the fabulous band the Mac was. We moved Mick's drums out into the center of the studio with John standing next to him, with his amp in the "Stevie Nicks Memorial Vocal Room," as Richard had nicknamed it, where Stevie was doubling and harmonizing with Christine. Playing her Yamaha electric piano, Chris was in the area just left of the control room and Lindsey played near Mick in front of the control room glass with his amp sequestered in the iso room to the far right.

Since the only live sound being made out in the main room was coming from Mick's drums, we put a pair of AKG 414s spread wide apart and far back from the kit to get a full room sound to add to the ambience of the drums. We were able to cut the whole basic track in about four hours, and then it took another two hours to perfect John's bassline on his Alembic. You can always tell a live track by the feel, and this one was brimming with it. The song has great energy all around from kicking off with Mick's snare-fill intro and John's lightning-fast bass fill that introduces the vocals, to Lindsey's fuzzed-out Stratocaster propelling the song all the way to the finish with a trademark Fleetwood Mac vocal choir outro section supported by a little Hammond organ to spread the pop gospel.

We experimented a bit with "Think About Me," using the Chamberlin set on Vibes, a pump organ, a 12-string acoustic, and a few guitar parts before Lindsey just laid down a blazing lead part and a few fills to bring the song home (you can hear him excitedly letting out an "Owww!" right before it). We decided this was just a rock-and-roll song, plain and simple, and there was no need for clutter or doing too much. Here was an all-too-brief cameo of the *Rumours* formula and the so-called Fleetwood Mac sound in all its pop glory.

February was turning in to a very productive month, probably the one that the Mac and us had tracked and overdubbed the most songs, and definitely the longest-running period of good cheer, with no heavy crossfire, and positive collaborative spirit. Now that much of the heavy lifting had been done, the band had loosened up its visiting policy. Many friends, hangers-on, and free riders visited Studio D, some drawn by the word of mouth that the Tusk *sessions were an ongoing party, others by real curiosity at seeing firsthand the top recording studio in town, and others who were authentic guests that included artists close to the band. Among the latter, we had Eric Clapton, Peter Noone of Herman's Hermits, Bob Welch, Stephen Stills, and one that Lindsey had begged Dennis to bring in: Brian Wilson.*

Lindsey had huge respect for Brian Wilson as one of his main inspirations. The Beach Boys' founder is widely considered as one of the most innovative and significant songwriters of the late twentieth century, a master vocal arranger, and also a revolutionary of out-of-the-box recording techniques and music production. By this time, the former Beach Boys leader had gone from teenage prodigy to tragic LA cult figure. Lindsey always felt that much of Brian's most important work had been overshadowed by his surf hits and that many of his best songs were underappreciated. Much of Lindsey's search during Tusk *had a kindred spirit in Brian Wilson's jour-*

ney on Smile. *Thus, Brian's arrival in Studio D had a powerful effect on Lindsey, and all of us that recognized his genius. Brian was accompanied by a chaperone since he was in recovery from long psychiatric treatments with the notorious Eugene Landy. Brian was heavily bearded and looked good, wearing an Adidas tracksuit. Someone remarked that he had lost a lot of weight, and he explained that he had taken up jogging and was no longer on a cheeseburger diet. The fitness craze was already in full swing in LA by this time.*

It was a visit with surprisingly little spoken, but high in significance and emotions. After a few minutes of chitchat and showing Brian around the studio, Lindsey asked him whether he would play some songs. We still had the upright tack piano from "Sara" in the studio, so Brian sat down and started playing "Sloop John B" followed by "Caroline, No" his famous falsetto a little worse for wear, but still tender as ever. The magic of the moment flowed among us, along with some tears too, especially from Lindsey. Brian's short and sweet visit left us full of good vibrations.

These feelings from Brian's visit manifested in the recording "Think About Me." It was another grand occasion to get the Mac in the studio to play and record together and recapture that vivid group magic that had given it so many great hits. "Think About Me" is the most straightforward rocking songs from the album, driven by the powerhouse rhythm section of Fleetwood and McVie's rock-solid kick-snare-bass steamroller, coupled with Lindsey's riffing closely with Christine's bluesy shuffle on her electric piano.

"Think About Me" has that bouncy midtempo reminiscent of "Don't Stop," including the dynamic duet lead singing of Christine and Lindsey, with Stevie on the harmony, as if the Everly Brothers had a sister. One of the key ingredients of the Rumours *sound was background vocals that functioned as lead harmonies, and here it was again, that same sexual electricity.*

So, by the time Ken and Richard had the basic drums tuned and equalized, getting the band's performance was short and sweet.

A bad sign of when musical ideas were not clear during Tusk, *of which there were many, was when we took hours testing drum kits, tuning the snare or toms, varying microphone positions, and dawdling over the infinite selection of guitars and pianos. This could sometimes last a full session. Everyone would call it quits and agree to continue the next day. This is why "Think About Me" felt wonderful—spontaneous even. In a mere afternoon, the band and crew were running the song down with perfect feel, groove, and sound.*

The band got a good headphone mix from the control room, which is crucial to a happy band and music making. For example, Mick might have wanted a mix where he could hear his drums dry with his kick and snare getting a splash of reverb, and for his listening pleasure, only John's bass and a touch of Christine and Lindsey to make sure he kept the pulse and groove. And so on with the rest of the band. A diverse and idiosyncratic headphone mix is essential to a good recording session. In Studio D, the original design included individual headphone stations for every musician, pioneering a concept that today has very elaborate brands selling this unique product.

Christine and Lindsey always had an unspoken mutual respect and bond that was evident when they worked together on a song. They regained their mojo as duo lead singers and song arrangers, which was obvious that day as they instructed Mick and John on the details of the song. Inside the control room, Ken, Richard, and I talked about facilitating the session and giving them all they needed as fast as possible, knowing that a minor distraction or problem could dispel the magic. Christine sat at her electric piano and sang into an Electro-Voice RE20 with Lindsey facing her a few yards away with a Shure 57 for his voice.

GET TUSKED

The results came in fast as they cut the song in only four takes, deciding after careful listening that Take 2 was the one. Another pointer of when a song idea was clear and structured had to do with the fact that when recording it with the basic instruments and a vocal track, it would stand up straight right away, calling for overdubs that only reinforced the quality and strength of it. Working with Fleetwood Mac taught me that when the original basic track needs more elements to stand up musically, it's a sure sign of weak song construction. Many producers correctly point out that the extreme acid test for song strength is strumming on an acoustic guitar while singing it as if it was just a get-together of friends.

On "Think About Me," you can hear the full extension of the sonic quality that Studio D had to offer Tusk, and of course, the engineering talent of Ken Caillat and Richard Dashut when they helmed the console. The song was structured like some of their classic hits and played in the studio with that feel and intensity that the only a band recording together in a live room can summon. The best acoustic design of the time, the best microphones and outboard gear available, and most important, one of the best Neve analog consoles ever built all performed their jobs flawlessly. The advantage that analog still had over digital was the preamps built into the console with its big transformers that colored sound in a special way. With its wide and open transient response, the advanced equalizers in the Neve included center frequencies that always hit the sweet spot.

With the basic track already solidly in the pocket, building the overdubs was an easy path for Lindsey and Christine, including a piano to accent some of the runs with an early rock-and-roll feel, a Moog synthesizer to double the bass and push those low frequencies, a track of lead guitar where Lindsey unties himself to deliver a short solo reminiscent of "Go Your Own Way," and finally, an exuberant set of background vocals that harmonized *in the final lines of the verses before fusing in the choruses with an emphasis on Lindsey's voice.*

The vocal session flowed really well with the singers' usual high proficiency that made their blend a rainbow of sound. The call of Lindsey's anguished soulful cry, "Baby, baby, once in awhile!" to the response of "Ooooooh, think about me!" during the vamp unveiled a really nice switch of perspective, an understated sense that this was a duet, of both lovers' separate yearning for attention.

During some rare time off, I caught another break with Diane. Her boyfriend was a talented musician and singer-songwriter named Jay Gruska, who briefly sang with Three Dog Night. He was part of the Village gang that always came over to party. I had a few friends up to my place in Tahoe, and one morning I had to pick up my business manager, Brian Adams, at the airport. Jay had told me the night before that he had to pick up Diane at the same time. When I knocked on his bedroom door to wake him, he muttered that he was too hung over to pick her up and would I mind doing it? My face broke into a huge smile, "Why, not at all. It would be my pleasure."

Off I sped to the airport in my little Ferrari. I easily spotted the lovely Diane standing outside in front of the terminal. I pulled up to the curb in front and she happily jumped in. I shouted and waved over to Brian who was fumbling with his luggage and asked Diane to sit in the middle to make room for him in my little two-seater. She had on a little tennis skirt and a halter top and had to straddle my gearshift, so every time I shifted into second or fourth gear, I would say "excuse me" and smile.

A quarter mile from my house, I noticed a highway patrolman clocking me with a speed gun on the opposite side of the road. Naturally, I was speeding. With his being on the other side of the busy twisting highway with traffic shooting by, I decided to show off a little and do something I had done in Malibu a few times before. As the patrolman got back into his car, I apologized again to Diane, downshifted into second gear, and punched it.

Vrooom!

I shot around the next curve at full speed and made the turn onto my street while the cop was trying to cross the grassy highway divide with his lights spinning. I whipped my little Ferrari up the driveway, behind the house, and out of sight. We held our breath for a few seconds as the siren screeched by my street.

We were safe.

We laughed at the thrill of our little act of civil disobedience. Diane was impressed and still delights in telling the story to this day.

Shortly after, it was Jay who was throwing a party at his place in Topanga Canyon. During the party, I wandered off and discovered Diane was sitting alone in her bedroom. She said she wasn't in a party mood and that she and Jay were probably breaking up. I ended up spending most of the party in the closet of her bedroom sitting on the floor among her shoes and getting to know her better. Sitting in the serenity of her little walk-in closet, I confided that if she didn't have a boyfriend, I would be definitely applying for that position. She hinted that that position might very well be open to somebody like me. The best part was when I stood up to say good-bye to her, I gave her a hug. And, as luck would have it, it felt so good hugging her that I just kept on holding her and it became one of those magical hugs the lasted almost a minute. Fate had set in motion a relationship that would change my life.

14

EVERYTHING YOU DO HAS BEEN DONE

> We are perfectly capable of not spending that amount of time, but we're learning more and more, as we should be, in the studio. Not necessarily learning how to get more technical, but perhaps less and less technical, using very sophisticated machinery in the proper way without letting it use you.
>
> —Mick Fleetwood

As I was preparing to leave my house for the studio, I heard the phone ring and hesitated a few seconds before picking up the call. Ken's voice on the line was tense, as told me that today we were going to work on another of Lindsey's songs, an issue that I know made him anxious. The good thing was that Lindsey was coming back to Studio D to record one of his songs with the band, specifically with one of the best rhythm sections of rock and roll, Mick Fleetwood and John McVie.

Walking to the Village from my home a few blocks away along Sawtelle Boulevard, I noticed how one of the most typical LA landscape images, the palm trees, were rocking dangerously. The image reminded me of so many opening shots for movies or TV series where the action takes place in LA, so I started singing "LA Woman": "Took a look around to see which way the wind blow." I wondered what the day had in store. I couldn't help but wonder where Lindsey's push for "no more of the same" was going to take us, not only musically but sonically. He had already thrown curveballs to the band and our recording team, leaving us out of his songs, and pushing Ken to accept the unacceptable in terms of sound quality. Today wouldn't be any different.

It was only a few minutes after me that Lindsey showed up with a JVC "ghetto blaster," making us think he was listening to new music on the radio, or that maybe he had a demo of his new song. The mystery was resolved quickly as he had us listen to the cassette played through our deck and the big JBL speakers in the control room. What we heard was a raucous recording with Lindsey's voice loaded with rage and accompanied by a pumping piano. The song he selected for this comeback was the scathing "What Makes You Think You're the One."

With his usual diplomacy, Richard commented on what a good song it was and how much it was going to gain with Mick and John in the studio on it. Ken didn't comment on the noise attack that we had heard; instead, he cut to the chase and asked Lindsey for his ideas on how to record the song—maybe his vocal and piano together with Mick and John in the live room?

Lindsey was sitting by the $400,000 custom-made Neve console, puffing out a cloud of cannabis. "Well, I want this JVC deck to be our main input recording device. I like the vibe it gives this song. I like the edge and distortion it adds."

"But, Lindsey, are you joking?! That's good for a demo, but not for a record. Is it a crime for it to sound good? It'll be compressed to hell," Ken responded in utter disbelief.

"I don't want something that's too cute," was his only reply.

Lindsey may have been half baked, but his decision was well cooked, because he liked the distorted roomy sound that he associated with old proto-rock recordings, such as Chuck Berry's "Maybelline." The plan was to place the JVC deck in the middle of the room, after carefully checking the music balance and making sure that, through its little, five-cent microphones and cheap electronic capacitor-limiter circuitry, all the instruments and voice were present. This deck had a set of L/R audio line out RCA connectors that fed the audio signal when the cassette deck was placed in Pause-Record.

So, Ken and I spent a good deal of time going back and forth between the control room and the live room, moving the boom box until we got a decent pickup of this unique trio. Lindsey sat in the piano sideways like Jerry Lee Lewis, screaming his vengeful vocal lines, as he directed across the room Mick to hit his drums with a wild, tribal fury while John played a punchy, sonorous march that never kept still. It's one of Mick and John's best moments on the album.

In spite of Lindsey's dilettante desire to record through only the boom box, Ken pushed for a parallel setup with our superior array of studio microphones to ensure clarity later on, if need be. This call from Ken would be key in getting this song sounding right yet still preserving its raw, "lo-fi" character.

Another important consequence of having Mick and John back in in the studio playing "What Makes You Think You're the One" was that Lindsey realized that with the proper musical direction, this superb British rhythm section could demolish any of the young bands he was listening to the time. This session brought Mick and John back to his songs, a key development to realizing these songs live on the Tusk tour where some songs, such as "Not That Funny," would run nearly ten minutes. A highlight was Mick's remorseless thrashing of his trash can drums and his array of cymbals, especially the 18-inch Paiste China, providing a rhythmic counterpart to Lindsey's primal screaming, reminding me of John Lennon on "Mother" and "Cold Turkey."

The darker side of "What Makes You Think You're the One" was rooted in the lyrics and performance that revisited Lindsey's feelings toward Stevie and their past as a couple, a breakup that was only two years old at this point. If there was any doubt of who the song was about, Lindsey did his best to imitate Stevie's distincive vibrato, giving it a bleating, goatlike quality, and her rudimentary piano playing, which he knew made her self-conscious. This only served to exacerbate Stevie's feeling of mistreatment by her ex, in a very dysfunctional way that I was about to discover directly from her. Stevie provocatively described her experience making Tusk as being like one of the hostages in Iran held by Lindsey as the Ayatollah Khomeini who had seized power of Studio D. To Lindsey's mind, he felt forced to work on Stevie's songs and use up all his best ideas even when he had no desire to. Regardless, their exchanges became more aggressive, with Lindsey throwing his anger and sarcasm around in the studio, and onstage when he literally hit her with his guitar. Life imitating art imitating life.

At this point, the band had worked on over half of the twenty songs that would eventually become *Tusk*. Each of the writers had brought forward and tracked at least four songs apiece, enough for an album with all three writers equally represented. *Tusk* would later be accused of being a Lindsey solo album since he would garner the lion's share of songs. Those claims were valid. No one told Lindsey any of his songs weren't up to snuff. Chris would bring in only one song that wasn't used, and quite a few of Stevie's that Hernan recorded along with "Sara" would go unused because she was so dependent on others to bring her songs to life. Unfairly, Stevie, the brightest star of a band full of stars, had to campaign more, and she wasn't always able to do that. This is why some of Stevie's more vicious answer songs to Lindsey such as the potential classic, "Smile at You," which predated *Jagged Little Pill*, didn't see release until thirty years later, by which point it had lost its bite.

"Lindsey's Song #6," better known as "What Makes You Think You're the One," would be one of the harshest songs on *Tusk*. It's the sound of barbarians at the gates, with a martial drum beat built around the snare and kick and straight-ahead, ham-fisted piano chords that just pounded the song's vindictive lyrics forward like a battering ram. The lyrics detailed how much resentment Lindsey still felt about how much of his life Stevie had revealed on *Rumours*, how much fame she had received as a result, as well as some not-so-veiled criticism of her work. After every damning rhetorical question that Lindsey spat, a jury of tape-saturated electric guitars would back him up, the volume swelling up like a screaming mob. I didn't tell him so, but it was one of my favorites of his, and had a lead vocal performance that was as thrilling as it was corrosive.

"What Makes You Think You're the One" could just as easily be an angry charge leveled by the band at Lindsey and the pressure he was under to be its savior. Although we were all as supportive as we could be during the sessions, it was clear he had a persecution complex fueled by the drugs that his girlfriend was feeding him and that we all took to keep working our balls off. Lindsey wasn't the only paranoid person in the room, but he was the one whose songs we were being paid to record. The full band played through this ragged march, and at the time, we were at least a little bit optimistic about Fleetwood Mac's playing as a band again. Sure enough, when the band played the song live for the *Tusk* tour—one of the few it played from the album that the tour was supporting—all of its members would really sink their teeth into it, the song's bloodletting serving as each night's group therapy and Lindsey's absolution.

After all that angst, I needed to take a break from the studio. Without saying a word to anyone, I ducked out of the double doors and into the sunlit hall. It was strange not seeing Diane anymore. Next to her old reception desk was a hippie lounge, a mirrored room with pillows covering the floors. It was just outside Studio A, where Steely Dan were having problems of its own recording *Gaucho*. I was a huge fan of Steely Dan, especially *Countdown to Ecstasy* and *Katy Lied*. I even went so far as using the last half of the intro of "The Boston Rag" for my answering machine. I sat there alone in the flop room, numb to the world, my ears ringing from listening to loud music all day. One of the guys from Studio A came in and collapsed across from me. We both sat there for a few minutes, letting our ears cool off.

Then suddenly he said, "You're Ken Caillat, aren't you? I'm Gary Katz. I'm the Steelys' producer."

"Wow; hello, Gary! It's a real pleasure to meet you," my mood lifting.

"Dude, we can hear Fleetwood's kick drum in Studio A."

"Oh, shit; really? Sorry!"

"It's all right. Hey, can I ask you a question?" he said. "How do you get such amazing bass sounds for Fleetwood?"

"What?" I exclaimed. "I was trying to copy *your* bass sounds!"

"No, seriously; what's your secret?" He smiled.

I wanted to pinch myself.

"Well, I generally prefer to use John's direct bass signal more than his bass amp, and other than that, it's probably that John is always needling me that his bass isn't loud enough, the bastard."

"The squeaky wheel!"

We both laughed.

"Hey, why don't you come over to the session, meet the guys, hear what we got?"

"Gary, thank you, but I have to take a rain check—I can't listen to loud music right now."

"I know what you mean. Well, happy trails." He got up.

I eternally regret never going over to Studio A to meet Steely Dan and listen to its work. What was I thinking?!

As I watched Gary trundle back to his studio, the permanently calm Ray Lindsey came to get me. He looked panicked, which was rare for him.

"Hey, Ken, come quick! There's something wrong with Mick!"

I shot up and walked briskly past the gold records on the wall to Studio D. Ray told me that while I was gone, Mick declared that he was going to snort the longest line ever, which he then proceeded to do.

This was trouble.

I swung open the doors and sprinted into the control room. "What's wrong with Mick?!"

"He feels really sick and thinks he's going to pass out." Hernan looked at me, worried. "The line was as long as the Neve!"

Mick was lying down on the sofa in the studio lounge, pale as a ghost, and all the girls were talking on every available phone to get advice on what to do. Mick, the father of two girls, was only thirty-two but starting to bald, and suddenly looked old beyond his years. *This is it*, I thought; *Mick has finally snorted himself to death; here comes the heart attack*. I pitied the guy.

Everyone peppered Mick with questions, "When did you eat last?"

What did you eat? Are you hungry now? Do you feel lightheaded?" Mick just lay there, nodding incoherently.

They rushed in an "emergency" dinner from Central Park and got Mick to eat something. As it turned out, he was hypoglycemic, meaning he had low blood sugar. As all the girls and crew doted on our fallen leader, engineering took a beer break, relieved that we had dodged a bullet. For the next six months, Mick was put on a very strict diet consisting of small, balanced meals served at regular intervals of every three hours. The fridge in the lounge would be full every day from here on out with veggie plates.

Mick was sitting up on the couch loading up on protein and carbs and drinking orange juice instead of his usual beer, which probably had been the cause in the first place. He said his neck was killing him from the fall. Gabrielle at the Penguin office had some experience with low blood sugar and explained that Mick's body was reacting to no food, lots of cocaine, and too much Heineken.

"Where's LB?" I asked.

"He got fed up and went home to work on his songs more," Christine said forlornly. "It's still not the way he wants it. I think we're never going to finish this record, I'm afraid, if Lindsey can't figure out what he's looking for."

Throughout the room came a simultaneous guttural tone from everyone agreeing with Chris. Mick, always managing, said that Mickey Shapiro, the band's lawyer, had gotten him an appointment with his doctor the next day, so we could call Lindsey and tell him to stay home and work on his songs there. Then, Mick said, when he was better, we could get back to recording, thereby putting all the blame on himself.

EVERYTHING YOU DO HAS BEEN DONE

Probably many music lovers wonder why artists, producers, and recording engineers take so much time and become so obsessive in the search of the perfect take or sound. Why go through such a lengthy process to be satisfied with it, polishing it to the point where sometimes the original demo is nearly unrecognizable? When nonindustry people get a glimpse of what it takes to do a record, they cannot believe the patience and persistence that musicians, producers, and engineers display to achieve some sense of perfection. Of course, the particular circumstances that surrounded the making of Tusk *added elements to this OCD behavior that became a pitched battle during those thirteen months.*

Mainly, it had to do with the relative balance of sounds to one another within a song. By the time that we were recording Tusk, *there were already some set ways on how to record and mix a rock or pop song. Our team of recording engineers on* Tusk *weren't dogmatic about these rules, but they were conscious of them—some things you didn't do for very good reasons. But Lindsey, both as a striving artist and a fledgling engineer, was all about "possibilities." He was very much in favor of experimenting with the balance of a recording and confounding expectations about how something should sound, to say nothing of the pop song format.*

One of his favorite obsessions at the time was guitar distortion. He was fascinated by the effect of distortion on guitar amplifiers and the reaction it received from baby boomers that impacted the status quo of manufacturers in the early days of rock and roll. The use of distortion in guitar amplifiers occurred as an accident that changed the landscape of popular music, as young proto-rockers started overdriving their amps beyond the manufacturers' recommended volume gain. Meanwhile, the manufacturers, which were mainly small shops located in the Midwest, threatened to stop selling their equipment to stores that catered to rock-and-rollers. Eventually, they saw that this was the future and caved to the massive demand of aspiring rockers and distorted guitars became the soundtrack to a cultural and musical revolution.

To Lindsey's mind, overdriving a cheap, Japanese ghetto blaster to get the same guerrilla distortion made sense, a nod to the old days and to the DIY ethic of his own time. Anybody could do this. You didn't need an outrageously expensive console or Mesa/Boogie stack to get this sound. In the context of Tusk, Lindsey's vendetta to get away from the sound that millions of people around the world adored, revolved around his belief that rock musicians were not an exclusive membership club. Pure rock and roll was the bastard son of blues, folk, and country: born in the fields, grown in basements, and matured in dingy clubs. It belonged to the people who didn't question the aesthetics of their favorite music, but judged it by their heart, when it touched them and changed a few minutes of their day.

A week after Mick's collapse, Diane brought her sister Kristy and her husband, Craig to meet me and maybe a few members of the Mac. I was leading my guests down the hall and into the inner sanctum, but as I got to the studio door, Lindsey burst out of it and saw me and said "Caillat! This mix is fantastic! You're worth your weight in gold!" and threw his arms around me, almost picking me up off my feet in a bear hug, which was impressive since I outweighed him by 30 pounds.

"You're a fucking genius! You figured out how my song should sound!" he said, as he put me down and rubbed his hands together in approval.

I introduced him to Di's family. Craig was beside himself with pride, seeing a rock star praise me that way. This was our first meeting and he was already picturing free concert tickets and the rock-and-roll lifestyle for him. The strange thing was that I hadn't even been working on "What Makes You Think You're the One." Apparently, Lindsey had gotten in earlier than me and loaded his tape on and was listening to my setup from the night before of a different song, and probably being stoned, he put two and two together and got eight, and I got a bear hug.

I considered correcting his misconception, but I knew it would embarrass him to point out his mistake in front of everyone, and let's face it, I could have used a pat on the back from Lindsey. Di stayed about an hour with everyone in the control room and then left. Before she departed, she asked me whether she could stop by later, after the session, as she had something she wanted to ask me. Sure, no problem, of course.

It always seemed to work out that some days just become guest days and it goes out there into the universe that Fleetwood Mac is open for visits. Luckily for me, everyone had left at around nine that night, just before Diane arrived. I was cleaning up a few things and Diane was sitting in the lounge of Studio D, talking to Carla Frederick, my favorite Village assistant engineer, who was taking a break from one of the studios. She and Diane came into the control room. I gave them both a kiss and asked them whether they wanted a beer. Diane jumped up and offered to go pour them.

"Wow, she looks great," I said after she left.

"You know she's not with her boyfriend anymore?" Carla confided.

Oh, really? I exclaimed, my eyes wide. "Well, thanks for stopping by, Carla. I'm sure you've got to get back to your session! You can take your beer with you," I said, laughing.

Di brought back three cold mugs of beer, and after a few minutes,

Carla drained her mug, excused herself, and left. Meanwhile, Diane and I had been talking so much, we'd hardly taken a sip. Diane joined me on the couch, making just enough room for Scooter to join us. She came to tell me that her birthday was coming up and asked whether she and her sisters and her mom could use my house in Tahoe to celebrate. "Absolutely," I said. It was a pleasant sensation being at the studio with a beautiful girl and not working.

"I hear you broke up with your boyfriend?" I said, trying to conceal a slight smile on my face.

"Yes," she said; "he wasn't ready to get serious."

"Well, he's an idiot! A complete idiot! The last time I saw him here at the studio, I warned him that if he ever let you go, I'd be all over you!"

"Really, all over me . . . ?" she said, leaning in to kiss me.

I turned toward her, put my arms around her, and kissed her long and firmly.

I made out with the most beautiful Diane. I instinctively and unconsciously reached under her sweater and put my hands on her breasts, and she took an immediate deep breath in, the wind passed over my tongue when she exhaled, and her warm breath filled my lungs. By this time, I was red hot and she could tell she needed to slow things down.

She kissed my cheek and said, "I can't stay any longer; I have a modeling interview early in the morning."

She stood up.

I rearranged myself quickly as I stood up with her. I told her that she could pick up the key a week or so before her birthday and to call me so we could do this again.

"Or you can come over to my house and bring it to me," she said.

"Let's do that!" I said. "What about this Saturday?"

"Sorry, I can't. I'm going to an event with my stepmom at the Playboy Club."

"Your stepmom?"

"Yeah, she's the erotic novelist Raven Touchstone."

"Can I come?"

"Bye, Ken!"

15

MISTRESS OF MY FATE

> We have three writers. I write all the time. Lindsey writes a lot. Christine writes. And to have waited three years to have three or four songs . . . I mean, I write three or four songs in in three months—or more than that. One isn't enough for me. Wasn't enough for Christine. And most certainly was not enough for Lindsey. So we had to do a double album in order to be true to the fact that we are our own writers.
>
> —Stevie Nicks

I woke up late the next morning to the sound of heavy motors in the distance. I was still high on my romantic studio encounter with Diane. I hopped out of bed and pulled back the curtains to behold another bright, sunny day in Malibu. I slid open the glass door out to the small, oval, concrete porch on the edge of the slope, and yawned as I stood naked, peeing into the sunrise. I could see, through the thicket of pines and sycamores, a bulldozer clearing boulders and rocks off the Pacific Coast Highway. I didn't really think much of it. The Big Rock Mesa area of Malibu had been shifting for the last few years, to the point that most of the pipes in the area had been moved aboveground until the area settled down. The heavy rains this winter hadn't helped, either. The trees were probably the only thing keeping the mountain from sliding into the ocean.

I whistled for Scooter, who was out doing his business, and went back inside my bedroom. *Boy, I wish Diane was here*, I thought, I was pretty sure she was the one for me. I decided to call her and invite her to come out and spend the day together. As the phone was ringing, I worried I was rushing things, but she answered before I could hang up.

"Hel-lo," her sleepy voice crackled, trying to get it together.

"Hi," I said sheepishly, "I'm sorry if I woke you," trying to think how I could undo this call. "Ummmm, I was just looking out at this amazing day from my bedroom window, and I . . . thought . . . how you'd probably enjoy the view, too, and I . . ."

Just spit it out, Caillat, I thought.

"I think you should come over here and spend the day with me. My pool is heated and I've got steaks we can barbecue?"

"Okay," she said, cutting me off. "I had a really nice time last time. I guess I could stand to spend a *little* more time with you."

"*Great!*" I shouted. "Don't forget to bring your bathing suit, or *don't* bring one. It feels great to swim in that warm water, naked!"

She laughed.

"Good-bye, I'll see you soon," and she hung up the phone.

"What just happened, Scooter? Did I just sound like a big girly girl?"

Scooter tilted his head sideways, like WTF? My heart raced as I bolted down the long, open hallway and out onto the brick patio and nudged up the temperature of the pool heater. The pool house had been closed up for a while and it was like a sauna inside; all the glass doors were covered in condensation, which gave it a nice effect, but made it hard to see the ocean.

I went back into the kitchen to check my supplies. I had Champagne, vodka, margarita makings, steaks, hot dogs, everything a well-stocked bachelor pad should have. Now all I had to do was to shower and wait for my new girlfriend to show up. I was feeling giddy. Just then, the phone rang and it was Judy Wong from the Penguin office, calling to tell me that Warner Bros. had booked a five-person film crew to spend about a month in the studio with us, shooting a film of our making this album.

"*Five people? A month?!*" I yelled. "Does Mick know about this?"

"Yes, Kenneth, they all know. I just wanted you to know so you can be prepared to give them what they need."

"When is this supposed to happen?" I asked

"In a couple of weeks, around the end of March."

"Okay; that should be fun," I said sarcastically.

"Behave yourself, Kenneth. They won't be in the Bubble for long." She hung up the phone.

"Crap! More people in the studio. Just what we need!" I told Scooter and headed back in to shower and get ready for my date. I looked at my bed and realized I should probably change my sheets. Before jumping in the shower, I put the stereo on my favorite San Diego radio station and picked out my nicest Hawaiian shirt.

Then, there was a hard knocking on the door, which surprised me.

I knew there was no way Diane could have gotten here so quickly. Since I was still stark naked, I grabbed up my dirty sheets and hastily fashioned a toga before I approached the door. I opened it up a crack and said, "Hello?"

A motorcycle cop straight out of *CHiPs* was standing on my welcome mat in his helmet and mirrored aviators.

I felt a shock. He looked at me a bit funny.

"Good morning, sir; sorry to disturb you," he began. "Do you own a blue, English Ferrari?"

Oh shit, I thought, *they got me. All those times blowing through speed traps has pissed them off enough to go door-to-door.*

"Uhhhhh, no, officer. I do not . . ." The Dino just happened to be in the shop.

He looked at me a little closer. My heart was thumping.

"Do you know whether one of your neighbors owns a blue Ferrari?"

"Not that I can recall. It's a maze up here. I don't really know my neighbors," which was the truth.

"Well, all right. If you see one, please call this number," and the policeman leaned in past the door and handed me a card.

"Will do, officer. Good day." I almost closed the door on him.

Jesus Christ! I thought, walking to my master bathroom, shedding my toga, *that was fuckin' close.'* I looked at myself in the mirror and noticed something odd. My nose was crusted with coke from the night before. I got in the shower.

The doorbell rang an hour later. I opened the door cautiously before swinging it wide to see the beautiful Diane with the flawless skin, standing there with a small travel bag in her hands.

"Hey, you!" She smiled.

"Wow, you look great!" I said, and she really did. I stepped forward and kissed her with my arms around her. "Care for a margarita?"

"Sure. It's the perfect day for it."

I blended up some drinks until the ice chunks were bite-size and there was a head of foam bubbling on top. As I filled our decorated glasses, my dryer emitted a large buzzing sound.

"Do you want me to get that?" she said.

"Um sure, it's my bedsheets."

"You're washing your sheets?" she queried, with a raised eyebrow.

"Yup, something every guy should do," I said, hoping she didn't read too much into it.

She came back with her arms full of my sheets, "Wow, I'm impressed. Come on, I'll help you make your bed. It's always easier with two people." I followed her back to the bedroom, where we both put the sheets on the bed. There was something very hot about her making my bed, the anticipation of it after all these months.

The next morning, we awoke and I asked her whether she wanted to go to the beach. She was up for it, but she had taken my advice and hadn't brought her bathing suit. So, we decided to take Scooter down and play Frisbee. She drove us down to Topanga State Beach and we walked out past the wind-bent junipers onto the sand and took our sneakers off.

"Can you throw a Frisbee?" I asked.

"Of course!" she said, looking at me as if I was an idiot.

"Great," I said, stepping back and creating distance. "Run toward the water!" I threw it perfectly to her, but she screamed and blocked her face with her hands and the Frisbee fell onto the warm sand.

"No worries," I said, laughing. "Now throw it to me!" I jogged slowly, parallel to the water, to make it easy, but when she threw it, she held on to it too long and it went behind her and into the water, almost killing a pelican. I looked at her, smiling.

"I ran track and I can do other things good!" she said in defense.

As it turned out, that was a very true statement. I laughed and waded out into the surf just before the Frisbee was washed out to sea. We spent the next couple of hours playing with Scooter and practicing how to throw a Frisbee. Eventually, she got the hang of it. We went back up the hill to my house and soaked in the pool, watching the sun go down. We woke up together that second morning without a care in the world, completely natural. She gave me a ride to work and it was as if we had known each other for years.

"Thanks for helping me unmake the bed," I said.

"It was my pleasure. See ya soon. We'll get the sand out."

On March 29, 1979, the five-man film crew arrived. It was headed by established documentary film director Tom Spain. He had two cameramen, a sound guy, and a black-and-white still photographer, Randall Hagadorn. They were booked to be with us every day for almost two months, until June 4, when we were scheduled to record the University of Southern California marching band at Dodger Stadium. Everyone showed up on the first day of filming dressed to impress. We all had a laugh when Mick, John, Lindsey, and Richard showed up in tweed outfits for their movie debut. Henceforth, they were known as the Tweed Boys.

As fun as being in a movie sounded, I knew it would all be a lot of work. Their sound guy wanted to get a special audio feed from our console for everything we recorded. On the first day, the guys came in with about 100 pounds of gear, cables, and lighting, which only made our control room already full of equipment, that much more claustrophobic. If you've ever been on a movie shoot, you know that even the simplest shot takes forever to set up, getting the lighting right and the camera angles perfect. Now, add that to the fact that they're filming a performance by the band members who have to get it right, too. So, everything now took three times as long for a process that was already meticulous and time-consuming. This documentary probably delayed the release of *Tusk* by at least a few months.

Much of the documentary was done cinema verité to an extent. It was interesting to me, seeing everyone playing nice with one another. The way they could switch it on and off. I remember one of the first interviews they did was with Lindsey talking about how much he loved working with John and what a creative musician John was and what great bass parts he thought up. Then, they asked John about working with Lindsey. I thought they both were going to choke on their words. John, as always, took a more humorous approach, saying he'd prefer not to say what it was like working with Lindsey, that he was a religious man and didn't want to lie for fear of being struck by lightning. They all laughed . . . sort of.

The first order of business was to recut, for the cameras, "Save Me a Place," to make it look like a band performing. We had John play his Gretsch bass. Mick, looking absolutely miserable and bored, played a single floor tom in a white linen jacket and neck brace, the result of his recent doctor's visit, where they said he might need a spinal fusion. Lindsey sang a work vocal softly into a Shure SM57 so not to have his vocal bleed into his guitar mics. He had his hands in his blazer pockets with the sleeves pushed up in the androgynous way that California guys adopted back then that was everywhere in the '80s. This was as dressed up as Lindsey got in the studio, still wearing his flip-flops as a reminder of his boho days.

GET TUSKED

I felt it was a nice gesture, on Lindsey's part, to have John play. And the way John played bass accents on the turnarounds was a nice change from Lindsey's straight bass playing. But I knew this performance would never replace our current master recorded at Lindsey's house. It was telling that the first line of this song used to be "I don't know why I have to win," which was reminiscent of "You don't know what it means to win" from "Never Going Back Again." Lindsey came from a family of athletes and could be very competitive, which often came out in his art, and in his personal and professional relationships, for better or worse.

By the end of March, we prepared to wallow in one of Lindsey's favorite songs, "Save Me a Place," a simple song recorded with his MCI 16-track at home and brought in for improvement at the Village. Ken and Richard, at this point, felt more empowered to speak more openly to Lindsey as coproducers of the album in music matters, and specifically on his songs. So, in spite of the fact that we all liked "Save Me a Place," they made it clear after a few playbacks that the song would be immeasurably better if it was attempted in Studio D with John and Mick. Lindsey had slowly come back to collaborate on the girls' songs and his presence in the studio was more continuous.

As usual, nobody except John McVie and me arrived at Village before noon. While I set everything up, John played his Gretsch to loosen up his fingers, looking fresh and happy to be back playing. The band's delayed arrivals always helped me complete all the tape machine and Dolby rack alignment rituals, and the basic setup of the microphone layout. Together with Ray, we set up Mick's full drum kit, Lindsey's Mesa/Boogie and Marshall amps and cabinets, plus six– and twelve–steel string acoustic Martins, in case they were needed.

Richard came in earlier than Ken that day, so he played a bit of drums in his Charlie Watts imitation, loosening them up before another the key ritual of tuning every piece that gave Mick such an amazing sound. Ken walked in at the same time as Lindsey and Mick. By then, we were all prepared for the session. We played the original home studio 16-track to remind Mick and John of their parts, and set the metronome to the correct pulse of 61 bpm. Then, it was out to the live room, where they went with us to help accommodate their sounds.

Lindsey's original home demo from October had a very simple drum track based on a strummed twelve-string and low-tuned snare, highly padded, so it wouldn't ring or crack. The drum thudded along on the 2 and 4 and Lindsey played a simple bassline that supported the downbeat with a hi-hat coupled with a capo'd acoustic guitar to get that double-time feel the song had.

In the live room, Lindsey used an electric guitar for structural reference, playing to what Mick and John were adding to the song, while offering his usual suggestions to keep it simple and minimal. Mick was to hit just his snare and John was to pluck nothing but root notes with no passing notes. After a few runs, it was clear he wasn't happy with their accompaniment, finally inviting them into the control room to listen and talk about how he wanted the feel of the song to be. Ken, Richard, and I could tell that we had come full circle back to Lindsey's one-man band mind-set. With a clear direction for the song and no patience for the "possibilities" that Mick and John might bring, tensions had risen again. John requested a second vodka tonic to make it through this calvary.

Neither Mick nor John complained, and Ken and Richard kept cool. Richard and I went out with Mick to retune the snare to fit the demo character of the song, which basically meant lowering the pitch and tightening the rattlers. As I was moving away the rest of the kit and microphones, Mick sang, laughing, "Do you hear the drums Fernando . . . ?" Even today, I still hate that ABBA song that somehow brings back some of the more traumatic feelings of working on Tusk, with its endless power struggles and the contempt that accompanied some of those sessions.

The three men ran the song down a few times to get a tighter sound before we hit the red button on the control deck of the beleaguered Studer multitrack. They did eleven takes, settling for Take 6 as the master. Lindsey wanted to get the rhythm structure going on the song, so he suggested Mick replace the hi-hat with brushes on a trash bin that were doubled. By the end of the session, Lindsey told John he didn't like his bass part, and invited him into the control room to try a few more takes under his guidance, which he did, switching to his Gibson violin bass as a way to change the sound.

Lindsey still wasn't happy, and by this point the vodka had done its job and John was in no mood to continue the struggle, so he dumped his Gretsch bass into the trash can. Together, Mick and John sat on the back couch, riding the bench, with gaffer tape on their mouths in an act of silent protest. The scene was tragi-comical and surreal at the same time. Lindsey, for his part, just took John's bass out of the trash, played a few passes that were to his liking, and then it was settled, to everyone's relief, that we call it a night after a long day of Tusking.

A few days later, to preserve the intimate, acoustic feel of his pleading ballad, Lindsey once again made use of the Andean charango I had given him. He retuned it before taking a couple of runs to nail a great take that can be heard in left side of the mix. Once the instrumental track was tight, Lindsey started to work on his backgrounds, which he did all by himself, doing a three-part quasi-barbershop harmony ensemble that explored the lower part of his range and blended with his lead vocal. The lyrics were classic Buckingham, concise and conventional, but effective. Lindsey was an exceptional singer, both passionate and technical, and on Tusk, he was at the top of his game. One example of this is when he went into the chorus and added full vibrato to the endings of all the voices, achieving the near impossible task of ringing at near perfect time, to create a deeper emotional mood.

"Save Me a Place" was one of the special moments of Tusk when the band gathered in the control room to listen to a rough mix after the session's long day. Somehow the vulnerable vibe of the song had managed to heal all the bad feelings that accompanied his exile of the band. We had dimmed the lights down to a minimum and just sat there with drinks in hand to listen. The mood turned from relaxed to melancholic and a wave of sadness crossed the room as the last sounds of the songs faded away. Lindsey was in tears, leading to Christine's weeping as well. The rest of us just sat in silence, observing the feelings that were embracing us all. No words were spoken, but it was clear that what had seized us all was a fragile Lindsey pleading through this confessional hymn not to be forgotten or left out by this family that was his own, too. Christine got up and walked over and gave Lindsey a big hug. I still keep this memory as one of the highest points in the making of Tusk.

When I think of the "The Dealer," one of Stevie's most underrated demo songs during Tusk, I remember an incident that occurred around that time. During the '70s, the drug trade was one of immense importance in the music business. It was represented by the friendly drug dealers that studios allowed to peddle their goods as long as they stayed cool and peaceful. They were dealt with like any local merchant, and they treated their customers accordingly. Village Recorder had a couple of dealers who catered to the bands that that we all knew and socialized with, even going to lunches. The drug business had yet to reach the all-out war that erupted during the '80s with victims of the Colombian and Mexican cartels splashed across news magazines.

Assistant engineers were good referrals for dealers, especially when an artists had an emergency. Unfortunately, we were also the connection to moving bigger amounts when artists decided to scale up and invest in bigger stashes than just buying a gram. I was approached a few times by dealers to be that middleman. It was known that Fleetwood Mac was a big client, and although the profit was tempting for someone making as little as I was, I never felt comfortable with the idea. Today, I'm happy not to have fallen into making easy money with the band and contributing to its addictions, since I'm sure would have ruined my life, as it did to other former colleagues and crew members.

One of those dealers was a Chilean friend, who one day showed up at the Village while we were recording Tusk, with an unusual visitor and proposal. Reception called that this friend wanted to talk to me urgently since he had a big artist with him who wanted to speak to me immediately. I looked into the pillowed reception room, and there was my friend with this weird and wasted-looking guy who looked familiar, but I couldn't place him.

My friend looked up at me and said, "Hey, Hernan, let me present Sly Stone."

I couldn't believe it.

"What an honor to meet you, Mr. Stone. I understand you did some recording at the Village some time ago," I said politely, trying to mask the shock on my face.

I thought that I had seen a lot by then, but it was hard to see Sly out of his mind and looking the way he did. I respected him as a songwriter and producer and loved his music. Here was one of the heroes of Woodstock, whose epochal performance had moved a generation, beyond fried. I knew my friend had become hooked on freebasing, so I realized then that Sly must be his new drug pal and they were still rolling from their all-night session

Sly broke the ice fast, saying "Hey, brother, just call me Sly, and I'm here because he told me about your experience in the music business and I would like you to be my manager."

I thought that this surreal moment could only have happened in Los Angeles. Of course, I was honored by the offer, but the magic spell was only going to last as long as the white tornado and whatever crazy ideas arose from it. I knew I had to get out of this situation and fabricated the quick excuse that I had to get back in the studio with the Mac, and that I was honored by the offer and would have to think about it and respond in a few days. And that was the last time I saw or heard from Sly Stone. His next album, released a month after Tusk was entitled Back on the Right Track.

It's strange how certain incidents and events are somehow connected in one way or another. Three years had passed since Stevie Nicks wrote "Dreams" at the Record Plant studio in Sausalito on Sly Stone's piano in an empty black-and-red room that had a sunken recording pit in the middle, and a big black velvet bed with Victorian drapes, which was much in her taste. Now, here we were trying to cut her song, "The Dealer."

The first time I heard the song was when we were cutting the demo of "Sara" and a few others that Stevie would use on her solo albums. Stevie played "The Dealer" on the piano a couple of times, singing it with intensity and cracking jokes, as the double meaning rang heavy in those days. She asked whether we liked it. I liked it immediately since the song had that Mac beat and witchy groove that characterized "The Chain" and "Gold Dust Woman," making it another good candidate to be cut by the band.

By the time Stevie brought back "The Dealer," several months had passed and it received a lukewarm response by the band. To this day, it's a mystery to me why her bandmates didn't give it a better shot, and why Lindsey's involvement, which was essential to its future, had been so minimal in comparison to what he had done for "Sara," or all of Christine's songs. But this always seems to be the case in the life of bands, the song that gets away. Only in hindsight, with the benefit of digital formats, can we look back and confirm such glaring omissions.

We approached the recording of "The Dealer" the same way it had gone with "Think About Me," with the whole band playing live in the studio: Mick's full drum set in his special area, John's bass direct to the console, Christine on her Yamaha electric piano in the iso room to our left, Lindsey on electric guitar through his Mesa/Boogie, and finally Stevie singing and playing keyboard live in the Hawaiian iso room. Here's a partial transcript of the 1/4-inch tape log:

STEVIE: *The chord changes in this are real subtle.*
CHRIS: *I know. You'll have to play a few times because, I mean, we just listened to it on a cassette once or twice.*
STEVIE: *It's real simple. Basically, the verses descend. I'd really like it to be rock and roll, y'know? As opposed to, I mean, it could be real kind of pretty, but I'd just as soon it not be. Got that, Chris?* (Laughs.) *Not. Pretty.* (In a small, worried voice.) *"I don't know how to play piano not pretty.*
CHRIS: *Yeah, I just want to know the chords.*
STEVIE: *I don't know what this chord is.* (Plays.)
CHRIS: *I think the rock-and-roll part is going to come from the bass, drums, and guitar. I might end up doing something similar to what you were doing except for the middle bits.*
STEVIE: *For sure. For me, I've always played it so simply that it's hard to keep the rhythm in the singing. It was written so much on that, when it changes a little bit, it's real hard to sing it.*

MISTRESS OF MY FATE

CHRIS: *Mick, you wanna play something or what? Mick?! Ken! Richard! Oi! Yeah, I'm sittin' in here, like, suffocating. Tell me what's happening? There's no air in here; what am I supposed to do while you guys are in there having a party?*

RICHARD: *We're trying to get together here.*

CHRIS: *Mick's poncing around doing nothing. Mick!* Get on the fuckin' drums! I'm in here suffocating! *Get on with it! There's no air in this room! Gimme a break. If you're going to have a party, let me know!*

STEVIE: *Christine needs a fan in there. Somebody go buy her a fan.*

CHRIS: *It's a stale air, anyway. We need fresh air. What I'm saying is that there's not much definition on this piano. But as long as I can just bash away, is that all right? Let's do it.*

STEVIE: *Do you think somebody can get my glasses out of my purse, because I can't see my words or anybody else.*

JOHN: *Absolutely ridiculous. I can't live with this. Absolutely awful. I mean, my god. Raymond!* (In German accent.) *Schnapps und beer und cigaretten und der Feuer.*

LINDSEY: *Also, do you have an extra beer or Perrier back there? I can't hear no fuckin' guitar in my cans at all.*

CHRIS: *Neither can I.*

JOHN: *Got any explanation for this, Hernan?*

Guitar comes in.

CHRIS: *Welcome to the solution, baby.*

MICK: *Air-nan is my special pal.*

LINDSEY, in faux Chilean accent: *Geeee-tarrr. Ready for another Blue Hawaii, Mick?*

CHRIS: *Let me answer that.*

237

STEVIE: *On the verses, it doesn't go like that, it goes . . .* (Plays.)

LINDSEY: *I know. I know. I listened to the song. I know exactly how it goes.*

STEVIE: *Yes, I know you know, but nobody else seems to.*

LINDSEY: *Oh, you're talking to Mick, right?*

STEVIE: *I know you know. Well, as long as you know it, then.*

JOHN: *I think I might be sitting in the control room.*

STEVIE: *My song is ruined.* (Laughs.)

JOHN: *Where is my bass sound?*

KEN: *You're plugged in direct.*

JOHN: *Is that good?*

LINDSEY: *Is that the "now sound," Ken? Okay, we're ready. Let's go.*

JOHN: *Stevie, I'll sit this one out. It's just a boggler.*

STEVIE: *Yes, darling, okay. Listen, if you sit right here, you can watch what I'm doing, which is very simple for those of us like me.*

JOHN: *If I sat there and watched you, if it makes no sense to fuckin' you, it might make more sense to me, I don't know what is what those black and white things* are.

STEVIE: *Neither do I.* (Laughs.)

JOHN: *My genius comes from here. Or the rear.* (Laughs, and starts singing "As Time Goes By" over Stevie.) *Suggestion . . . suggestion, as Lindsey and Stevie know it, and I have absolutely no idea what's happening, and Christine is floundering, why not do Mick, Lindsey, and Stevie?*

STEVIE: *That power trio of all time.* (Laughs.)

JOHN: *Well, two out of three's good. At least get it down.*

LINDSEY: *It's a new power trio dream.*

JOHN: *I just don't want to waste everybody's time. I'm not playing beats. I'm playing notes. If the notes are wrong, it'll sound nasty.*

The band jumps into a barrel-house boogie-woogie.

JOHN: *Richard, we're going to have to delete the bass.*

LINDSEY: *This is déjà vu from an hour and a half ago.*

CHRIS: *That's because we're no further ahead than we were an hour and a half ago.*

LINDSEY: *Why don't we play it?*

CHRIS: Exactly.

STEVIE: *Chris, that's far out because it kind of sounds like a saloon piano, y'know? And this song is kind of a saloon song.*

CHRIS: *Stevie, this piano costs sixty thousand dollars.*

STEVIE: *I know!* (Laughs.) *And my mother said I'd always be singing in saloons. I like the saloon feel. It's a saloon-gambling song. Think: gambling and cards.*

LINDSEY: *I wanna rock ya baby . . . rock you alllll nigggght looooong!*

The band falls into an easy, twelve-bar bluesy shuffle.

STEVIE: *What a* band! *I mean we could go back to England. Back to the pubs. Well, we never were there, but we could learn.*

JOHN: *Stevie, don't knock it when you're starving. We'd been through that for seven years.*

STEVIE: *No, I know. I like it.*

CHRIS: *I do, too.*

STEVIE: *Chris, you can come over to my house and we'll sing the blues.*

The band kicks into "Rock Me Baby." Christine sings lead and Stevie harmonizes.

STEVIE: *Chris, I liked it.*

CHRIS: *That's a real oldie oldie oldie.*

STEVIE: *It was a good harmony thing, too. Note the perfection in which I was following you.*

GET TUSKED

CHRIS: You were singing the right part, too.

STEVIE: I know. We'd be killer on a two-part blues number, Chris.

CHRIS: Stevie, I bet if we did that onstage, it'd go down a storm.

STEVIE: We'd kill 'em. I'm absolutely sure of it. But the other three would probably kill us first. I like it. Remember we never went through the blues years.

CHRIS: All right, let's do your song.

STEVIE: Lindsey, help me with the time. Should this be faster?

LINDSEY: No.

STEVIE: There's too much going on, I think. We're losing the rhythm of it somehow. Well, I don't know what it is. I just wanted it to be so straightforward, and since it's difficult, I don't know. What do I know? Nothing. But I know that it should be straightforward.

LINDSEY: NoTHING?"

JOHN, with German accent: You know nossING?

STEVIE: NoSSING? (Laughs.) Linds? Lindsey? I wish you'd play more. Or I just don't have very much of you in my phones, and I need it. Isn't it wonderful to be needed? I guess it's not.

LINDSEY: The key to getting this track is . . . not stopping.

MICK: Yeah, I just want to hear it back after we've done a few.

LINDSEY: Well, we've got to finish one.

STEVIE: Well, maybe the band has listened to it enough that they've learned it now. I mean, I don't know, y'know?

MICK: It really could be a real interesting thing, like 'Station Man' with a twist.

STEVIE: Richard, can you ask Ray if I can have some more COCA-Cola? Yeah, I'm off the heavy peppermint thing.

Band plays a take that breaks down.

STEVIE: *It dropped, didn't it? The tempo, when the drums came in? Lindsey's playing a bossa nova. Is it for real?*

LINDSEY: *I liked it.*

MICK: *It's not me.*

STEVIE: *Is it me?*

MICK: *It fuckin' ain't me. No.*

LINDSEY: *Start it faster then, if you want to do it faster.*

STEVIE: *Okay, well, I thought I did.*

MICK: *You're all going out of time.*

LINDSEY: *Maybe, you're just screwed up.*

MICK: *Oh, that might be it.*

Lindsey plays Chuck Berry licks and John plays "As Time Goes By" on his bass.

STEVIE: *Mick, do you wanna take a break?"*

MICK: *No.*

LINDSEY: *Is my pizza here yet?*

STEVIE: *Lindsey wants his pizza.*

RICHARD: *Not yet.*

STEVIE: *We're hiding it from him. Okay, I'll start playing, and then you start playing, and then we'll actually do it. I'm also out of my, uh . . . COCA-Cola.*

It was clear that Christine, John and Mick went through the mechanics of taking the song beyond its original demo, but without much direction from Lindsey on the arrangement, while Stevie was incapable of inspiring the others to focus on the task at hand. Lindsey trumped the song through a lack of enthusiasm. That much was clear as he went through the motions playing very basic guitar which never tipped the rest of the band as to where to take the song and give it energy and uniqueness.

"The Dealer" session provides insight into how a band works or doesn't work in the studio. Goofing off, complaining, fighting, passive aggression, and overmedicating are common symptoms that a band is drifting and losing patience. "The Dealer" had a trickier chord arrangement than Stevie was used to writing and required a host of dynamics to bring it to life. Stevie has said that the band never wanted her to make music lessons as they feared it would interfere with her gift, which made her dependent on them, and others, to properly groom her songs. Sadly, the band didn't rise to the occasion and Stevie didn't push them to. I still believe that "The Dealer" could have been a huge hit for Tusk, an album that needed a few more blockbuster Stevie songs. Stevie knew the song was good and tried to record it again for Bella Donna, but again it was shelved. Eventually, "The Dealer" came out as the lead single from an album of unreleased music years later, relegated to the "lost gems" pile of Fleetwood Mac songs that almost were.

16

A YEAR GONE BAD

> We're perfectionists to the point where it may be worth it to scrap something because it's gotten too perfect and try to get it until there's a good feel.
>
> —Mick Fleetwood

By this time, we're eight months into the album, and it's all become routine now. We all drive in to work, fully expecting to be there at least ten hours. We've become family, and not just the band and the crew, but the studio people, the food runners, the guys who park the cars. We've accepted that we're prisoners in the Village. It's a very tight-knit; everyone is in everyone else's lives. Richard has a parade of women coming through his life and into the studio. The roadies come and go, always keeping a few steps ahead of the band. Lindsey mentions he hasn't talked to his mom since Christmas. We have all begun to synchronize our lives. We all come in when we feel like it, and somehow we all arrive together. The ashtrays are full by midnight and empty in the morning. Every hour is consumed by our music. If you get tired, you can have a toot or go upstairs to Dr. Death's office to get a B_{12} shot. We finish one thing, and then someone says, 'Let's pull up this song and give a listen,' and so we do. We never seem to get tired of listening to these songs even after a year of hearing them over and over and over again. We may only spend an hour on a song, or it may become an all-day-and-night project. One of the new band mantras is "So close, but yet so far."

April was a month of listening sessions with some sporadic recording for the cameras. Sometimes, to help us see the big picture, we would do rough mixes of each song and listen to them all back to back. That would usually entail creating some sort of running order, such as two fast songs and then one slow song, ideally each from different writers so nobody felt left out. Superstars are children, too, and must be handled with kid gloves or be prepared to face the consequences. It can be very political. Every band member needed to know he or she had Richard's and my ear, and that secretly we might like that artist the best.

Big picture month also meant making mixes, adding a part here and there, then making more mixes until we had a rough album assembled, which unsurprisingly was not just one album, but enough songs for two albums. At this point, we weren't sure whether we would pick the best songs and make a single album, or God forbid, make a double album. I was excited to take the best songs and try to make one super album. However, with this band, that could be difficult. I could imagine how the conversation would go:

"You're not thinking of cutting out one of my songs are you?"

"Well, honestly, I was thinking we'd have to cut more than that if we want to make it a single album."

"Wait! Don't walk away mad! Don't hate me! But it was Richard's idea!"

I chuckled, thinking how that would go down.

When I raised these concerns to Mick one night, he, as always, had an answer at the ready, "Kenneth, imagine an album jacket that would hold two albums, but we only sell the single disc holding half of the songs. Then, six months later, after the fans have absorbed it, we release the second disc, and its jacket fits into the first package, completing the artwork and making picture whole!"

"That's brilliant! That way we keep each disc at the retail price of a single album at Tower because a double album would be too expensive for people to buy at fifteen ninety-eight," I reasoned. "Have you discussed this with the label?"

"Yes, they love it!"

"Great, because I'd hate to sequence a double album. Do you think we could put all of Lindsey's songs together on one side, for when people just want to binge listen to LB?"

"Let's see how it goes in the next few months," he wisely suggested.

It was a slow but productive month of April showers, making thirty rough mixes of all the songs, giving everyone a complete picture of what we had to work with and how much work we had left to do. Another consideration we had to factor in at some point was our budget with Warner Bros., which would run out in the near future, and the band would have to go back on the road to pay some bills and sell some records. We weren't worried. We could feel the homestretch approaching.

One of our mottos on Tusk *was "Never a dull moment." We could pass all the hardships just by stepping out of the control room and mixing whatever we needed for the moment. Although Studio D came complete with bar provisions, Fleetwood Mac comprised a serious bunch of drinkers, so they and their cronies could expect to find Dom Pérignon, Cristal (the Champagne of czars), Chivas scotch, Stoli vodka, Beefeater gin, Bacardi rum, Jose Cuervo tequila, Rémy Martin and Courvoisier cognac, Drambuie, among other* alcoholic delights, fully stocked at all times. The only piece of equipment that didn't always perform as planned was the tap that refused to deliver cold Heineken. The beast inside the beer machine was rebelling against its masters, often pouring out only a foamy, lukewarm brew, prompting Richard at one point in the evening to say in his impeccable John Wayne imitation, "This beer . . . tastes like . . . slime!"

Spring was upon us when Lindsey brought into Studio D several 16-track, 2-inch tapes of "I Know I'm Not Wrong," another one of his songs that was labeled "Lindsey's Song #1." This song wasn't unknown to us. It was one of the first songs we tried to record for Tusk on June 26, 1978. As the acknowledged music director, Lindsey had the authority and strength of vision to run the band through its paces to find the right tempo and feel, easily amping up his performance to become the dynamo that the others followed. Out of those original attempts to track the song, it had a far more basic rock-and-roll Rumours sound with some performances that were among their most inspired and hardest-rocking moments, Mick playing a straight beat and John filling the space with a limber groove that danced, Christine giving it color, and Lindsey screaming improvised lyrics. These scratch tracks were the palimpsest Lindsey endlessly erased and wrote over. The new versions from his home studio featured the now familiar arsenal of Kleenex boxes, fuzz guitar, pillows, bongos, toy piano, and bathroom vocals, practically a blueprint of his future work.

As we had done before, the 16-track tape was turned into a 24-track to facilitate overdubs that required many tracks beyond what even we had available. But thanks to a new technology available in those days, we used an Adams Smith synchronizer to get our two Studer 24-track tape machines to run together to get more tracks to fill with the overdubs and arrangements that Lindsey required. It would take a few runs to get the machines to sync,

Christine McVie recording a lead vocal

The Fleetwood Mac All-Stars

Halloween 1978

Bob Welch, John Courage, John McVie, and Ken Caillat

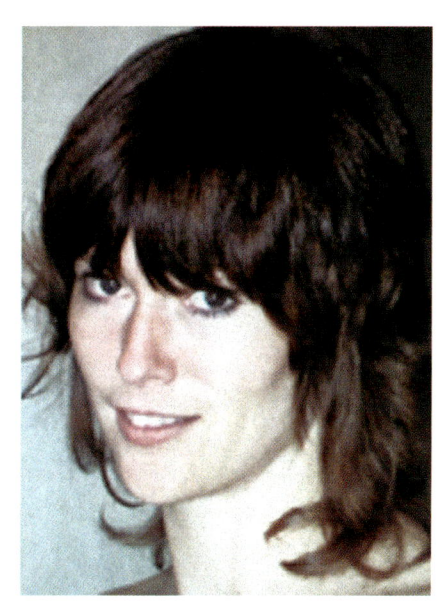

The lovely Diane

The Tweed Boys

John McVie at work

John dissatisfied

Happy Birthday, Warners!

Silent protest

Ken and Diane, Dodger Stadium

Lindsey works out "Walk a Thin Line."

Deep listening at maximum volume

Ken and Richard mixing Tusk

Stevie in Chile

Hernan and Stevie in Chile

Ken and Diane get married.

Get Tusked!

so to make the process easy, we would create a simple basic stereo mix that we would bounce to two tracks on the B-roll multitrack to facilitate overdubbing.

"I Know I'm Not Wrong" is one of the faster songs on the album, but is more elaborate musically, and the production value is higher than on "The Ledge," "That's Enough for Me," and "Not That Funny." The lyrics were typical of Lindsey—defensive, self-assertive, damning, and dominating, except for the evocative phrase of "somebody outside the door," which he would sing in both this song and "Not That Funny." Apparently, Lindsey and Carol had experienced a couple of terrifying break-ins at their Hancock Park house, which made him more paranoid than usual, and he obsessed on the phrase.

I would venture to say that "I Know I'm Not Wrong" might be Lindsey's favorite song, if only because he worked on it throughout the making of Tusk, taking weeks to settle on a chorus progression and phrase he liked. When it came to this song, Lindsey was indefatigable. Like Cézanne and his mountain, Lindsey experimented endlessly in search of the most complete and true representation of this song, spinning off a dozen different versions, from slow to fast, from shiny to distorted, to find the one that clicked and best exemplified his new approach.

One demo would be an ineffably gorgeous music-box instrumental. Another one made the song a bouncy, Ghanian highlife song with a catchy electric twelve-string figure and polyrhythmic drums similar to "Tusk." Another one would be a hard-charging rocker with layered reverbed voices singing over an insistent wood block and random snare hits. And yet another would feature a choppy rhythm with drumfills tumbling out of nowhere, tinkling toy pianos, and a different vocal sound. He even invited Stevie to sing on his baby to see whether she could unlock the magic he knew it contained, but even her tracks were scrapped.

GET TUSKED

By April, Lindsey had zeroed in on the guitar sounds he preferred, which offered all kinds of goodies, starting with his trademark, speeded-up electrics that sounded like a mix between an autoharp or a high-pitched ukulele, a set of doubled Telecasters playing a muted strum, and a doubled set of Ovation acoustics that mixed strumming, fingerpicking, and low bends. There were a couple of fuzz electrics that added low frequencies to the Gretsch bass he played, and an interesting last-minute double solo in the vamp that rocks it out with full throttle. Pure ear candy.

On top of all the above, Lindsey had a bridge section with a set of doubled harmonicas that he wanted to sound as horrible as Jack Benny playing his violin. To get that sound, Lindsey held a Beyer M360 ribbon microphone with the harmonica against it, and then used one of Ken's inventive tricks of feeding it to the live room through a pair of headphones and a Pignose 7-100 mini portable guitar amplifier to get the room ambience, both recorded by a Neumann 87 microphone. These signals were then compressed and equalized heavily through the console. Lindsey would continue to experiment on "I Know I'm Not Wrong" through the mixing stage of Tusk well into August before finally declaring it finished. After building the song up and tearing it down several times, he settled for something in the middle.

It's interesting to listen to "Go Your Own Way" and "I Know I'm Not Wrong" side by side to see how much Lindsey's direction was changing in only two years. Both are fantastic rock songs by the same band, but the way both songs express themselves production-wise couldn't be further apart. Whereas "Go Your Own Way" climaxes on a soaring '70s guitar solo that would make such bands as Boston, Journey, Foreigner, Styx, and Kansas proud, "I Know I'm Not Wrong" melds its solo into the general chaos with nary a bent note. It will forever be a mystery why Lindsey chose "Not That Funny" and not "I Know I'm Not Wrong" to be a single, and why, even though it was rehearsed for the Tusk *tour, it was never played live. Here's a partial transcript of the tracking session for "I Know I'm Not Wrong":*

JOHN: *How about a headline from a* Melody Maker *article? "Sid Vicious, the New John Lennon."*

CHRISTINE: *Sid Vicious? Jesus.*

MICK: *(Sings.) Give me the drugs. Give me the drugs.*

JOHN: *In your case here, difficulties are only . . . temporary.*

MICK: *I'm beatin' the shit out of my neck. (Plays drums.)*

CHRIS: *Ahhhh, fuckin' 'ell, that shit's loud. Didn't I just say that to you Richie?*

MICK: *It's fine. Keep playing. I'll keep you all locked in.*

CHRIS: *I should say so. Jesus. Don't get too cocky there, Mick, c'mon.*

MICK: *Not using both those machines, it'd be a nice idea to have all the tape on the other machine so you could cut straight over, so you're always loaded up and never run out.*

CHRIS: *We used to be able to put tons of takes on one reel.*

RICHARD: *That was at 15 ips. We're recording at 30 ips, which is twice as fast.*

MICK: *It's all right, Chris, we got two machines.*

CHRIS: *Well, all right, jolly good show.*

LINDSEY: *How was the tempo?*

MICK: *Sounds good in the cans.*

CHRIS: *Sounds a bit too chamber-y. Put a bit of chamber on Lindsey's voice, but not that much. It's way back there.*

LINDSEY: *(Starts singing again. Stops.) Less chamber. Less chammmmm-mmber. Okay, that sounds all right. Can you turn the piano up or something?*

RAY: *It's pretty close.*

CHRIS: *"Pretty close" isn't close enough, Raymond.*

JOHN: *What do you want to do? Go on?*

KEN: *Let's do one more.*

JOHN: *Use your discretion.*

MICK: *Do you think it's getting worse, or better?*

RICHARD: *I think the playing is real, real good.*

MICK: *I knooooow, Richard. So, keep throwing it out?*

CHRIS: *Let's do one more and go and have a listen.*

LINDSEY: *Huh? What is that, schnapps?*

JOHN: *I'll have a sip of it, Ray.*

CHRIS: *We rolling?*

RICHARD: *Yeah.*

The band starts playing. The track breaks down and Lindsey teaches the other musicians how to play "Here, There, and Everywhere" instead.

CHRIS, in a Scottish accent: *All right, this is it. I've got a feelin' in my booooones.*

LINDSEY: *Humbling ourselves right before cutting a track by playing the Beatles.*

CHRIS: *I'm sure they'd be very flattered.*

JOHN: *Bloody wonderful.*

The warm weather had started, and a new season of practical jokes had opened at the Village. Ken's new Jeep Cherokee was christened by being completely filled with duct tape. Frank Wolf's BMW bike was covered with honey in retaliation. Ken's Ferrari was not-so-mysteriously filled with chopped-up recording tape soon after. A waterfall from the fourth floor *drenched me on the way into work one morning. If that wasn't traumatic enough, shortly afterward, I was completely wrapped in duct tape and left at the door of Studio D. Removing the tape was a bit, shall we say, hairy, like being waxed to death. The water fights were also nonstop. This was how we relaxed and blew off steam.*

The Village Recorder, by that time, had become a home not only for me, but also for everyone else in the band and crew. Gary Starr was the chief engineer who had hired me and who, on occasion, drank with John McVie at a bar down the street during the down times. He and his crew of maintenance engineers were always available to help us if anything went wrong. And on top of them all was Dick LaPalm, the general manager, who was available to help us out and listen to our bitching when there was a problem or a special requirement. Sometimes it was way past his bedtime and I would be sent by Mick, Ken, or Richard to his hidden office on the fourth floor to explore whether he had a late connection that could help in getting the Peruvian magic white powder that was essential to complete the session.

We knew that when we had to reach out to him, it meant that we would have to sit and listen to his wonderful stories of the days when he worked as a music publicist and promoter in Chicago for such jazz artists as Nat King Cole, Count Basie, Peggy Lee, Sonny Rollins, and Sarah Vaughan, as well as Chess Records blues legends like Muddy Waters and Willie Dixon. Dick had a wild sense of humor, too, so sometimes these conversations took us completely out of the session, laughing till dawn.

After having an excellent day of overdubbing "I Know It's Not Wrong," it was decided we should take a break later on and go out to dinner later at Central Park. I saw this as a great opportunity to see Diane again. I called her and invited her to meet us at the restaurant. Richard called Lindy to come down the hill and join in the fun, too.

"Oh, Diane," I said, "you'd better wear something waterproof!"

"Okay, I have the perfect thing," she said, having heard the stories.

"A bikini wouldn't be a bad idea," I slyly suggested.

As I hung up, I heard Mick and John trying to figure out our schedule so John could undertake his annual sailing trip, when he took his 58-foot racing sloop from LA to Hawaii every year with all his sailing buddies, and anyone else brave enough to go. He always took along plenty of great food, and enough vodka and beer to ride out any emergency. John's predicament was he didn't want to cancel his trip or delay it when the weather was bad. I said, "Let's just try to get all your bass parts done early so you can go." John hated the studio and couldn't wait to leave, so he agreed, offering to come in early every day to examine all his parts. Of course, this isn't what I wanted, to have to come in early a day after we might go late, which happened often.

"Maybe we can have Hernan come in early one or two times a week?" I suggested, smiling.

Hernan shot me a look.

"Yeah . . . but we probably can't do that more often than that. He needs his sleep, too."

Hernan shook his head.

It was Friday night and Central Park was bustling with customers. The restaurant was in the upcoming enclave of Brentwood in West Los Angeles located along San Vicente Boulevard, its four-lane artery, just before it twists toward the ocean. Well-dressed joggers kept themselves in shape by running on the long median beneath its famous coral trees and shopping at the posh health food shops. This area had *yuppie* written all over it before that term existed.

I walked into the 2,000-square-foot restaurant that was somehow massive, yet intimate. It boasted thirty tables dressed in white tablecloths, with a single flower and candle in the center of each. The lighting in the restaurant was perfect—not too dim and not too bright. Right in the middle of the restaurant was our usual table, holding over a dozen of the Fleetwood Mac's family. We entered from the rear and front like an invasion of drunken rats.

As I walked into the room, Carla, the owner, welcomed me and showed me to my table. I took my seat and noticed that all eyes were upon us. Apparently, the word had gotten out that Fleetwood Mac frequented this establishment. About five minutes later, my new girlfriend Diane came in through the front door. We all laughed at her attire. She had on her high-waisted "sailor" jeans with a double row of buttons going up the front and a yellow vinyl Windbreaker with a hood, certainly not what you wear on a Friday night or a second date. Apparently, she was expecting rain.

These meals always started out innocently with glasses of water all around, then beer or wine or cocktails for everyone, then a loaf of bread for the table, then second and third rounds of cocktails, then the salad course, and then about this time, usually Lindsey or Richard would accidentally spill his water or cocktail on someone else, and then the food fight would begin. The excitement and anticipation rose as the evening wore on, knowing that, at any moment, a Kowlooning might unfold.

This particular evening, I remember Richard launching his salad at Mick. Not to be outdone, Lindsey grabbed the large salad bowl on the cart next to the table and tossed it all over Richard. Some of the lettuce landed on a table adjacent to us where a young couple was enjoying a quiet meal, but to my surprise they, too, emptied the contents of their salad bowl over Richard and Mick's end of the table. Diane, without missing a beat, zipped up her slicker and pulled the hood over her head, pulling the strings tight so that you barely saw her beautiful face.

I remember Lindsey, Carol, and Stevie saying almost simultaneously, "Wow, Di, that's brilliant! Why didn't we think of that!" Suddenly, from across the room, came several slices of French bread. We turned in the direction of where they came and saw another couple teaming up with the first. One guy handed his girlfriend their lobsters thermidor, which she lobbed toward us as if they were horseshoes, their cheesy, eggy guts spewing all over Lindsey. Di and I emptied our water glasses at them to buy time. Just to be clear, we weren't stupid enough to throw our cocktails. At this point, the roadies could not contain themselves, and it was all-out restaurant war. There were no survivors and no leftovers.

The owners, Bob and Carla, rushed into triage mode and brought fresh towels to everyone, and oddly enough more water glasses. I knew what was coming. I grabbed Diane's hand. She had water and salad dripping all down her slicker.

"Let's make a run for it! Thanks, Carla!" I yelled. "Just put it on our credit card!"

Diane and I ran the opposite direction of the crowd that was already emptying out of the once peaceful restaurant. We ducked out the back door and into my Dino, where Scooter was waiting patiently. I gave the pretty little circle of Diane's face a kiss and said, "Do you want to go back to the studio?"

"How about coming over to *my* house?

"Oh yeah, that's much better idea!"

I drove her to her beat up VW Bug and proceeded to follow her to her stepmother's house in the Valley. When we go there, she poured me a glass of wine and put on Shaun Cassidy's *Born Late*. I gave her a disapproving look and she explained that she grew up with a father who was a crooner in the same class as Sinatra, and that she had helped write one of the songs on the album, which had gone platinum, so now we both had something in common. I was impressed. When she'd said she did a lot of other things good, she'd meant it. We had a hit of pot while sitting on her bed. She had me get undressed and lay down for a massage. While her hands were on me, magic ensued and I blurted out that I wanted her to marry me after the album was finished. She kissed the back of my neck and rolled me over on my back, and we stayed awake all night, making love.

As I drove home that early Saturday morning I looked over to Scooter and asked him again, "Oh boy, Scooter, what have we gotten ourselves into?"

He tilted his head to the side and looked inquisitively at me.

"Diane could very well be the mother of my children and my future ex-wife." Scooter got up, put his front feet onto my lap, and licked my face in approval.

The idea of covering the Beach Boys' "Farmer's Daughter" had been around for a while, as Lindsey noodled it, along with countless others, on his guitar during breaks between takes, exaggerating its distinctive, twangy riff and singing the melody in his best Brian Wilson falsetto and getting Stevie to join in, which she was always happy to do. Brian's presence was always around in the studio. He was Lindsey's acknowledged mentor as a teenager, and through Dennis's visits to Christine, we all caught glimpses of some of that aura of studio magic.

We all took our places and readied ourselves for a productive day of overdubs, hoping to finish before midnight. Dennis and his buddy, photographer Ed Roach, popped in. Naturally, the conversation turned to Brian and his recent visit. Stevie and Lindsey were politely evincing their appreciation of the Beach Boys and what a huge influence they were on their music when they were teenagers. To prove it, Lindsey and Stevie started singing "Farmer's Daughter." Dennis turned to Ed and Christine said, "See, I told you we were good."

When Dennis and Ed left, a lightbulb went on and Lindsey asked Ray Lindsey to pull out one of his unique, vintage instruments, the Fender Bass VI six-string, bass guitar. He started playing the riff of "Farmer's Daughter" with a special grin on his face that we knew meant that he was cooking something up. He stopped playing suddenly, and high as a proverbial kite, did his characteristic hand rubbing and told the band:

"Hey guys, I have an idea . . . let's try recording one of my favorite Beach Boys songs . . . 'Farmer's Daughter,' and see where it takes us."

With that, everyone in the control room responded with a big yes! We knew right away this was going to be another one of those magical moments, everyone knowing that it had a deep meaning for Lindsey to be able to pay tribute to Brain Wilson, and a good occasion to bring back the group's camaraderie. So as the clock marched past midnight, we took off to new heights, completely taken by Lindsey's surprise bonus track.

"Farmer's Daughter" had come out in 1963 on the Beach Boys' first full-length album, Surfin' USA, and had a distinct Duane Eddy–influenced guitar line by Carl Wilson and David Marks that Lindsey loved. Lindsey went for the Fender Bass VI bass guitar that not only gave this version a lot

A YEAR GONE BAD

of character, but connected with the early experiments of recording songs with these baritone hybrids that that had a darker tone, being an octave below a regular guitar. He knew full well that Brian, who like him was a bassist turned composer/producer, had used a baritone guitar on "Caroline, No," but also that Duane had used a similar instrument on his album, The Twang's the Thang. *Again, even a simple tune like "Farmer's Daughter" embodied both an ambition to emulate and to point the way forward, as the next twenty years would be absolutely filled with detuned guitars.*

    Lindsey sat with us in the control room to record the song from the ground up by doing first a pass on the Fender Bass VI direct into the console through the wonderful-sounding Fat Box that Ken always had at hand. Lindsey built the basic structure of the song, quickly layering four more tracks where each new pass had subtle differences, such as muting or a change of pickups, or making the twang bending less obvious, and to this Ken added the amazing Neve preamp and equalizer, tweaked through an inserted Universal Audio 1176 compressor to give the guitar even more character. Mick abandoned the surf hi-hat and snare beat of the original and played compressed toms to lock in with the guitar and give the track a basic groove.

    A couple of hours later, the song was ready to be adorned with vocals. Lindsey sat at the piano with Stevie and Christine to work out the voicings, getting the perfect blend very quickly. When they were ready, Ken suggested they move into the control room to get more intimate sounding vocals. We placed three Neumann U49 large-diaphragm, tube microphones by the couch with a pair of extra-small Auratone 5C monitor speakers to be used for sound reference so the vocal blend would happen as natural as possible without the use of headphones. We dimmed the lights, brought out a full bottle of Courvoisier VSOP cognac, and started recording.

    Lindsey, Christine, and Stevie did a first pass in falsetto as in the original

Brian Wilson melody before doing two more complete passes, doubling and adding harmonies. Listening to them live in the control room was an intense experience for Ken, Richard, and me, as we heard every breath inflection and tone detail with the trio's eyes closed as they delivered some of the best vocal work I have ever heard. In a way, "Farmer's Daughter" was a throwback both to an older song and to an older production style: recorded and produced in a few hours, to be mixed right away and finished with wonderful results, as was done in the early days of the Beach Boys and the Beatles, as opposed to the painstaking lengths we went to during the making of Tusk, *either reaching for perfection or wasting our time in the attempt.*

Later that night, Dennis and Ed came back to pick up Christine. With tears in her eyes, she had us play back our cover of "Farmer's Daughter," which we had toiled over all night. Dennis broke down, hearing the musical vision of the brother he no longer had, which was heavy for all of us. We didn't notice that we had spent close to twenty-four hours in the studio by that time and it was early morning. We all left without saying much, quietly moved and full of the feeling of that magical moment, driving off in different directions into the gray of the early dawn.

17

A CHARMED HOUR

> You've got to play [*Tusk*] a lot. It keeps getting better.
> —John McVie

I turned the corner at breakneck speed and hit the gas as I came out of the turn. I adjusted my sunglasses and glanced back.

Shit.

Hernan was right behind me, and he was gaining. I could hear the high whine of his engine in my ears.

I pushed it as hard as I could until we were almost neck and neck. I couldn't let him win. He'd already won enough. I pulled my wheel hard right and sideswiped him. He veered off, surprised but unfazed, recovering just in time to keep up the pursuit. I knew that I bought myself just enough time to keep the lead and go all the way. I smirked with satisfaction. Along Butler Avenue, I could hear the crowd roar.

And then, the unthinkable happened.

I was in the home stretch, eating up the road, finish line in sight, when a car backed out of nowhere. There was nothing I could do, no chance to brake or brace for impact. My car smashed into it, shrapnel flying as I caromed off its rear, flying out of control until I came to an abrupt stop facing the opposite direction I had come. To my horror, Hernan was still barreling forward with no intention of stopping, the madman. The only thing between him and the finish line was me and what was left of my shattered car. I hit the gas and my engine shot to life for one last gasp before Hernan and I both collided head on. I spun left violently as his car rolled ass over teakettle like an Olympic gymnast. There's no way he could have survived that.

"I win!" yelled Hernan upside down and triumphant, "you owe me twenty bucks!"

"Whaddya mean?! It was a tie!" I retorted.

Sure enough, both cars were over the finish line, even though his was farther down the street. All bets were off on this one as jubilation mixed with groans. The remote control cars that I brought back from Japan during the Rumours Tour were now totaled. One of our favorite past times was no more. I could probably fix them, I thought, but the instructions were in Japanese. Oh well.

It was April 1 and it was a festive day at Studio D. Mick had brought in his two adorable daughters, Amy and Lucy, who had a ball running around the studio and playing with all the musical toys we had lying about. It was also time for our annual April Fool's Day joke on some unsuspecting Fleetwood family member. This time, it was its accountant, David Bloom. Christine decided to make her faithful business manager sweat a little. She picked up the phone and called David, who was relaxing at his home that Sunday. Now, David wasn't your ordinary accountant. He was a big thinker. He was the mind behind John and Christine getting in on the ground floor of Hawaiian Telcom. This proved to be an investment that would pay off big for them.

"David, I've decided to buy the *Queen Mary*!" she commanded ada-

A CHARMED HOUR

mantly. "I don't care how much it is. I have my heart set on it; just buy it for me! *Now!*"

She muted the phone with her hand so he didn't hear her laughing. I was surprised he didn't catch on.

"Uh, all right Chris; let me call you back." He hung up the phone.

Chris laughed so hard that cigarette smoke blew out of her mouth so fast that it made her cough.

"That was cruel, Chris," Mick said, laughing, "David must be freaking out right now, trying to figure out how to talk you out of it."

"Oh, Mick, I'm just having a bit of fun. Last year I told him I wanted to buy London Bridge," she said.

She picked up the phone again, gulped her glass of Champagne, called David back and had everyone in the room yell out: "April fools!"

She had a good laugh, "You know, David, I love you; you're always such a good sport!" Rounds of "We love you, David!" circled the room.

"All right," I said, "enough hijinks. Back to work. At three hundred dollars an hour, this record isn't going to finish itself, you know!"

"*Yesssssss, Ken* . . ." came the disapproving response along with a few Bronx cheers.

Since our schedule for the month was packed. We started off next with a complete tracking session of "Angel," a Stevie song with the full band, reminiscent of a northern soul tune in straight 4/4, which was fun from the first bar due in large part to John McVie's bass playing. Conjuring the ghost of James Jamerson, "Angel" is easily John's spotlight on the album, and could easily double as his epitaph. The song itself is a bit of an anomaly. It's infectiously danceable, grooving non-stop from beginning to end, and yet the lyrics are anything but disco. The band treated it much in the same manner as "You Make Lovin' Fun," and it made a fabulous, up-tempo addition late into the making of the album, even if it had Stevie's trademark darkness, as she explained to the film crew:

> I wanted to write a rock-and-roll song. And so it started out being much sillier than it came out. It didn't end up being silly at all. It ended up being very serious, actually. But when I started it, I thought, for me, because I write so many intense, serious, dark songs, that I wanted to write something that was up. And it starts out that way, and it is up, but there's a definite eeriness that goes through that song, too, that I didn't realize was there until just the other night.

As we were in the midst of recording "Angel," a funny event related to Stevie made the news. An FM station accidentally played the Atlanta Rhythm Section's "Imaginary Lover" at the wrong speed of 45 rpm. Favorable calls began to light up the switchboard, so the disc jockey let it play. Speeded up, the song sounded unmistakably like Fleetwood Mac, with Stevie Nicks on lead vocals. News quickly reached Stevie in Los Angeles. She rushed out to buy the record and brought it to Studio D to be played at the wrong speed. We played it and she said it gave her chills; it was like something she'd sing, and the same way she'd sing it. We decided to prank Christine and mixed it in with some other demos for Tusk. *Christine loved it and complimented Stevie on her new song. We heard later that the Atlanta Rhythm Section didn't find it as funny as we did.*

After Christine's delirious prank on her business manager, we all wanted more, so while doing background vocals with Christine, Lindsey, and Stevie on "Angel," ideas came and went until we all agreed to play one on my

A CHARMED HOUR

girlfriend, Kris. Since it was a Sunday and we had decided to take it easy, it was a perfect excuse to invite a few selected friends to come over for an album preview. Kris had already met the band and team, so she was no stranger. It was decided that seven in the evening was perfect for some cocktails and the private listening party. Stevie and I were going to be the pranksters; after what had happened with "Sara," we had a level of closeness that would assure a good result.

Before the appointed time, Stevie went out into the studio to play the piano and rehearse "Angel," the song that we were going to work on for the next few days. Lights were dimmed close to darkness in the live room, and we had set open microphones on the piano, so that in the control room all sounds and conversations from the live room would be heard. I went out with mixed feelings to assume my role, expecting Kris at any moment to go in the control room where Lindsey, Carol, Mick, John, Ken, and Richard were lounging and waiting for the trap to spring.

"When you were good, baby / You were very good," Stevie sang as she played the piano, varying the speed to fit the lyrics.

"Hernan, do you like the way the words flow? I'm not sure whether I should slow it down."

"I love it, Stevie . . . maybe a little faster, so that the fans can tap their feet. I like the way the verse builds up to the chorus. Yeah, definitely a cool song!" I said, looking with the corner of my right eye into the control room to see whether Kris had arrived. There she was with her back to the live room, chatting with the lads. So, I winked an eye to Stevie to let her now that we were on.

Stevie had no trouble becoming the best of actresses as she assumed her role. "Oh, Hernan, you are so sweet! Come sit next to me at the piano, so I can run through some more of the lyrics and hear how they sound."

She continued singing with me very close to her, shoulder to shoulder at the piano: "I still look up / When you walk in the room."

She stopped suddenly and looked at me in the eyes, as she said with that purry voice that only she can do, "You know, Hernan, you have been so sweet to me that I have started to like you more and more."

My heart was pumping and my head was swirling, feeling at that point that the joke was becoming quite real as the sexiest female singer of those days was singing in my ears with no time to respond. At that point it was obvious that Kris was listening in the control room, not believing was she was hearing, but not reacting in fear of being considered not cool.

Stevie continued, "I wrote part of those lyrics while sitting in the studio as you walked passed me, and many times we crossed eyes while we were working together, so, yeah, they're very real. I cannot pretend anymore." Stevie put her hand over my shoulder and looked straight into my eyes, playing her part too close to reality.

I didn't know what to think or how to handle myself anymore. I knew it was just a joke, but my improv chops were not advanced enough to just follow her lead with a cold heart. The thought of Kris's feelings made me come back to reality, so I continued playing the part of the innocent, insecure object of desire.

"I like you, too, Stevie, but you know that it would be crazy that you and me would get together."

By then, Ken and Richard were supposed to act completely surprised and comment that they have no idea what's going on, and so sorry for leaving the mics open. Just before this happened, Stevie put her other arm around me and gave me a loud kiss that was interrupted by Ken's voice over the talkback of the live room saying: "Hey, Hernan, Kris is here!"

Stevie and I looked at each other in full complicity and walked back to

A CHARMED HOUR

the control room to announce, "Hey, Kris, Happy April Fool's Day!" Kris didn't look too happy, but she was a good player and finally laughed big, saying, "You guys had me for while!" That evening came to an end, leaving me with a feeling of disarray, as this little charade had opened unsuspected new spaces in my "good friend" status with Stevie, and left some cracks in my relationship with Kris.

"Angel" was a Stevie Nicks rocker with a pop twist. The band was happy to gather again in the studio to do what it did best, playing live together. This was also the last song to be recorded and selected for Tusk, making it the last official album song cut at the Village. "Angel" had a basic 4/4 rhythm pattern, built around Christine's bluesy shuffle electric piano, Lindsey's electric guitar riffing, and the perky funk of John's Motown bassline. Ken and Richard were happy to have the band once again in the live room that, after all, had been built especially for these types of sessions, instead of spending eighteen hours trying to find a particular, undefined sound.

We discussed and planned the setup to get everyone as close as possible without any sound leakage into Mick's drum microphones. Ken, Richard, and I discussed what overhead mics were better for this song, settling on a pair of AKG 414s, and adding an AKH 451 on his metal snare bottom to catch the harmonics as well as a D12 on the kick. Richard did his tuning process on the Tama drum set, while Ray set up Lindsey's Marshall stack in the iso that we called the Brazilian room due to its fine wood walls. John's bass was injected straight into our Neve console and Christine's Yamaha electric piano was in the center with visual contact to the Hawaiian iso room where we had Stevie's vocal microphone. We all knew she could nail most of her singing live.

One of the delights of having the band playing all together with its full instrumentation was that the initial sound layering and equalization process happened quite fast, as the faders that had the drum microphones were brought up and everything fell into place with the kick and snare sounding good, adding then John's bass, Christine's electric piano, and Lindsey electric guitar strumming and riffing, to finally be crowned by Stevie's unique voice. The band did a few runs to make sure all the parts were there and to allow us to balance the headphone mix to each musician.

The song trailed a bit at first while Lindsey struggled to find his way into the song, and some adjustments were made to pick up the pulse. His initial disengagement was a stumbling block, and key production elements of the song began to fall through the cracks. "Angel" was a unique song that needed real surgery to cut it to a working length. It also presented a challenge because, like "Dreams," the song basically had just two chords that required a powerful groove and dynamic lyrics to keep the listener's interest.

First, we had to bring it pulse up to really get it to rock. With these changes, Mick's drumming and John's bass playing got more dynamic. Stevie already had a complete set of lyrics that were equal parts Ovid's *Metamorphosis*, Welsh *Mabinogion* myth, Gothic poetry, and personal diary, married through her gift for melody, and delivered in a low, conversational contralto that rose to a R&B shout at the end. With one verse, one bridge, two long prechoruses, and two short choruses, "Angel" had a continuous, unpredictable arrangement that made a five-minute song sound like a tight three. We rolled from there and had the song down in six takes, of which the last was the master.

As I drove back home in my new blue Alfa Romeo GT Sprint Veloce, I couldn't help remembering what a famous LA psychic had told me a few years before, on how I was going to have a blue Italian sports car and work with a big British rock band where one of the singers was a girl, and that I was going to have a love affair with her. She added that I should be careful *with what could happen with this love affair. During the tracking session that Monday, I couldn't help thinking of the joke on Kris, and how Stevie's acting was too real, or my intuition was correct in telling me that some of her energy had a second intention. She met my eyes a few times while singing in the iso room, and felt I might be right.*

"What was that?" I asked Diane, lifting her pillow to expose her long eyelashes surrounding her almond eyes and a very sleepy face.

"What did you say? she asked.

"Did you hear that? It sounded like thunder or something, but it felt more like an earthquake."

I walked out onto my patio. All I could see was bumper-to-bumper traffic heading into town, and occasionally, Caltrans vehicles with their yellow lights and annoying beeping.

"Crap, this doesn't look good," I said. "Looks like some kind of accident down there may have closed the PCH [Pacific Coast Highway]. I better go and see whether I can find out anything."

"Okay, I'll take a shower while you go see. Maybe take Carmen so you don't get stuck down there," she suggested.

I hung around until I knew she was safely in the shower, and then Scooter and I cruised down the hill to the PCH to see what all the fuss was about. Before we got to the bottom of the hill, I could see that there was a mess ahead. All the southbound cars were using my intersection to turn around and go back north. Hundreds of cars were making U-turns, ignoring what the traffic light was saying.

I pulled over in a small turnout and contorted my tall frame out of the VW Bug and walked down with Scooter to see what we could see. As I crossed Big Rock Drive and walked in the direction toward the

GET TUSKED

supposed accident, I was shocked at what I saw. There was no accident at all. The entire mountain above the PCH was completely covering the highway, making it completely impassable with dirt, bushes, and gigantic boulders everywhere, and a few sinkholes to boot.

Scooter and I headed back up the steep hill and Diane was unfortunately already dressed.

"We're so screwed!" I said. "The whole fucking mountain has slid down onto the PCH! You should see the size of some of the boulders on the road!" Thankfully, it was Saturday and I didn't have to be at the studio that day.

"There's helicopters hovering above," Di said. "Turn on the news!"

All the local stations were covering the "Big Rock Malibu Slide." They predicted the road would be closed for at least a couple of days.

"That was lucky. Hopefully they're right and it will be open next Monday and we can enjoy the pool house without a lot of traffic noise."

"If they don't open it before you have to go back to work, you'll have to drive all the way around the slide," Diane said with foreboding.

"Yikes, that means I'll have to drive north to Malibu Canyon, go north over the 101, east all the way to the 405, then south through Brentwood to the studio! That's horrible! My twenty-minute, oceanside commute is now a forty-mile freeway suicide mission! Not to mention the price of gas! The gas lines are already bad enough! This is going to suck big time."

Diane handed me a beer.

"Let's just hope they clean up that mess before next week. I'm sure they will," I said, ever the optimist. So, we stayed home and tried to enjoy ourselves.

We didn't get much peace and quiet that weekend. They were using

A CHARMED HOUR

dynamite to break up those big boulders and to loosen the rock up on the steep hill. The news reported that one boulder was estimated at 116 tons. Throughout the weekend, local news kept us updated on Caltrans's progress cleaning up the slide.

We were interrupted Sunday night with another familiar rumble followed by sirens. "*Oh, crap!* Looks like I'll be going the long way around to work tomorrow," I said.

"Me, too, I have a modeling job out in the Valley, and Ventura is going to be *jammed*," she gasped.

This slide was worse than the first one, proving that the mountain was very unstable and geologists would be devising a long-term fix that could take weeks or months and would probably require some sort of giant retaining wall solution. It was a case of enough was enough. Big Rock had been unstable since the '40s, periodically closing all or part of the PCH. I prepared for the worst and planned to make the long trek around and through the most congested part of Los Angeles for the next few days or forever how long it took. Even driving a Ferrari doesn't make that drive enjoyable.

The first Monday after the slide, I arrived to the studio late, and naturally I got the business from Dashut, "Mr. Malibu pays the price for his fancy pool and view! Looks like the landslide brought you down! So yeah, hey, Cutlass, you're welcome to come stay with me until they clean that up."

"That's very nice of you, Richard, but I don't think it'll last too long. Perhaps if we have a really late session, I'll take you up on offer, but I have a live-in girlfriend now." Cue the sound of catcalls from around the control room.

As the days went on, more and more people came to the same conclusion that I did and eventually parked their car on either side of the slide. It got crazy. Hundreds of desperate people started parking down the center of the PCH, and soon my twice-daily walk became more than a mile. So, it was time for a new plan: roller skates. I went and bought the best roller skates I could find, and then I didn't care how many cars parked on the highway. I could simply skate on by them, sobriety permitting

Speaking of, that Thursday night, the film crew was roped into trying to do a spot for Warner Bros. Records' twenty-first birthday. The guys wanted no part of it and Christine and Stevie were volunteered to deliver the birthday greetings. All they had to do was say, "Happy Twenty-First Birthday Warner Brothers Records!" This was the end of the night, and the girls were in transcension mode. In their condition, they weren't able to even do this. But bless Tom Spain and his crew; they were patient in the hopes of capturing something. But it was not to be. It was like herding cats. This moment now lives on YouTube, and it is very entertaining. Christine was completely schnockered and Stevie wasn't far behind, but the affection they had for each other and the laughter were completely genuine.

As I drove the direct route home that night, I noticed there must have been another five hundred cars more than the usual. To make it worse, the California Highway Patrol and Malibu Sheriff's Department had joined forces to give every one of the parked cars a ticket. Not just the cars double parked in the center median of the highway, but all the cars on either side of the highway, parked chaotically, any way they could.

Now this didn't seem right to either myself or Diane, who had decided to come by the studio and ride home with me. We both had our skates and a buzz on, so we thought it wasn't fair that these good people

A CHARMED HOUR

should have parking tickets. We got out and took every ticket off each car and stuck them in the cyclone fence where they would be seen by the authorities. There must have been five or six of us rabble-rousers who stood up for our fellow man that evening late in mid-April.

By the time the slide was finally repaired properly in May, we were nearly done filming and only doing final touchups on the record. Under serious public pressure, Caltrans dwarfed our budget by spending $7 million dollars on 800 feet of road.

The film crew included a still photographer named Randall Hagadorn who we all befriended more than the rest, as he was closer to the rock world and already had a taste of all the craziness happening in Studio D. By mid-May, he had to spend a few days in Hawaii for another shoot before returning with a wonderful gift for all of us: magic mushrooms. Of course, it wasn't a gift to be left unopened, so it was decided by all that we would partake of them and let flow in the studio in whatever manner each would feel and act.

It was a day of overdubs for "Angel," so that as the psilocybin kicked in, the studio became a personal tripping ground for all, forgetting our chores and focusing on individual psychedelic experiences. Stevie grabbed her Spanish castanets and twirled inside the live echo chamber. Mick played his new African talking drum, which was probably talking to him. Lindsey held his Martin acoustic guitar and fingerpicked Django Reinhardt. Christine and John were not in the studio that day, but Ken, Richard, and I joined in the psychedelic feast, wandering through the rooms and wondering whether we should be recording all of this. I wish we had. The scene made me think of Aldous Huxley's The Doors of Perception *that I read as a teenager, which had opened my appetite for expanded awareness of the mind.*

After a few hours, when our feet were relatively back on the ground,

Lindsey said he was ready to work his lead guitar for "Angel," a task that normally would have been simple to set up. But this time the recording team and crew were tripping out, including Ray, who was entrusted to set up the amp rig and electric guitars. My mission was to get the 2-inch tape and multitrack ready as well as set up microphones and outboard gear into the Neve console, a task that took forever as I perceived the whole studio environment and equipment as a large playground covered in glue. Finally, Ken and I managed to get things going as Ray got Lindsey all hooked up, ready to go. Richard tried to be the spokesman, keeping the momentum going with his eyes two black slits.

In spite of the spaced-out start, Lindsey fully connected to the song and let loose his creative juices, giving us many takes of his trademark leads that weave through "Angel," riffing throughout before finally breaking out with an epic solo that crescendos with Stevie in the vamp. Since "Angel" bore a groove-heavy resemblance to "You Make Lovin' Fun," Lindsey played in a similar fashion with fuzzed out lines on his white Telecaster that snaked throughout Stevie's lyrics. One of his talents as a lead player was his ability to play a careful call and response with the singer. For example, in the bridge, Lindsey stopped playing entirely to emphasize Stevie, and when she sang, "I've the same wide eyes / they tell a story," he lightly tremolo'd two high notes to accentuate the scintillating look of a woman. It's a very subtle effect, but it's there.

Afterward, Lindsey and Stevie spent time at the piano working out their vocals together before trying "Angel" out as a duet. The end result was a compromise where certain parts of Lindsey's vocals appear at unexpected moments to either augment Stevie's lead or fill in for it. Featured in the Tusk *documentary is a segment of Stevie taking one of her lead vocal passes at "Angel," and you can see the sheer power that she could deliver a rock vocal-*

A CHARMED HOUR

ist, which was always a performance to behold. She danced and marched in place in her platform shoes and pink leg warmers the same way she would perform it speeded up live on the tour, bringing the same excitement to the microphone that Lindsey would in his wildest frenzy. Stevie said playing "Angel" live reminded her of being an old-time dancehall girl, which she would enact, cutting the rug across the stage with her long flapper scarf. This would be the last classic, '70s-style rock song Fleetwood Mac would record.

As the session for "Angel" was finishing, Richard called me to a corner of the control room to tell me that I should be aware that Stevie was hot on me, and that she was probably not going to stop that evening. Apparently, she had confided her intentions to seduce me that evening. A thrill went through me. In spite of Richard being constantly funny as hell, he also had many moments when he allowed for deeper conversations. I couldn't help remembering when we had talked about being insecure and shy, and how he had learned so much from Alan Watts's book The Wisdom of Insecurity, understanding that being shy or insecure also meant sensitivity, concepts that helped me through those days.

Most of the band and the crew left Studio D exhausted from the long tracking day, with only Stevie, Richard, and Mick's roadie, a black ex-marine named Randy Woods, with whom I had a good relationship, still in the control room. As I was wrapping the session, putting away microphones and equipment, I heard Stevie purr:

"Oh, Hernan, I would love to listen to 'Angel' one more time before we leave."

"Sure, Stevie," I answered, knowing where this could lead.

I loaded the 2-inch tape into the multitrack player and went to Take 6 of "Angel" to get a good rough mix going. Stevie didn't drive, so the fact that she had sent her girls home was another sign that she was committed to getting me one way or another. I felt her energy behind me, as she danced while singing harmonies and answers to the lead vocal she had cut earlier. She got a joint going and a bottle of Courvoisier cognac to indulge in, passing them to me while I was fine-tuning the details in the mix. Richard wisely exited, wishing us a good night, loaded with humor, laughing at his role as Celestina.

The night was unleashing a new scenario that I just couldn't predict where it would carry both of us. Stevie asked me to bring her voice up and add more reverb, and to blast the volume. Randy, too, already had read what was going on, and discreetly said in my ear, "Don't worry, bro, I'll guard the door so nobody goes in the control room."

I felt Stevie's hand rubbing my neck as she danced, singing with that voice that had me mesmerized:

"And to those that I love like a ghost through a fog / Like a charmed hour and a haunted song."

The little hit of sinsemilla and sip of Courvoisier were doing their job at freeing any apprehension and releasing all stops on me, and certainly for Stevie. For the next few minutes, I fumbled the mixing, moving the faders with no direction, trying to act professional. Stevie by then had moved closer, putting both her arms around my chest from behind while singing close to my ear.

At that point, I just stopped being the responsible engineer and let go of my inhibitions, taking her by the waist and sitting her on my lap, kissing her passionately while feeling her warm, intoxicating lips as our tongues searched for contact. "Angel" played on a loop during our close encounter in Studio D. The risk of getting caught only intensified the feeling. With no sense of time, and abandoned to each other, Stevie and I went on like two adolescents, caressing, kissing, each reaching for the other's body and coming very close to making love on top of the console, until we realized that it was better to move to a more intimate space.

"Wow . . . this is wild!" came out of my mouth as I tried to come down to earth with my heart still pumping fast, and not sure what the next step was going to be.

She smiled and said, "You know what? Let's go to my house and I'll make you the best Mexican omelet ever, my specialty."

Her warm tone of voice and inviting words created an intimacy that, as the minutes and hours flew by, were significant in generating familiarity and confidence between the two of us very fast, and then through the days, weeks, and months to follow, made our very special romance a fun and loving experience that is hard to put in words.

We tidied ourselves for our exit past the reception desk, and jumped in my blue Alfa to drive to her house. As we drove down Santa Monica Boulevard, Stevie flipped through the dial to KLOS where Jim Ladd was playing Led Zeppelin's "Going to California," one of my favorites of their acoustic songs and somehow an inspirational hymn: every time I heard it in Chile, it helped keep my dream alive of someday taking the leap to California. My heart was so full of emotions and the fresh experience of making out with Stevie. Through the window and into the chill night air, Robert Plant's voice wafted.

18

UNDOING THE LACES

> Please toe the line / But no one was listening
> —Lindsey Buckingham

Driving in the early hours of that Tuesday down Santa Monica Boulevard, all of the familiar LA characters from the movies were roaming its streets, bohemians and revelers getting a last-minute fifth at the local liquor store, the occasional teenage runaways on the move, nervous cops rushing through the dark alleys, and low riders and hotrods cruising amidst the Ferraris or Lamborghinis racing towards Malibu. Passing through Beverly Hills, Stevie and I made a left at the Troubadour past the Sunset Strip, ascending the curves of Doheny to Stevie's magnificent Tudor-style house.

Stevie was quite animated and told me how she had worked as a waitress while pursuing her musical dreams. She asked me whether the way she pronounced my name was correct as she caressed my hand while shifting the Alfa. The stories and her warm, amorous voice made those initial moments a close affair. As much as we had allowed ourselves to let go in Studio D, what the future held for this possible love affair was a mystery to me. It was still dark when we arrived at her house. It was five a.m. and

Stevie stood there cooking breakfast. The Mexican omelet was the perfect delicacy to quench the munchies.

When we were done eating, and our initial rush had dwindled, we were quite sober and mindful of our next moves. I asked myself whether this wasn't just a wild moment of passion that we could have both laughed and forgotten about the next day. She invited me to go upstairs, leading the way through the den and big living room that had her unique decor that included colored scarves filtering the beautiful art deco lamps; magical objects, including crystal balls and Welsh mythical figures in bronze; a couple of Spanish guitars; and some nice classic sofas with fluffy pillows.

We hugged and kissed up the long staircase on our way to her bedroom, where we dropped onto her antique, four-post, Chinese canopy bed, picking up where we had left off in the studio. It didn't take long before we were kissing with even more intensity than before. The small canopy bed added sensuality to our entanglement as we slowly moved closer. At that point, Stevie stopped me with a serious expression on her face to ask me with solemnity:

"Hernan . . . before we make love, you have to think of the implications that this moment can have on your life. I adore everything that is happening, but our next move can change your life completely. And I don't want you to be hurt. Whatever decisions you make, consider the consequences, please."

Her words rang deeply in my head that moment; I didn't know whether to retreat or defy the odds. I was in the eye of a storm, and her warning reminded me of all the good omens, synchronicity of events, and signs that preceded this encounter to finally lead me to this moment.

I had come a long way from the shy kid that loved rock and roll and dreamed of being part of it in California. And this precious moment was there to be taken no matter what dangers lay ahead. Looking at Stevie's pretty face, framed with those blond curls, and her sensuous body language, her charm had gotten hold of me. I felt bold and gallant, undoing the laces and entering an unknown dimension that was so alluring. In spite of the warning flashes triggered by my mind, such as how to tell Kris, how to face Lindsey and the band, how to deal with her fame and rock star world, I knew there was no stopping. Her solemn tone guided my mood as I searched for meaningful words:

"Stephanie . . . I would never forgive myself if I dodged the call of passion. Whatever has to happen, let it happen."

"Are you sure, Hernan?"

"I couldn't be more sure. I just realized that this moment is not accidental."

"Okay, Hernan; let it be, then."

We opened the gates of lovemaking. Everything around us just shined and flowed, making that first rendezvous very special.

Eventually, I looked at my watch and realized that it was already early morning, and I had to make it home and check in with Kris before she went to work. I kissed Stevie good-bye, leaped down from the bed, and in a rush with a full heart of emotions, left her to sleep soundly.

Going back to the Village the next day had a special feeling, as I noticed that something inside me had changed, somehow fulfilling Stevie's initial predictions. As I walked into the psychedelic, mirrored reception area, I couldn't help but notice how dazzled and high on adrenaline I felt. When meeting Richard, he looked at me with a wink of an eye, signaling that we were in cahoots on the affair. Moments later, Ken came in to the control room where Richard and I were commenting on what had happened, so I let him know the whole story.

Ken counseled me, "Well done, Ernie; just be cool and careful with how you guys handle this."

During the following days Stevie shared the story with her friends and Christine, and eventually Mick found out. He approached me during a session and put a strong hand on my shoulder, saying, "Wow, Fernandez; what have you gotten yourself into? Stevie is a wild woman!"

From that point on, my life was absolutely crazy, running from the studio after a full day of work to Stevie's house for a night of lovemaking, to my home to rest for a few hours, then back to Studio D. It started to become a blur, but I'll always remember coming home as the city started to move and the sunrise chased away the mystical night birds. The singing of the night birds at dawn became part of these encounters, reminding us that it was time to fly away

It got tougher and tougher to leave Stevie, as our affair drew us together more and more. Secret rendezvous were part of the adventure, so planning them was fun. Just after the Big Rock slide, we ran away to Ken's house in Malibu a couple of times to live our affair to the max, listening to some of my favorite Brazilian music that Stevie loved so much. We even danced away while drinking Ken's special margaritas.

Stevie wrote me a passionate letter that showed the intensity of our romance, enjoying every minute as if there were no tomorrow:

> *I don't know what is happening, but it's happening fast, and the feelings are heavy and flying . . . When we are holding each other, there is nothing else to me!*

We went on like that for a couple of weeks before I decided I couldn't take the situation anymore and opened up the whole affair to Kris. I felt bad for her, but there was no turning back. I found a temporary room at a friend's house to move into, but by then, Stevie and I spent most of our time together. Our love affair had gone beyond a one-night stand, and she invited me to move in so we could be together more freely and make it easier on our long hauls across the city.

And the show had to go on, as the making of Tusk continued its long and twisting parade into heavy overdub mode, going from one song to another as the mood and ideas came and went. Tom Spain's film crew coexisted with the band and us, capturing the studio process with each member of the band, our jokes and conversations, and special stagings of the songs to re-create their dynamics. The first few days of the crew's presence had made everyone self-conscious of the cameras in our personal working space, but as days went by it, all became quite natural and part of the norm.

Fleetwood Mac was a group of performers, and they were at ease being interviewed and goofing off, especially Mick and Richard. Mick's recently deceased father had been a wing commander for the Royal Air Force and one scene that didn't make it into the documentary was when they filmed a cockpit sketch at the recording console as the pilot and copilot, respectively, of Air Maybe:

CAPTAIN MICK: *First Officer Dashut, what does the altimeter read?*
FIRST OFFICER DASHUT: *Thirty thousand feet, captain and holding steady.*
    All systems normal.
CAPT. MICK: *Are you quite sure?*
F/O DASHUT: *Quite sure, captain.*
CAPT. MICK: *Dammit, man, I just saw the wing fly off an hour ago.*
F/O DASHUT: *I doubt it, captain, I would have noticed.*
CAPT. MICK: *Are you calling me a liar, Dashut?!*

GET TUSKED

F/O Dashut: *(Lighting a joint and handing it over.) No captain, just stoned.*

Capt. Mick: *That may very well be, but we must not tell the passengers. We don't want a bloody panic on our hands. This is a fixed wing aircraft, now go out there and fix the wing or we'll keep flying in circles. And don't let anyone see you.*

F/O Dashut: *Yes, sir, I'll hide in the lounge cart.*

Capt. Mick: (Handing joint back.) *Very good, Dashut, and bring back a few bottles of tequila. I'm thirsty.*

F/O Dashut: *Captain!*

Capt. Mick: *Yes, Dashut?!*

F/O Dashut: *We've lost another wing!*

Camera starts shaking violently.

Capt. Mick: *Good God, man! Emergency maneuvers!*

The lights flicker as both men fight to regain control of the aircraft, flipping switches, pressing buttons, and pushing faders.

F/O Dashut: *Captain! I don't think we're going to make it!*

Capt. Mick: *Whatever you do, don't tell the passengers! And destroy the black box!*

F/O Dashut: *I can't!*

Capt. Mick: *Why?!*

F/O Dashut: *Because that's where I keep my stash!*

Capt. Mick: *Quite right. Quite right. Damn luck that. Send out an S.O.S.!*

F/O Dashut: *An S.O.S., captain?*

Capt. Mick: *Yes, Save Our Stash! Now grab the parachutes!*

F/O Dashut: *But there's only one, captain!*

Capt. Mick: *For heaven's sake, man, why don't we have more parachutes?!*

F/O Dashut: *Because this is an error plane, captain!*

CAPT. MICK: *Then you must give me the parachute for Queen and Country.*
F/O DASHUT: *It's been an honor, captain.*
CAPT. MICK: *The honor has been all yours, Dashut, but don't worry, I'm going to get help.*

Stevie and I managed to rob some kisses hiding in the dark corners of the studio and lay low somehow, putting off the pending disaster when Lindsey would find out and react in a way that Stevie feared was going to be fury and rage. But I assumed whatever consequences would arise from our affair and was ready for the moment of truth, which eventually came a few weeks after on one evening as we were finishing some vocal overdubs and winding down from a long day.

Lindsey walked in from the lounge looking overrefreshed. He came straight up to me with a bottle of Chivas Regal that he had been drinking while doing his lead vocals, saying with a slight slur:

"Hey, Ernie, I would like to talk to you now. Let's go out to the studio."

"Sure, Lindsey," suspecting the worst.

Lindsey got straight to the point. "I know you've been seeing Stevie in secret."

I took a deep breath and wondered whether it was too late to do live sound for Captain & Tennille.

"Why didn't you guys tell me?" He looked honestly offended.

"Well, Lindsey, we thought it was better to keep it private for a while until some time had gone by."

"Why? Did anybody else know?"

"Only Richard and Ken, eventually Christine."

"Yeah . . . Chris told me . . . it bothers me to feel like I was the only one shut out. I care for Stevie and don't want her to get hurt."

"I understand, Lindsey, sorry to have shut you out. Our secret was meant to be kept till we were sure of what we were doing," I said as my semipanic started to fade. Lindsey confided his feelings that I realized mainly had to do with our not trusting him, and also how much he cared for Stevie's well-being in spite of all the past wars waged among them directly and through songs.

"I like you, Ernie. Have a sip with me of this wonderful Chivas so we can talk!" He passed the big bottle of scotch. I took a giant gulp.

I realized that he was quite boozed up from doing vocals most of the day with the help of these Scottish spirits that had him open and sensitive to the situation. He also reaffirmed that he liked me and considered me a good person, closing with: "Of all guys, I rather she goes out with you than those other guys she sees."

This last line changed my perspective of him and his place in Stevie's life. From that day on, Stevie and I were deeper and more committed, liberated from the constant anxiety of how Lindsey was going to react. In spite of our new open secret, we were careful not to act out as love puppies in the studio, which would interfere with task at hand.

Lindsey made a call to Richard early in the morning; he wanted to do "Song #3," or what would become "Walk a Thin Line." Immediately, I knew this was going to be a very long session. During *Rumours*, the entire band would usually get together and play whatever the new song was together. Everyone would contribute whatever ideas came to mind. But, Lindsey was on a quest of his own to find his new self, and the studio habits had to change accordingly. Most of his songs that we worked on would now be one big experiment.

For example, "Walk a Thin Line" in a manner similar to "That's All for Everyone," was a study in repetitious chord progression. Lindsey's new songs for *Tusk* reminded me at times of an Andy Kaufman bit, wildly provocative and punctuated by long pauses. How far could he push his audience before losing them? Or was the whole point not to care? But we did care, and our goal on this song was to make sure we filled in the stark structure with as much musical filigree as we could so that, lyrics aside, translate the song into visual sound.

Lindsey would approach each song a section at a time, interchanging his found sounds until he got exactly what he was looking for. He didn't care whether his songs contained instruments that weren't played in time with one another. He didn't care whether they were distorted or out of tune—the rawer, the better. This made collaborating with him on *Tusk* a challenge, to say the least. Lindsey, along with others, such as Paul McCartney, Pete Townshend, and R. Stevie Moore, was developing the vocabulary of home recording on professional gear, a privilege that most folks didn't have.

Richard and I were nominated for a Grammy for Best Engineered Album for *Rumours*, so our good sound was our trademark, our passion. Normally, sessions would progress as the band improved their performance of the song, take by take, before figuring out overdubs to embellish the master take. We approached Lindsey's songs very differently; they were always compartmentalized works in progress, never the band trying to collectively catch lightning in a bottle. We started "Walk a Thin Line" in early October, but we didn't finish putting the last touches on it until late April.

"Walk a Thin Line" was typical of Lindsey's *Tusk* songs as it was a built song with multiple layers of found sounds from around the studio, jigsawed into the song's unique arrangement. Notably, "Walk a thin Line" featured a quirky, double-tracked toy piano arpeggio hook. Lindsey, at this time, was somewhat infatuated by the toy piano. He first suggested it during our recording of Bob Welch's "Sentimental Lady," a song that Welch had done earlier with Fleetwood Mac but always felt was a lost hit, and so it was, with Lindsey's help. Next, Lindsey used it again on Walter Egan's hit song "Magnet and Steel" that Walter wrote about Stevie. Eventually we swapped the toy piano and upgraded to a much nicer baby grand. Lindsey plinked the piano with one finger at half speed, so when the track was sped back up, it became even more jangly and lifted the chorus even higher.

It was remarkable how loose all the parts were. The low chunks that Lindsey played on his Gretsch were doubled, but they weren't played in time with each other, something very uncharacteristic from his earlier work where everything would be laid down perfectly. On *Tusk*, even when Lindsey was playing it "straight," he was letting in just enough chaos to trick the ear. His lyrics on this song, and his others on *Tusk*, generally concerned risk, loyalty, self-affirmation, and justification, often veering between accusation and identity, his songs surfed the line between successful art pop and self-indulgence. The days spent looking for just the right sounds to fit the mosaic in Lindsey's head, would vacillate between being extremely fun to extremely tiring.

In the following weeks, "Walk a Thin Line" received multiple overdubs from Lindsey, such as two Ovation acoustic guitars played at different octaves that replaced the hi-hat's part, and a set of doubled piano tracks replaced his rhythm guitars with long sonorous left-hand chords, as Lindsey kept his foot on the sustain pedal throughout. For the minimal bridges, he took up his Fender Stratocaster and adeptly invented a figure with his tremolo and volume pedals for a synthesizer effect, which took the song to an entirely different place and made you forget that you'd been listening to the same two chords over and over again. "Walk a Thin Line" was now a doo-wop song on acid.

"Walk a Thin Line," in particular, served as either Lindsey's mission statement or a literal plea for mutual understanding. It's not as well known, but Fleetwood Mac had counted amongst its numbers four highly talented singer-guitarist-songwriters in Peter Green, Danny Kirwan, Jeremy Spencer, and Bob Welch, well before Lindsey Buckingham joined. Not even the Yardbirds could top that. Everyone thinks Fleetwood Mac was one type of band before Stevie and Lindsey joined, but the truth is it had played, and could play, all types of music very, very well. Furthermore, this band was used to departures and emotional issues that would have broken up any other band.

Tusk was going to be the Mac's twelfth album, and as such, it wouldn't be the band's first departure from what its fans thought it was. People thought Fleetwood Mac was just a London blues band until it released *Then Play On*, its most progressive album until *Tusk* ten years later. If any band could back up the experimentation of a guitar player going mental, it was Fleetwood Mac. The only genre of music Fleetwood Mac didn't play in its long history was uncommercial, outsider music because the band didn't like that type of sloppy music, and neither did Lindsey per se. Yet Lindsey was a weird guy, and he wanted to explore the underground, so things were gonna get weird. If the band wouldn't let him leave, then fine, he was going to drag the band along with him, kicking and screaming, if necessary.

The month of May proved to be very productive on overdubs, which gave the band and us a closer musical outlook on how the songs were finally going to be mixed, especially for the girls' songs. Lindsey was still trying vocal melo-

dies, new lyrics, and in some cases, changes in the structures of the songs. The fact that we were doing vocals required that I reserve the best microphones at the Village Recorder for our sessions, something that not always appreciated, since the other studios down the hall were busy with other important projects.

Given that it was strategic mission entrusted in me by Ken and Richard where I could not fail, I had to use different tactics to assure the availability of the best tube large-diaphragm condenser microphones, such as the Neumann U47, Telefunken M250, and AKG C12. The quality of sound and their tonal warmth made these microphones a must to our sessions, although for many of Stevie's vocals we used her favorite dynamic microphone, the Sennheiser 441, which cost a few thousand dollars less.

After putting "I Know I'm Not Wrong" to bed, "Walk a Thin Line" was paramount to Lindsey's agenda. After having a relatively scant number of songs on the previous albums, and he had written a bunch on the Rumours tour with a Tascam 8-track in his bag, and he wanted his creative renaissance to be well documented. We listened again and again to Lindsey's ninth song for Tusk. Gradually, his face had a sign of curiosity that I believe had to do with his mind's crunching new possibilities for the song. The mystery was resolved when he told us that he wanted to try a fresh version of the song from scratch.

We began with Lindsey's home version of "Walk a Thin Line" as a template. The song was a study in juxtaposition. It had a military drum beat that marched slightly faster than our heart rate, and a doo-wop vocal arrangement underpinning lyrics that centered on individuality and marching to your own drummer, which was literally what Lindsey did. The starkness and rawness of the recording stemmed from his home experiments, as he explained his process on "Walk a Thin Line" to the film crew:

UNDOING THE LACES

What I'm basically trying to do is take a track that we cut in the studio, which has very, very dry sounds on it, no ambience or echo at all, and selectively, say, take the snare drums and the vocals and run them through these speakers and mike the bathroom, which is right across the hall, and which has an amazing sound. I mean, 1927 bathrooms, believe me, are rock and roll all the way. I mike what's being recorded in there and record it back onto some empty tracks, so the whole song takes on a more atmospheric sort of feel to it.

For the next five hours, all of us started block building the drums, aided by a click track set to 69 bpm, a slower tempo than his home recording. Despite the doo-wop vocals, this song did not swing in any way whatsoever. The special drum sound came from wiping the hi-hat and instead layering a bedrock of kick drums and snares that eventually were combined on a pair of stereo tracks. The different takes of kick and snare were treated to different microphone models and distances to get drier or wetter takes, creating a wall of sound, much in the style of Phil Spector, but with a wider degree of tonality and outboard gear treatment; that is to say, equalizers and compressors.

The fact that the two kicks and fours snares weren't precisely in time with one another, especially in the stuttering press-rolls on the snare that Lindsey borrowed from the Rolling Stones' song "Sway," which gave the song a feeling of naïveté, like a child playing an instrument for the first time. After building a barren set of drum tracks, devoid of hi-hat, cymbals, or toms, Lindsey recorded a simple, but effective, bassline that doubled his Gretsch's crunchy strum to imaginatively evoke an eighth-note feel.

Bringing his tracks into the studio was fundamental in Lindsey getting what he wanted to hear. With Ken at the wheel, the song took on a deeper *musical tone and character. Lindsey was a fan of double or triple tracking his vocals just like John Lennon, in addition to having his vocal sound altered. We would VSO Lindsey's voice up and down to create additional timbres, and with "Walk a Thin Line," we added tape delay on everything to accentuate Lindsey's experiments in off-time backgrounds that had a kind of comic Beach Boys* Smile *feel. Lindsey would get down on his hands and knees in the Brazilian iso room and sing into a microphone taped to the floor to make his vocals sound as different as possible from one another. We used a slave 24-track to have more tracks and build enough passes to achieve that massive swarm of voices.*

The next time Hernan loaded "Walk a Thin Line" on the 24-track Studer, we were working with Lindsey on finding a slower speed for the song. I was immediately struck at how much different the track sounded. It had become a dreamy, trancelike stoner ballad that now ran to nearly four minutes. I couldn't believe my ears! We set up a M-49 and a few others that Hernan managed to purloin for us to do Lindsey's background vocals. Lindsey wanted to make all his vocals lush.

He started slowing the whole track down before doubling his lead vocal with very breathy "Taaaaake your tiiiiime." This track was VSO'd even more so for literal effect, making it sound very ethereal, or as Lindsey put it, "Mickey Mouse-ish," for those three words, pushing his already high-pitched voice to the edge of helium. Then, beneath those words, Lindsey sang four pairs of vocals, "Ooh wah, ooh wah, ooh wah, ooh wah-ahahh," and each pair had a different VSO speed for an out-of-phase rock choir. When Lindsey's lead vocal finishes the title phrase, "I walk a thinnnn linnnnne," the eight background vocals come back in and completely bury the word "line" in a monk's chant.

UNDOING THE LACES

After the second verse and chorus, the lead drops out for that gauzy, spaced-out instrumental section where Lindsey experimented with more harmony vocals, all done by him. They were mostly mouth noises with Lindsey changing the shape of his mouth from "ahh" to "ooh," almost like vocal warm-up exercises, singing one continuous note and back before finishing with the extra-long chorus. When we were done with the vocal, Lindsey was elated and mentally spent.

I was very proud of him for showing off his softer side instead of deliberately distorting the track, which is what I was expecting. I knew that this song would be a joy to mix, making a perfect sonic painting to complement more the girls' songs than his previous efforts. "Walk a Thin Line" reminded me of one of Lindsey's expressions that artists were "insecure overachievers" and the vulnerability that so many artists must have to be able to do what they do. I was very excited by the finished track and the feeling of camaraderie that comes with a good day's work in the studio.

Although the Fleetwood Mac family played a lot of softball, a soccer challenge between the Brits and the Chileans was bound to arise. Our neighbor, Argentina, had just hosted and won the World Cup the previous summer, so this was a grudge match of sorts. It took a while to organize, but we finally settled on a park in Encino. It was hilarious to see the Brits—John McVie, Mick Fleetwood, and John Helliwell and Dougie Thompson from Supertramp—in their soccer shorts with some of the road crew as plugs, going up against a group led by my friend Gerardo that included guys who had played rugby and soccer for our British school in Chile. The appointed time for the match was high noon, with the rock stars showing late with the help of some good brews, tobacco, and Peruvian dust. We played a fifteen-minute-a-side game that had many casualties with the final score of 6 to 1, Chile. Unfortunately, nobody took photos of our momentous victory.

Saturday, May 26, 1979, was Stevie's birthday and my dad's as well. He was in Lake Tahoe enjoying four years of early retirement, but it was also an exciting day for me, his namesake. We had, through Judy Wong, been able to bring on "the Penguin," the all-star third baseman for the Dodgers, Ron Cey, as head coach for the Fleetwood Mac softball team. We had set up a secret practice session on the top lawn at Pepperdine University in Malibu to prepare ourselves for our games against the Eagles, REO Speedwagon, and our ultimate nemesis, the Messiahs of Money, our business manager's team. We were bringing in some ringers of our own, some sluggers from Wally Heider's Studios to bolster our team's batting average.

The morning started out innocently enough. That weekend, the lovely Diane arrived at my hillside home with her VW Bug filled with her clothes, her guitar, pictures, and her faithful German shepherd, "'Sky." Sky was getting older and pretty much did only what she wanted to do. As I helped her unload her car, I said, "What's the deal with all the stuff? How long are you planning to stay, anyway?"

She passed me with her arms full of stuff and just gave me a kiss on my cheek and said, "Don't laugh. Your bachelor days are over, young man!"

"Okay by me!" I said. "Just get inside and get your clothes off. The pool is steaming and we have a game to get to!"

All the families and friends of Fleetwood Mac showed up to Pepperdine University with their blankets and picnic baskets to watch the team practice their moves and clear out the cobwebs that had gathered over the long winter months. The first to arrive were the road crew and their families. Then came the office staff, then the attorneys, and finally the team itself. Diane and I, Lindy and Richard, Sara and Mick and his mom, "Biddy," and the kids, Carol and Lindsey, Julie and John and their daughter, Christine and Dennis, and Hernan and Stevie and her posse. It was a beautiful spring day in Malibu and Ron Cey was coaching us on the proper techniques of catching and throwing a baseball (without a beer or a joint in our hands). Poor Ron realized soon enough that for some of us there was no hope at all, so he did what he could.

I was a frustrated pitcher, wanting to throw overhand like the big leagues, but limited to using a softball and pitching underhanded. As the morning warmed up, bottles of Champagne and cans of beer could be heard popping all over the field and in the stands. The spectators were seated around the practice area shouting out words of encouragement and off-color jokes. Even though we were worse than the Bad News Bears, we tried our best to be serious.

"Somebody remind me, whose idea was this baseball thing?! It's too hot!" Richard complained.

"It was yours, Dashut, you putz!" came a resounding chorus from nearly everyone in earshot.

"It's not my fault you drank the Kool-Aid! You guys will thank me when we kick everyone's pompous asses!" was his satisfied retort.

In the distance, we heard the low rumble of something approaching. The noise got louder and louder and suddenly we noticed a large shadow crossing over the field above us. I looked up to see a large, blue Bell Jet Ranger helicopter cresting over the coast and rising above us. I couldn't believe my eyes.

"What the hell?!" I yelled over the incessant *chup-chup-chup-chup-chup-chup-chup-chup*.

It was directly overhead now and just as I took a step forward to get in its shadow to see better, I felt something just skim the hairs on the back of my head and down my back and into the green pristine grass that was blown violently flat.

"Oh my god, it's a water balloon! Diane exclaimed, "and it made a big hole in the grass!"

"Huh?" I grunted before I came to my senses. "Watch out, everybody! They're dropping water balloons from the helicopter!"

Everybody on the field looked at Di and me, so I pointed to the large divot in the lawn and said, "This one missed me by an inch! Cover your beers and your children!"

Instantly, everybody realized that this was a real danger and started waving at the helicopter to call it off.

"Who *are* those assholes?" I screamed.

I could barely hear Richard's reply over the noise of the rotors.

"It could be only one asshole . . . Brian Adams, the ringleader of the pencil pushers!"

Mick put on his stern British demeanor and signaled to one of our attorneys to do something. And then things got very serious. It was as if Mick had called *atten-tion!* to his troops. After we had got the attention of a helicopter, it landed and we confronted the culprit. It was none other than the dastardly Brian Adams. He insisted he was only trying to disrupt the enemy, but after he saw so many angry mothers, he offered helicopter rides to the kiddies. This brought our first official baseball practice to a close with mass disarray. The last thing Ron Cey said as he left was, "You guys are fucking nuts!"

UNDOING THE LACES

Another day in Fleetwood Macland, I thought, throwing my glove in the car.

Stevie's birthday came up in the middle of the hustle of finishing Tusk. *We expanded our studio schedule into the weekends, but we took that Saturday off for the FM All-Stars practice. After the helicopter attack, Stevie and I left early to celebrate her thirty-first birthday at the chic and trendy entertainment industry French restaurant Le Dome. It was a fun night with plenty of good Champagne. We were joined by my sister Carolina, who had flown down from the hippie mountains of Santa Cruz.*

Carolina and Stevie connected fast, laughing and telling stories of our parents, as the night progressed and got louder. It did us well to get away from the studio and the FM bunch. In the middle of the celebration, our waiter brought us a bottle of Dom Pérignon from the table across the way. It was sent by none other than James Bond in person, Sean Connery, who very sweetly waved at Stevie while singing "Happy Birthday" in his thick accent. We went to his table to pay our respects. Bond was my father's favorite character and Sean Connery his actor of choice, so it filled us with emotion to meet him. He told us when he first heard of Fleetwood Mac, he thought it was a Scottish band.

19

NAIROBI TO LOS ANGELES

Tusk is more like a puzzle. You get the feeling that if you
spent enough time with this album, and this band,
you could figure out how and why the pieces fit
together. Or at least why you wanted them to.

—Daisann McLane, *Rolling Stone*

Monday, June 4, 1979, was the historic day we finally arrived at 1000 Vin Scully Avenue, Dodger Stadium, with our piecemeal recording of "Tusk," to perform the mammoth task of recording the largest one-and-a-half-minute overdub in pop music history by the University of Southern California Trojan Marching Band. This was a very exciting day for all of us. For me, as an Angeleno, I'd been to Dodger Stadium many times, but obviously I'd never had it all to myself. My fantasy was to pitch from the famous mound that so many of the greats had pitched from before, such as Sandy Koufax, Don Drysdale, Don Sutton, Bob Welch, and soon Ken Caillat! I was happier than hell in Blue Heaven.

We arrived early in the morning to Chavez Ravine, located in the Elysian Park area of Los Angeles and horseshoed by the San Gabriel

Mountains. It was a gorgeous morning without a cloud in the sky. We parked in the lot behind center field, and I walked in between the outfield pavilions like a gladiator with my baseball glove and sexy new girlfriend. I looked up at the Three Sisters palm trees in left field and up at the two futuristic, hexagonal scoreboards and my heart raced.

The Dodgers themselves were on a road trip, but the ground crew was just finishing up its meticulous ceremony. After marveling at the rows and rows of empty yellow, orange, and blue stands, the first thing I saw was the Wally Heider's recording truck parked just off the infield grass on the dirt sidelines leading toward the bullpen. This would be my office for the next few hours. Next to the truck were over twenty cases of Heineken stacked up into small mountains, with lakes of iced Champagne in their shadow.

Growing up at Heider's, I'd spent five years learning how records were made, both in the studio, and especially in live venues. I assume it's a bit like being a farmer: you really have to love it, because it just gets in your veins. Placing a microphone in front of an instrument you just met, hearing what its particular sonic characteristic is, and then picking the right microphone to capture its tone becomes an art. Each mic becomes my friend and has its own personality and I can "feel" which mic is needed for each instance. As with players on my sports team, I know their capabilities and limitations.

The first thing that happens when recording at a live event is to "pull cables" for power and audio, visuals, and communications. Finding a source of "clean power" is not always easy. You have to locate the power box and hope you can tap into a clean source, one without air conditioners, photocopiers, or other noise-creating equipment, because their clicks, pops, and buzzes will absolutely ruin your recording. The truck's tech was skilled at locating power sources, and at Dodger Stadium it was easy to interface with the building's power.

The Heider's crew, who were all my personal friends and FM All-Stars teammates, unloaded and stretched out twenty-four pairs of 250-foot audio cables, meaning each cable would be connected to our console in the truck to twenty-four microphones several hundred feet away. A second "snake" had to be run to completely cover the entire marching band, which we were told numbered as many as 112 musicians, featuring marching trio drums, snares, bass drums, tubas, trumpets, mellophones, trombones, saxophones, French horns, clarinets, flutes, piccolos, clarinets, bassoons, and bells.

This was the earliest I'd seen the Fleetwood Mac awake when not on tour, but everyone was exhilarated and a party atmosphere prevailed. Stevie remarked to Christine, "Who are we to deserve the USC marching band to play for us?" To which Chris responded with typical English archness, "Stevie, don't be so humble." None of the finer points of the recording had been discussed yet; we just planned to arrive and wing it and record whatever they had. We had made a feeble attempt to provide enough headphones for the marching band. I told the Heider's crew to bring as many headphones and headphone junction boxes as it could find. The crew also brought big playback speakers in case we had to do it the old-fashioned way.

At first, we sat back and let the marching band and its director, Dr. Arthur C. Bartner, who was dressed in USC colors—loud cardinal red blazer and gold shirt and tie—start their rehearsing separately. The trumpets were in left field, the trombones in right, and the saxophones were in the dugout. For the past few days, we had been mixing and editing "Tusk" to be ready for today and had sent a mix over to Dr.

Bartner, so he could compose the score for our great experiment. This was our first chance to hear what he had come up with, and he did a fine job, especially with the countermelody played by the flutes and piccolos against the main riff in the fadeout. We were all surprised to hear our peculiar baby arranged for a marching band.

Once the band had limbered up, Mick and Lindsey asked the team in the truck to play back our mix so everyone could hear the new marching band arrangement played live with our track. This meant that Richard and I had to continually run from inside the truck to the infield where Lindsey, Mick, and Dr. Bartner were, so we could coordinate. Eventually, we were able to rustle up some walkie-talkies from the Dodger management so we could remotely coordinate their playback needs: "*Squawk!* Okay, guys, hold it. *Hold it!* Can you play it again from the top, and just keep playing it until we tell you to stop?"

The big speakers boomed the basic track of "Tusk" and Dr. Bartner listened and started assembling his band around him arranged by sections. For each section, Mick would be stomping his foot to the beat to indicate the correct timing to the band. Regardless, the band would rush the beat at times, especially when the tubas entered. We went through the song's arrangement, section by section, with Lindsey commenting on problems he heard and Dr. Bartner scribbling the appropriate changes to his master score, which then had to be communicated to the scores that the marching band had attached to its instruments. This process was painstakingly slow, and during their second set of rehearsals, we started setting up clusters of microphones around the different sections of instruments and getting levels.

Meanwhile, Richard and the crew were fulfilling their fantasies, too, smoking joints inside the home dugout in between sipping on longnecks and eating sandwiches and Dodger Dogs. Of course, that meant that the sweet aroma of good bud attracted every pothead in the stadium, including Stevie, Lindsey, Richard, Judy Wong, the Heider's crew, and a few of the more daring members of USC marching band. I decided to wait until we figured out how we were going to record this before I indulged.

If you weren't a member of the recording team, you were having a really good time. Spirits were high and the outdoor location served as a release for all the tensions that had accumulated during the year we had spent in our dark rooms. We had sent John off on his boat trip to Hawaii, and Judy had a life-size John McVie cutout made, which only added to the surrealism of what was taking place. Everywhere you looked, there was John, standing and saying nothing, which wasn't too different from the studio, as he could be very soft spoken. I found it funny to see Christine carrying him around in one hand with a glass of Champagne in the other.

Stevie, to everyone's great amusement, started twirling a baton she had brought, reliving her cheerleading childhood and hamming it up for Tom Spain and his cameras, only too happy for the spontaneously entertaining footage. Dennis Wilson, Stevie's friends, and the Fleetwood Mac Road Widows were roller-skating around the terraced concrete pavilions high up overlooking the playing field as the music blasted around the stadium. Mick was sporting his blue Dodgers T-shirt and Lindsey was adorned in a Trojan helmet in a gesture of solidarity and command. Both Lindsey and Mick stood on the field, instructing Bartner and his assistants and chatting good-naturedly with the students and invited journalists.

The magic of the occasion quickly evaporated for me as I was ultimately responsible for the problems that needed to be figured out

GET TUSKED

before we could call this session over and claim victory. Today's primary challenge was how to record over a hundred orchestral instruments all playing near one another without having them bleed into the next closest microphone. Unfortunately, all our microphones could hear the reference track we were playing the band, too, since you can't baffle a baseball stadium. The leakage from the far away speakers was too severe. We had to come up with Plan B, and fast.

I knew we would have to use headphones for this recording, but we only had about forty and not enough power to drive them all, let alone the fact that we needed three times that. If we could solve the headphone issue, it would give us two benefits: we would get a clean recording of all the instruments in the marching band, and if we needed to edit the recording, we could freely do it without worrying about what the leakage was doing.

I went over to talk to my old buddy Biff Dawes, the truck's head engineer, about the headphone issue. He and I were methodical and efficient to a fault and had a history of troubleshooting scrapes like these, including saving a Procol Harum live album in Edmonton through our own mutual meticulousness.

"Yeah, I figured this would become mission critical and we'd need to go to headphones. I already called the studio and told them to go find more or rent some if they had to," Biff said.

Just then, Richard came over to me and told me of a new problem. "Cutlass, bad news: the marching band said they can't play properly unless they're marching!"

"You're shitting me?!" I fired back. "We're going to have to follow them with our mics? We don't have lines long enough. How are they going to walk with headphones on?"

Things just went from bad to impossible, and everyone was getting really frustrated. I was glad I hadn't smoked any pot yet. I needed to think, and quickly. Richard and I walked over to Dr. Bartner to discuss our pending emergency.

"Art, can we talk to you for a second?" I asked, "I just heard about a potentially big problem. Is it true that the band must march while they play? That just can't be true."

"Well, typically, they all play while marching. They're a *marching* band. That's what they do," he said, casually, as if this should have been obvious.

One of the college kids overheard what we were talking about and blurted out, "How about if we just walk in place, sir? Would that work?"

"You may have just saved the recording, young man," Richard said, bowing slightly in deferential honor of his suggestion.

"That would work perfectly!" I agreed, "but you guys are serious? You can't just stand in one place and play?"

"If they stand, they tend to play a bit fast, moving ahead of the beat," Dr. Bartner explained.

"Art, we have one other issue to discuss, I don't think we're going to have enough headphones for the entire band. We may have to give them to only some of the musicians. Which ones would you recommend we give them to?" I asked.

"I'm the orchestra leader. Why don't you just give one to me? I can conduct them and keep them in time with your track," he suggested. "I do it all the time. I think we're ready to record now. We've made all the changes that were needed. I'll have the band take their normal performance positions and you can set up their mics."

He turned around to the band leader and asked him to have the band fall into performance positions. I told Biff via my walkie-talkie that the band was going to get into its performance formation so we could start moving our mics into position. Since the marching band had to be marching to perform, as I feared, we were picking up feet noise in the grass. Biff suggested we use shotgun microphones.

"You brought some?" I asked, surprised.

"Sure, you never know when you'll need them. Better safe than sorry!" Biff shrugged.

"Genius!" I said, relieved. In a matter of twenty minutes, the marching band was in position and its mics were held in the proper positions, allowing room for the musicians to march in place.

Soon we were ready to run the tape from the top and hear the orchestra play along. For simplicity, we left the speakers on so everyone on the field could hear the track. We did a complete take, recording all the instruments. It sounded good, but I could hear the leakage of the track blasting from the speakers, bleeding into all forty mics. Now for the real test: we needed to see whether the musicians could all play their parts in time with our track by following only Art's baton.

Back in the truck, I hit the talkback button and my voice boomed out into Dodger Stadium like a game announcer: *"You're sounding really good, everyone! If you're ready, let's try it without the speakers, following Dr. Bartner's baton."*

Hernan handed Art the single pair of headphones from our truck.

"Art, can you hear me?" I spoke to him directly into his headphones. He was now standing on a ladder that someone from the stadium brought him and he held up his hand with a positive thumbs-up.

"He's ready," Hernan confirmed over the walkie-talkie.

NAIROBI TO LOS ANGELES

I pressed Record.

We had a four-bar intro click track preceding the beginning of our little "Stage Riff" from six months ago.

"Here we go, boys; let's see if we can make history again," I said out loud to everyone in the truck. Richard, under his red USC visor and sunglasses, took a long hit off his joint, presumably for luck.

To my great surprise, when it was time for the band to enter, it nailed the take perfectly, and the big "Voice of the Theater" Altec 604 speakers filled the truck with the USC marching band's sweet sounds. We kept speakers putting out the track at a distance close enough for them to hear it, but far enough not to bleed into the small marching path captured with movie-location Sennheiser 415 shotgun mics attached to long cables that were carried by Wally Heider's engineers. Those tracks were coupled with the always unrivaled Neumann U87 and U47 for mid and ambient recording, including some that we placed in the highest bleachers. Thus, we not only captured the band on the infield, including the "How are the tenors, Tony?" snippet, but also wonderful reverberating ambience with leakage from the speakers that we later treated and used as the crowd effect that runs throughout the final mix on the fade-in and background.

Despite our best efforts, we found out when a marching band plays, it's not always on the beat, which we discovered when we got back into the studio. The overdub was still out of time with the track. The marching band would have to be manually synchronized onto our already bizarre and troublesome track. Even still, you can hear several times in the final mix that the marching band is speeding up or slowing down to get back in sync. We knew this at the time and felt resigned that it only enhanced the oddness of "Tusk." It certainly made a fantastic live song, especially when the Spirit of Troy band joined the Mac onstage for a few nights at the Forum that December. We made sure all its members all got free albums, and Stevie, Lindsey, and Mick returned the favor by joining the Trojans on the field during their half-time performance for homecoming.

When we mixed "Tusk," we were forced to synchronize two 24-track machines together, playing at the same time. "Tusk" has the highest track count on the album by a great deal. The song lent its name to the album and was given pride of place as the first single from Fleetwood Mac since "You Make Lovin' Fun" two years earlier. The band's fans couldn't have been more shocked, but that didn't stop the song from shooting to no. 8 in the charts and being one of the strangest songs to occupy that coveted real estate. I took some pride when twenty-five years later, Gwen Stefani took a page from the "Tusk" playbook with her first no. 1, "Hollaback Girl." To this day, both USC and the University of Alabama use "Tusk" as their unofficial fight songs, and I've heard it at countless other football games since.

When most of the recording was done, the band members plus Cardboard John sat down together, hooting and hollering behind the dugout as the marching band and color guard, in full uniform, performed for them around the field. Since we had enough usable takes, I decided it was time to have some fun myself and pitch from that famous pitchers' mound, and you know what I discovered? It's a lot farther to home plate than it looks. My first pitch barely made it the 60 feet, 6 inches to the plate. My second pitch, I had to throw so hard that I felt something in my arm hurt. My third pitch was a strike. "That's it; I'm done," I said. "I'd better quit while I'm ahead!"

I walked over to my proud girlfriend and we put our arms around each other. "Diane, I think you bring me good luck. I think we should get married!"

"Well, maybe," she said with a wink.

Fleetwood Mac's single, "Tusk," was indeed unique, but also very much a by-product of the rich cross-pollination of cultures in the late '70s, a period when many post-punk and New Wave bands were starting to look at Africa and Jamaica, among other exotic locales, for inspiration. The concept of primitivism was a well-established one in Western art ever since Picasso's Les Demoiselles d'Avignon, *and found new cachet and practitioners every decade. From Conrad to Coppola, Bowie to Basquiat, primitivism was hot once again. The "Tusk" day at Dodger Stadium symbolized this era and summed up the duality of the song itself, a tribal chant from the Dark Continent played by a village band in one of the sunny cathedrals of mid-century modernism.*

A month later, the Bee Gees would sell out Dodger Stadium, and five days later Comiskey Park would host the notorious Disco Demolition Night. The times were, indeed, a-changin'. In 1979, music fans were confronted with the Pop Group's Y, *the Talking Heads' African rhythms on* Fear of Music, *and the Slits dressed as half-naked, mud-caked tribeswomen on* Cut. *Even Elvis Costello & the Attractions, which didn't dabble much in African sounds, released* Armed Forces, *the cover of which featured a stampeding herd of elephants. The trend would continue as New Wave bands, such as Bow Wow Wow, took up Burundi rhythms and the new genre of "world music" crossed firmly over in the 1980s with Peter Gabriel and Paul Simon's use and promotion of African musicians and styles.*

The art design for the Tusk *album was also a departure from the band's two previous albums, taking its cues instead from the visual imagery* associated with the title song. The band hired the cultured and eccentric photographer-diarist-artist Peter Beard to create one of his multilayered, African-themed collages for the inside gatefold. Beard loved all the Polaroids we had around the studio and took a number of photos himself, which he set in collages that included his own African photographs, such as Machine in the Garden, Tsavo, Kenya, *found objects and ephemera, and ink writings and drawings.*

Beard took special joy in placing Ken's dog not only on the cover, but throughout the gatefold collages, including placing Scooter's head on the nude body of Magritte Rammé straddling an elephant tusk. Beard was a fun guy and enjoyed pot almost as much as Lindsey, regaling us with stories about Andy Warhol and the Rolling Stones. Beard lived a dangerous life and would later be near fatally attacked by a herd of elephants. Like the album itself, it's important to remember that a tusk may be smooth and elegant, but is also a fearsome and deadly weapon.

The band wanted its California identity preserved as well, choosing a moonlit gazebo on the coast of Santa Monica below the pier as the background of their group shot by famed, South African photographer Norman Seeff. In addition, the band used the up-and-coming Pacific Wave graphic designer Jayme Odgers to represent a distinctly modern Los Angeles feel with his mixed-media photo designs. Odgers's color palette for Tusk's backgrounds evoked both the khaki savannas of Africa and the sand dunes of Malibu, both elementally earthy and artificially avant-garde. The finishing touch came with the album title Tusk *in a small, bathetic font. Two years after* Rumours *won the Grammy for Album of the Year,* Tusk *was nominated only for Best Album Package, and still lost to Bob Seger's* Against the Wind *and a herd of airbrushed horses.*

Shortly after the Tusk tour, Mick and Richard would jet off to Ghana to work on Mick's solo album, *The Visitor*, where he and his band collaborated with local musicians in the spirit of mutual discovery. One of the songs they chose to record was "Walk a Thin Line," with Mick's brother-in-law, George Harrison, the original pop music explorer. Lindsey, for his part, would write a "Tusk" follow-up song with "Bwana," on his first solo album, which he released as a single. Later, Fleetwood Mac would return to this theme on Tango in the Night, *with an album cover inspired by proto-primitivist Henri Rousseau's iconic African-themed paintings. For all of the "out there" dismissals and observations about the* Tusk *album, it was, in a sense, very much of its time, if critics and fans knew where to look.*

20

LAST CALL FOR EVERYONE

> We had this concept called "*Tusk* mixing." And *Tusk* mixing was when there were mistakes made in the mixing process that you just left because it was an accident that happened that way and you just left it . . . On one of the Lindsey Buckingham songs, right at the very tail end of the song as it's fading out, there's a cymbal crash and somebody mutes it, and then they unmute it. And it's like, "Why on earth did they leave that in the mix?"
>
> —Jonathan Segel, Camper Van Beethoven

LA's hot summer nights had a good effect on our spirits, giving all of us a chance to find more time to go out as the mixing schedule depended more on Ken, Richard, and me than the band. Stevie and I took full advantage of the free time to enjoy our wild romance, sometimes going as special guests to shows like James Taylor at the Greek Theater, or just hitting some cool restaurants on Sunset. Stevie also found time for live duets with her friend Kenny Loggins on "Whenever I Call You 'Friend.'" Stevie would also do backgrounds for Lindsey's production of John Stewart's Bombs Away Dream Babies *for the hit single "Gold," which I noticed bore a small resemblance to "Sisters of the Moon."*

GET TUSKED

One of the wild adventures Stevie and I had together was an express trip to Phoenix, Arizona, where she was a special guest of John Stewart at the freshly inaugurated Compton Terrace. It was an outdoor amphitheater built by her father, Jess Nicks, next to Legend City, which was an Old West–themed amusement park. We took off for Phoenix after a long session at Studio D with no sleep. Upon arrival, we were taken to the amphitheater to do a sound check and get to know the brand-new venue, which was stunning with its desert backdrop. Stevie and John surprised me by asking whether I would do their live sound, something I had never done on a large scale. I had only been a house mixer on a couple of occasions in a small club. The adrenaline of the moment hit me hard, and the lack of sleep evaporated as we started doing the sound check.

We hung out at the beautiful Camelback Inn before the gig with an entourage that included some of Stevie's friends and my Chilean pals sipping some wonderful margaritas and some other delights until the time for the show came. When we got back to the Compton Terrace, the last lights of the evening were fading, painting the surrounding desert with magical shades or red, purple, and orange. When the spotlights hit John Stewart, he had a slightly similar look to Elvis, banging the acoustic guitar and singing in a fine baritone.

When John introduced Stevie to sing "Gold," the full-capacity audience of more than twenty thousand went wild cheering. But the Welsh Witch's presence couldn't go unnoticed by the spirits in the sacred grounds of the Pima and Maricopa American Indian tribes, the original settlers of that desert land. Lightning struck in the distance and wild Sonoran desert winds started to blow from behind the stage, getting stronger by the minute, finally becoming a full sandstorm that started taking down microphone stands first, followed by instruments, lights, sound rigging, and part of the stage. The show was over and sand was everywhere. We headed back to our hotel and partied until dawn before flying back to LA.

Life in the fast lane with the hottest female rock star in the world was challenging, with all the highs and all the trials that the role had. It was a fact that my life had changed completely since the affair started with Stevie, but I tried hard to make sure that this new status wouldn't make me a conceited idiot. Stevie was no ordinary girl, of course, but she had managed to preserve her warmth with everyone around, without giving herself airs of royalty that many other rock stars had. The practical challenge was that we were working hard at the Village nearly every day. We expected to have a peaceful environment to rest when we got home in the wee hours of the dawn. But Stevie's entourage had other plans, waiting for her to come home and party no matter what. Very few had any real function aside from hanging out and leeching. Stevie's true friends were wonderful and knew better than to distract her from her music.

That said, Stevie's house on Doheny was a party hangout stop for old friends who would show up in the middle of the night, expecting action, something that also was hard for Stevie to say no to. One night, J. D. Souther showed late to court her while I was still in the studio, giving her an exquisite mother-of-pearl-inlaid Ovation guitar as a present. He'd been after her for years, and I don't know how I was confident enough to think I was the only one. Stevie wisely and thankfully reacted to this situation by suggesting we move out of her house to the exclusive L'Ermitage hotel in Beverly Hills to regain our privacy and enjoy our free time to rest and relax.

A few days later, Stevie; her new Afghan dog, Branwen; her whole chiffon wardrobe; and I moved into our new suite. Stevie immediately created ambience by draping her fine silk scarves on the lamps to dim the light and create a more mystical mood to match my Brazilian record collection. The *move proved to be excellent for our mood and intimacy, as well as work, especially since Stevie still had lead vocals to record and many sessions of background vocals for her songs and the rest. After a year in the studio and two months together, we had become very close, enjoyed our mutual company, and shared similar sensibilities, in spite our both coming from vastly different worlds.*

Since she was without proper management, Stevie trusted me during that time to fly with her brother, Chris Nicks, to New York to meet with Danny Goldberg and Paul Fishkin who were courting her for their label, Modern Records. When the meetings were over, a limo pulled up, chauffeured by none other than Gene Simmons, who drove us all over the city and parked anywhere he liked. We were given the five-star treatment and got to see the Jam play at the Palladium, the Cramps at CBGB, and even had our heads turned around by meeting and hanging out with Bruce Springsteen. Paul and Danny were adamant about getting Stevie signed to a solo record deal, knowing full well that she was disgruntled and getting too big for Fleetwood Mac to contain.

Life back in LA resumed with little to no sleep. I had to be at the Village early, many times rushing through traffic to make it in time. On one of those races, Stevie was with me and we were driving quite fast on Little Santa Monica in Beverly Hills. A lady suddenly turned left in front of us and hit the Alfa Romeo on my side, making the car take a spin that I managed to control. The crash felt strong, made a lot of noise, and made me worry right away about Stevie. I had an enormous responsibility carrying the Queen of Rock and Roll in the middle of the making of Tusk. Thankfully, she was wearing her seatbelt. She was shaken and nervous as people gathered, but she was fine and I managed to get a taxi fast and took her to the Village right away. It was a big scare that made everyone reflect on their own personal welfare, and had John Courage advising me on how I should exercise full responsibility in preserving one of the jewels of the crown!

Most of the tensions from Tusk had been put on the back burner by August, since we were now full bore into mixing, with all the songs in the can, except for minimal overdubs on such songs as "Angel" and "Brown Eyes." Lindsey was a different story with his songs, still unsure of some of the lyrics, arrangements, and tempos, changing course during the mixing of his songs.

During Tusk, we had a saying that Mick or Lindsey would repeat as a mantra: "So close, but yet so far." Producers and engineers know that when a project is in the home stretch, it could turn into the most frightening moment as insecurity hits the mind-set of artists, resulting in the interruption of the mixing process with more overdubs. It can be a disastrous for the project as its artistic direction can be lost, like a movie stuck in reshoots. Tusk hadn't precisely been an album where direction was clear from the beginning, with all of its disparate and eclectic tracks. But whatever was already printed on those twenty-four multitrack tapes was the crumpled road map to mixdown that was moving all of us very close to the finish line.

Mixing the girls' songs was relatively straightforward, but Lindsey's aesthetic and technical approach to his own songs was not the standard, so they all had to carry his seal of approval all the way through. Ken, Richard, and I would start doing the basics of mixing a specific Lindsey song until he would show up and start stirring what already had been in progress. Many times Ken's patience was tested to the limit, with Richard trying to mediate unsuccessfully.

During all of this, Lindsey would sit over Ken's shoulder and turn the volume pot all the way to the right to blast the music as loud as the speakers could possibly go, unloading 2,000 watts of power on us through our monster dual JBL, three-way monitors. When the Village remodeled Studio B next door, they floated the whole room on sand because our playbacks were so loud. Ken, out of frustration, asked some of the Village techs whether they could secretly lower the volume internally, so that instead of going to 11 it would go to 7, but it was useless. As a compromise, Ken demonstrated the equalizer knobs to Lindsey, so he could tweak them to his liking.

On some occasions, they would compromise, but there were times when it was left as Lindsey wanted. Today as I listen to some of Lindsey's songs, some of them could have had much better dynamics, structure, tonality, and all-around results, especially among the fast ones. "I Know I'm Not Wrong" and "That's Enough for Me" are good examples of excellent songs that could have benefited from a more elaborate mixing process. A few years back, Warner Bros. asked Ken to remix Tusk in 5.1 for its Tusk Deluxe Box Set release, and you can hear the difference in the mixes.

On the opposite end is "The Ledge," with a mix that we worked deep, resulting in its own character. One example on this song is the effect of drying the vocals at the end of the choruses. I'm sure that today some of these songs could have a second life through remixing, which would produce some surprises and a new perspective. The slower and more intimate songs from Lindsey, such as "That's All for Everyone" and "Walk a Thin Line," received an excellent mix, as he eased his iron fist and trusted Ken and Richard. On these songs, there are many details that only careful playback on headphones will help the listener to appreciate. While tracking, Lindsey was big on possibilities, but for mixing, it's a matter of perspectives.

In the case of Stevie and Christine's songs, listening to them today is a wonderful experience as they have preserved the luster intended for them, with the girls' voices, their velvet timbre shining with emotion, as well as

LAST CALL FOR EVERYONE

Lindsey's work with some of the most beautiful and well-layered guitar and background vocals in the history of Fleetwood Mac, probably up there with the highest production quality of the Beach Boys, the Beatles, and Pink Floyd. "Sara," "Over & Over," and "Brown Eyes" were headphone gems, where the mixing process just made them shine their brightest.

The process of mixing involves making decisions and prioritizing the individual sonic space, tonal quality, character, and relative volume of each track that makes up a song. When the mix is ready, it gets recorded or transferred to analog magnetic 1/4- or 1/2-inch tape or a digital medium, such as a hard drive, that becomes the master from where all further processing is done, including the key process of mastering, to then copy and download from, to eventually be distributed and marketed to its final users.

The mixer's virtual space or sonic image where he or she has to display the mixing process is what is called the stereo image, which has been in use in the music industry since its inception in the late '50s, although its massive commercial use started in the mid-'60s with the 33 1/3 vinyl LPs. This stereo image is played back an illusion of multidirectional audible perspective between two speakers or, in modern days, between two headphones. The basic sonic positions of that stereo space go from a left to center to right image, which the talent of a mixer works to create depth and a perspective closer to how we listen in the real world.

Mixing a song is a highly creative process where the analog technology and tools of those days had a very important role in what was required to achieve sonic enhancement of what already had been captured on the multitrack tape. Mixing a specific song is a balancing act between the artistic vision of the creator and producers, and the high sonic standards needed to achieve it. That was the challenge that our award-winning duo engineers, Ken Caillat and Richard Dashut, were about to embark on for the weeks

GET TUSKED

to come in Studio D at the Village, where we had some of the best tools and equipment to accomplish that challenge.

Mixing is the make-or-break part of the recording process. A killer mix can propel a song into the Top 10. A bad one will sink it. I always picture my speakers as my canvas and my console as the tool that helps me create a sonic image that's as high, wide, and deep as possible. The way I see it, there's a mix space extending about 8 feet beyond the speakers. My sound field extends up to the ceiling and down to the floor, with the bass and the kick drum down at floor level, and the cymbals and the guitar harmonics at the ceiling. My big secret: I pan as many of the instruments left and right, preferably hard left and right, so as to leave plenty of space between the speakers for the vocals, especially the lead vocal. Don't be afraid to have the lead vocal be the loudest instrument in the mix.

If the speakers are 10 feet apart, the mixer has about 80 square feet of space to work with. Modern consoles allow you to adjust each instrument's or track's volume in real time, its speaker position, and the amount of bass, midrange, or treble that an instrument has (which becomes the sound's character). You can add effects to a track, too, such as reverb to a vocal to make it sound angelic, or a delay to the echo to make it more pronounced. You can also add delay to an electric guitar and place the delay on the opposite speaker from the guitar, to make it seem much wider and more powerful.

You can even add multiple effects at the same time. For instance, sometimes I add high frequency to a snare drum to make it *sss-nap* or add bottom end so that it has more impact together with the kick drum. I helped make the character of "Dreams" darker during mixing by placing more emphasis on the bottom end of most of the instruments. Then, I gave some instruments more top end to make them stand out, such as the phasing on Mick's hi-hat or the sibilance of Stevie's vocal.

Most of the time, an instrument also has a rough spot that needs to be taken down a little. For instance, in "Silver Springs," the kick drum was always powerful, but it had an annoying bump in its upper bottom that caused the speaker to make a nasty popping sound when it was turned up too loud. Picture all of the instruments as brush strokes. EQ can change the shape and color of each stroke so that everything fits perfectly together and jumps out at you and becomes a symphony to your ears.

Finally—and most important—are the song's dynamics. As instruments are added to a song, their relationships change. Some instruments' volume or dynamics need to be controlled. That is why the closest thing to an engineer on the console is the faders. This allows the engineer to "'ride levels," which means that he can reach out and move the volume sliders up and down as he sees fit. For me, this is the most fun part of mixing, but it's the barrier to entry for some who can't stay as fluid as the music they helped to create.

The engineer before me had relied on computer-assisted faders to remember his moves that first day, to make them for him, but when his computer died, he was in trouble and I got the gig. A good mix is rarely static. It's fluid, always changing. Back when I started learning to mix, a lot of the fun came from the fact that we didn't have computers to help us ride levels or to move faders for us. Like everyone who'd come before me, I had to learn how to do it myself.

When it came to mixing *Rumours*, it took us a long time to perfect each song. We'd listen to each one for six to eight hours, and everyone in the band offered suggestions. When the EQ, the effects, and the panning were perfect, and we had all listened to the four-minute song over and over, each of us—including every member of the band—made suggestions, such as, "Ken, where's the beef in my kick?" or "I don't like my vocal sound" or "Ken, can you add some more fairy dust to my vocal?" We weren't finished with a song until all of the mix changes were resolved and everyone was happy with absolutely everything.

At this point, we had all of the faders marked for their optimal positions, and it was time to play the console. I usually handled guitar and vocal levels, and Richard handled the drums and the bass. Each of us kept those instruments prominent so that they didn't get lost in the mix. Then, when we were ready, we hit Play, and I would ride the vocal up if one of the words got buried when a hot guitar lick came in during the first chorus. I'd push it up louder to make it jump. Then, Richard answered back with one of Mick's tom fills or John's basslines. When the guitar solo started, I tried to make it tear off everyone's heads. Richard pushed up the rhythm section in response. With my other hand, I supported the guitar solo with Christine's keyboards. By the next chorus, everything was back at its starting mark, and I shoved up the tag chorus vocal for a big finish.

On some mixes, we needed more hands. Mick, Lindsey, or Christine would reach in and help. Richard conducted. "Okay, Chris; mute that key part," he said. "Mick, now here it comes—ready, three, two, one." When we all had our fader performances and the high-fives were flying, we'd load up a two-track and record the mixes, stopping when someone made a mistake or pushed something up too far. Eventually, we got it right. Then, we listened to it to see whether we liked it. We called this process the "group grope."

LAST CALL FOR EVERYONE

Of course, today computers assist engineers, remembering each of the rides so that the engineer can work on other aspects of the mixing process. Yet computers can't replace how dedicated we were to our music. After we finished each song, we usually made cassettes for each of the band members so they could listen to the mix in their cars or at home. We left the mix setup for the next day so that we could listen to it with fresh ears, fixing any small problems in the morning before going on to the next song.

But that was then, and three years later, mixing *Tusk* on our brand-new Neve console, we had everything that a band could ask for. Its EQ or tone controls were broad and fat sounding, similar to a tube amplifier. It also had automation that could remember every move that we might make on the faders. If we made mistakes, we could go back and make corrections, but it had to be in real time, unlike the modern Pro Tools recording systems of today where you can look at the whole song displayed as a wave for each of its tracks or channels. But in 1979, our Neve was a huge improvement over our *Rumours* console at Producers Workshop in Hollywood, not necessarily sonically, but in functionality and in automation recall.

It all started at the console, a custom-made Neve 8078 that is still one of the best audio machines built, with its 31105 Input/Equalizer modules and its transformer colored signal path. It also featured a custom moving fader system called Necam, based on servo-assisted motors. This system allowed for all volume moves to be registered and automated, making it possible to make changes and updates on any of the prior moves.

As volume and muting were the only factors that could be automated in those days, all the rest of the variables involved on a mix had to be reg-

istered on paper notation, a responsibility that fell to me. This included all the parameters of the Neve equalizers, effects sends, panning, outboard gear such as compressors and limiters, outboard effects such as analog and digital reverb, slap delay through 2- and 4-track tape machines, and so forth, Today we can automate every aspect of a mix, but back then it was all by hand, memory, and timing.

The two main parameters that a mixer deals on a mix are volume and panning of a specific track. The other parameters that get worked on for a mix as it progresses are: equalization (tone control/harmonic coloration); compression and gating (dynamic manipulation); and such effects as reverb, pitch, delay, chorus, and flanging (altering of the acoustic environment, pitch, and time). The fine-tuning of these key components in the mixing process are so important that, beyond the musical quality of the song and its recorded performance, a bad mix could risk its possibility of becoming a hit.

The work of a mixer is similar to an orchestra conductor. In that process, the mixer makes volume decisions and positions the sonic panorama based on some of the cultural conventions that have been in practice in popular music. These traditions have changed through time, like everything in music, based on genre trends. In the era of crooners and big bands, such artists as Frank Sinatra had their voice well above the instruments for intelligibility and full enjoyment of their timbre. With the eruption of rock and roll, this relationship changed to have the lead vocal balanced in such a way that he or she feels that it's part of the band.

Together with the volume of a track, the mixer defines the position it has in the stereo image, center, left, right, or any place in between. Modern consoles incorporated a knob called the pan pot that places the track in the stereo panorama or soundfield. Panning is interrelated to volume perception, so for example moving an electric guitar track to a side could add clarity to the lead vocal that in turn would sound stronger as it sits in the center by itself. Moving the electric guitar during the solo could create excitement, such as on some of the earlier Led Zeppelin songs.

Tusk *was a collage of the long evolution of rock, with Lindsey searching for the roots of rockabilly in the age of punk and adhering to his own artistic vision, while Christine and Stevie were moving from blues and folk to chamber pop. Thus, the task of mixing such an eclectic album as* Tusk *was quite challenging for Ken and Richard. They were faced with the challenge of making the album sound "de-luxe" as Mick always intoned while standing in front of us with his arms on top of the Neve. All the while, Lindsey's sat shoulder to shoulder with his engineers to promote his "lo-fi" tendencies and do away with any unwanted studio finesse.*

During mixing, Lindsey wanted radical equalization, relative volumes, panning, reverb, ambience, delay, compression, among other variables, for the different tracks in his songs. All the demands he made at the start of the album came back during mixing, in every variable of the sonic palette, such as drying up the vocals and placing them lower in the overall mix, making them compete with the guitars and other instruments, or diminishing their level for lesser intelligibility. He also wanted that vintage panning from the Beatles and the Beach Boys days, with hard panning in the kick or bass.

We knew then if we went along with his ideas, the album would sound very thin and a special low-end compressor in mastering would have had to be used to prevent the cutting stylus from skipping. Not to mention, the sonic differences between his songs and the girls' would have been too extreme, beyond the fact that all the songs were already very different stylistically, easily the most radical of any Fleetwood Mac album. The Beatles' White Album *might have been wide ranging in genres, but at least it had great sound. Ken fielded Lindsey's requests and opinions with his usual diplomacy while simultaneously getting everyone excited with his own campaign that* Tusk *was going to surpass* Rumours, *at least with its cutting-edge digital sound.*

With the mixing phase of the *Tusk*, we were looking at how to make the songs better or find out whether we'd missed the mark and had to go back to fix things. Although at this point, after all the rough mixes we'd done, we were now basically polishing the songs to their brightest. It was also time to see what our digital recorder could do and make some history. Even though we were still making vinyl records, Dr. Thomas Stockham had convinced us that this digital format was noiseless perfection, recording *exactly* what we were hearing and forever playing it back with perfect fidelity. He said it would change the world, and I was all in for that. He promised albums would soon be available on credit cards!

At the start of the mix day, we assembled a variety of speakers to listen to our mixes, ensuring they sounded great on every listening system. We also arranged to get a link to the finest natural echo chambers available: Capitol Records. Back in the 1950s, when the iconic Capitol Records building was built near Hollywood and Vine, it commissioned guitarist and home recording pioneer Les Paul to design the echo chambers. To create reverb, he built eight trapezoidal echo chambers underground.

We arranged with the phone company to rent us a pair of "Class A" phone lines to connect the Village directly to Capitol's Chamber #3, available to us 24/7 for the duration of mixing. The Village also had several newer, German-made, 600-pound EMT echo plates which could emulate many classic spaces, such as Carnegie Hall, the Berliner Philharmonie, or an empty Grand Central Station. Additionally, we had our own replica of the Capitol chamber right inside or own Studio D. We were able to tint all of the vocals on *Tusk* a different treatment to make them stand out one another.

Part of the preparation then was to have all the echo options hooked up to our console. We had knobs for adding delay, not just repeat delay, but also echo delay, which would feed an instrument delayed into an echo chamber, guitars and vocals primarily. Then, we had every sort of expensive compressor and outboard equipment (not part of the console) to help control or modify each track or instrument. We recorded our mixes for *Tusk* to state-of-the-art 1/2-inch tape machines running at 30 inches per second. The tape is twice as wide than before, so the sound was twice a fat.

In addition to all that, we had the Soundstream digital machine connected to the output of our console, so it could get the same feed that the tape machines were getting. The Soundstream recorder was set up in one of our iso rooms, so we didn't have to hear poor Rich Feldman suffering since it had a mind of its own. He would feverishly adjust some control pot with his magic screwdriver to keep the machine running to spec. He had to keep watching an oscilloscope, making sure all the wavy lines were where they were supposed to be; otherwise, the machine would just stop in defiant protest.

Richard, Mick, and I would go out and watch the event as Rich wrestled with his machine. It was somewhat like watching a rider try to stay on a bucking bronco. Meanwhile, he'd be swearing up a storm under his breath. Afterward, Richard would go over and massage Rich's shoulders like a prize fighter and raise Rich's right arm, declaring, "The winner! And still the champion!"

When we would start on each song, usually Richard and/or I would take a stab at spreading the song out across the speakers, focusing on maximizing stereo spread and impact. Once we had a stereo sound field we liked, we would adjust the bass and treble of each instrument for that song, hopefully to take the breath away of each listener and to maximize the sonic quality on every speaker system out there. Finally, a major part of every mix was that we would use an audio compressor on individual instruments, and the overall mix, to help contain the instruments in the mix so an errant peak didn't come flying out and damage anyone's speakers or ears. We used compressors and limiters, such as the Urei 1176, the Universal Audio LA 2-A, our built-in Neve compressors, and the classic Fairchild 670 tube limiter/compressor.

After we all had perfected our mix by using our console's automation, it was essentially done. All we had to do after we gave the mix our blessing, was record it onto our analog tape machine and simultaneously to our digital machine. We couldn't switch to another song while mixing because even though we had our fader moves automated, nothing else was. This meant that through the course of mixing, which may have taken anywhere around ten hours, we were constantly making EQ changes, compressor changes, and manually adjusting our outboard gear, so we could change anything.

Now, you would think we surely must be done now, but you'd be wrong.

Ordinarily, we would have to edit together all the 1/2-inch master takes onto blank reels, that number equaling the number of sides of vinyl there would be, in this case, four sides. We had to imagine a running order that would cohere and sound good, taking into consideration tempo, genre, vibe, tone, singer, and potential intertextual dialogues, such as the segue from "Sara" to "What Makes You Think You're the

LAST CALL FOR EVERYONE

One" into "Storms." Lindsey called it a "study in contrasts," although we had two of Christine's ballads giftwrap the album.

Hernan was able to cut that together in about thirty minutes, including inserting the proper amount of spacing between each of the songs to feel natural. But to do this digitally, we were shocked to find out that we had to take all the digital tapes to Salt Lake City to use Soundstream's mainframe, where Dr. Stockham was still a professor at the University of Utah. The girls had no problem deciding that this would be a boys' trip, so Lindsey, Hernan, Richard, Mick, Ray, Rich, and I all flew out together.

The trip to Utah was planned for September while I assembled and made safety copies of all the masters in case anything happened on the way there. When the day arrived, we all piled into a limo to our private flight from LAX to Salt Lake City. It was all rock star style: cold beer and drinks waiting at the plane, with no hassle about Lindsey's joints. The pilot was an ex-Vietnam air force guy, so as soon as we took off, he asked us whether we wanted to take a small detour to fly over the Grand Canyon. Of course we all said "Yes!" in unison.

As we approached the area, he asked us whether we wanted to fly low into the canyon, and again, a loud, resounding yes echoed in the fuselage. It was a wild experience as this Learjet was small enough to get quite deep into walls of the Grand Canyon, turning and maneuvering at high speed. Then, he pulled straight up and our stomachs stuck to our spines. In the middle of this exhibition, he asked us whether we wanted to do a full 360-degree loop. Nobody dared say no and everyone prepared for one of the most extreme body-and-mind experiences, hoping not to barf while at it. The jet climbed at full speed before collapsing behind itself with our heads following down almost in a free fall. It was mind-boggling, for sure, with all of us breathing deeply at the end of it, our faces whiter shades of pale. I'm sure the pilot enjoyed laughing at his cargo full of hippies.

The trip that had started on such a high note quickly slowed down to a tedious rhythm that we survived as usual by making jokes, drinking beer, and smoking pot while the computer scientists fumbled around and tried to ignore their wildest bunch of clients ever. We found out that every step of the assembly process required either inputting or outputting through digital encoding that included very slow, hard-core processing. The Honeywell-based mainframe computer used by Soundstream, the most sophisticated of those days, had CPUs based on an Intel 8086 chip running at only 8 MHz with a processing speed of 0.8 MIPS (million instructions per second), versus today's 49,360 MIPS.

When we got there, we soon found out that we would be playing a waiting game. So, we had to spend about a week there while their huge washing machine–size computers ingested all our music and processed it, which as it turned out was no simple and quick task. It took all day for them input all of our songs. We went out to lunch before going on a hike in the magnificent, snow-covered hills of the Wasatch Range while the guys in lab coats whispered and calculated.

The next morning, they played back our whole double album of twenty songs, but something was wrong. The spacing between the songs was only one second long, with no spontaneity. Back then, we listened to each "'spread" between the songs and determined the right amount of space by feel. Everyone looked at me, so I told the scientists, "The next song should start right here," indicating where "here" was by dropping my chopping my hand down on the beat.

LAST CALL FOR EVERYONE

They said, "When?"

"Play from the end of the first song, 'Over & Over,' and when I say 'now,' mark the tape and put the beginning of the second song *exactly* there, just as we do in the studio."

They looked at one another as though I was from Mars.

"How many seconds of space do you want?" they asked hopefully.

"Do you have a stopwatch?" I asked. "We'll do this another way."

They gave me a stopwatch and played the ending fade of "Over & Over" until I felt that "The Ledge" should start, and I clicked the stopwatch.

"6.67 seconds!" I announced proudly! Mick nodded in approval, "Start 'The Ledge' exactly 6.67 seconds after you hear the last note of 'Over & Over.'"

The Lab Coats said, "Our editor tool can only work with exact seconds."

My head dropped in frustration. "Really? Music isn't measured in exact seconds. It's measured by feel. It must be exactly 6.67 seconds!"

I could see they were frustrated, too. Normally, they're not used to having to assemble albums but, rather, whole live performances.

"There's a really good restaurant just outside town called the Quail Run where the Mormons will let you guys drink all you want. Why don't you boys go have a nice lunch there on us and when you come back, we'll have all this worked out," a voice came from the back of the room. It was the 'father of digital recording,' Dr. Thomas Stockham, himself. He's the guy who discovered that the 18.5 minutes that were missing from the Watergate tapes was not an accident. He heard the frustration in his techs' voices, and in ours, and knew exactly how to fix it.

GET TUSKED

When we got back from lunch, he had installed a "Now" button for us to mark the precise time for our digital spreads. By the end of the day, all the songs had been marked and we went home for the night. Meanwhile, the computer would be making the necessary changes overnight while we slept. The next morning, we arrived early and they had the entire album ready to play.

I remember being there forever as their processing felt slower and slower, increased by our changes, especially from Lindsey's changing mood. Finally, we sat down to hear for the first time, all four sides of Tusk in order, an experience that was heartfelt and full of meaning. It had been more than thirteen months of blood, sweat, and tears, making and recording music, where we all put in all we could. We'd laughed, quarreled, created, explored, battled, loved, drank, smoked, and dined like Vikings on a raid, with moments of despair and frustration, inspiring epiphanies, confessions, and a powerful willpower to see the mission all the way through.

We listened and were pleased. They made us a cassette and reel-to-reel tape to take home for reference. We came with digital and left with analog. They would eventually send us a digital tape that we could master the vinyl album from. When we got home, Hernan made listening copies for everyone to scrutinize. Two days later, Christine called me and said she wanted the fade on "Never Forget" to be longer and more gradual, ending at the same time. "Okay, that's ea-sy, except for the fact we're dealing in digital now. I'm going to have to go back to Salt Lake City to make that change," thinking that I was off the hook. To my surprise, Christine glibly said, "Okay; I'll call the office and let them know."

Shortly later, the Penguin Office called to let me know that a limo would be picking me up in thirty minutes to take me to the airport. I was at the Village finishing up the album when the limo arrived. I jumped in with only my jacket. I figured this shouldn't take very long. As the limo was pulling away, I saw my friend Frank Wolf leaving the studio. I rolled down the window and said, "Hey, Frank! Wanna go to Salt Lake City with me in a Learjet, right now?"

"Let me go home and get a change of clothes!" he said.

"There's no time! And you don't need any clothes! We'll be back in the morning! You can buy some tooth paste there!" He jumped into my stretch limo and we headed off to the Van Nuys Airport where our very own Learjet was fueled and waiting for us. This was pretty exciting stuff.

I said to the pilots, "Don't be afraid to show us what this baby can do!"

Frank looked at me with the stink eye, "I'll get you for this, Caillat. If I throw up, it's gonna be on you!"

As it turned out, while we were coming in for final approach, we hit some very rough weather. It got very turbulent. The little plane was bouncing from side to side and up and down violently. All sorts of automatic alert systems and warning bells were going off in the cockpit. *Oh my god*, I thought, *we're flying Air Maybe*. I thought we were about to be tossed out of the sky by the storm and that this was the end, "Damn you, *Tusk*! I hate you!" I swore out loud.

The pilots were lined up on the main runway when they got a call from the tower to change runways immediately to a parallel runway just to the left of the main one. The pilots banked hard. I was sitting right behind both the pilots and could see the other runway jump into view in the rainy distance. The pilots looked at each other and said, "Let's do this! Hold on, everybody!"

They pushed the throttle hard forward and at the same time pushed the nose of the little jet down to aim directly at the close end of the runway. The jets' power propelled the plane down through the storm's turbulence to the end of the runway. Almost as one, one copilot lowered the landing gear and the other guided the buffeted plane to the landing hot, holding the nose against the tarmac slowly, and powering back the jet until we made solid contact on the ground.

I saw my life pass before my mind. I saw Cheryl. I saw Lindsey walking in on the first day with his new haircut in what seemed like forever ago. I saw myself flying off a speedboat on Lake Tahoe. I saw Dennis Wilson's driving me at top speed down Butler Avenue. I saw a house full of monsters. I saw a cop standing in front of me. I saw Diane in the morning. I saw Mick and John with tape over their mouths. I saw water balloons crashing to the ground. I saw enormous boulders on the PCH. I saw myself pitching at Dodger Stadium. At the end, though, I saw that I survived.

We taxied through the rain down the runway to our gate. I leaned forward and asked, "Um, would you guys call that an aggressive landing?"

They looked at each other with big smiles on their faces and then back at us and said, "Oh . . . Hell . . . yeah!"

"You guys did a great job landing this bird; thanks."

Well, I thought, *I guess that's one way to end this album.*

21

TUSK IS HERE

> You cannot make friends with rock stars . . .
> these people are not your friends.
>
> —Lester Bangs, *Almost Famous*

By the end of Tusk, we were all exhausted and needing a break urgently, so I came up with the off-the-wall idea of inviting Stevie to travel with me to Chile to unwind. She didn't give it a second thought and said yes, without knowing really where she was going, beyond the stories she had heard from me. We were daredevils, behaving like teenagers, driven by spontaneity and the desire to run away from LA and enjoy the free time, without even thinking of the threats and risks involved, especially for Stevie. She was the only child of a corporation president and one of the biggest stars in the world. It's a sign of how different those times were that neither family nor friends nor management expressed much worry about our trip beyond wishing us well and a generic, "Take good care of her." Just the idea of a big rock star traveling without a security detail to an unknown destination would today be considered insane and out of the question.

This trip presented Stevie with the opportunity to get away from all the attention that being a rock star carried, such as not being able to go to public places, and the ability to relax and enjoy outings without being harassed. This was 1979 and pre–John Lennon, and no rock star had been assassinated or violently attacked, but there was a growing series of menacing actions to them. By then, Stevie had received threatening mail and been approached by stalkers during tours. The Lennon assassination a year later completely changed the security level for the entire entertainment industry after that horrible event.

After the mixing trip to Utah, with all my duties for Tusk finished, I informed the studio management of my trip. The spell of the affair with Stevie put me in a different dimension, as if there was no tomorrow. I was completely oblivious of my working future. I realized in my last-minute preparations that I forgot to call my family in Chile to let them know of our voyage. I called my mother, Maria Teresa, and told her that in a couple of days I was landing in Santiago with my girlfriend, who was a rock-and-roll singer by the name of Stevie, and to please have a room ready at my old home. She hadn't received news from me for a while beyond a few telephone calls to say hello and know how she was. My mother had a sweet and loving nature, telling me right away that she would be very happy to receive us.

Stevie was always writing songs, so she also brought a Hohner electric pianet, a set of mini speakers, a Nakamichi portable cassette deck, a Sony electric microphone, and a Spanish nylon-stringed guitar. Stevie brought the diary my sister gave her, where she wrote poems, drew funny pictures, and narrated her days.

Luckily, we booked the first flight available that happened to be the inaugural jumbo 747 nonstop flight from LA to Santiago from Braniff International. We landed at dawn with part of my family waiting for us, including my cousins, who had organized a surprise party that same night. Stevie was in great spirits, a little tired from the eleven-hour flight, but

TUSK IS HERE

ready to begin this new adventure so different to the environment that surrounded her in LA.

Chile was known for having the most stable democracy in Latin America with little or no government corruption, also for its two Nobel Prize–winning poets, Pablo Neruda and Gabriela Mistral, and for its long coast with gorgeous snowy vistas of the Andes Mountains. On September 11, 1973, an infamous military junta backed by the CIA toppled President Salvador Allende's disarrayed elected socialist government and began a reign of terror.

When we arrived, the capital of Santiago was still under tight military control: there were soldiers armed with machine guns in the airport and along key streets and locations. For Stevie, this state of siege went unnoticed, and I didn't want to scare her with any stories I'd heard. We were rushed out of the airport by my father and cousins to get some rest and start the fun. I was very excited to be in Chile with Stevie, like the prodigal son coming back from the long journey full of stories and success in the music industry and a beautiful songstress whose real fame nobody suspected.

After resting all morning and a family lunch in the afternoon, we prepared ourselves to party all night long before citywide curfew. My cousins had invited some of my old musician friends without telling them who my special female guest was. The party was held in a log cabin on the slopes of the Andes toward the outskirts of town, giving it a special vibe. By the time we got there, it was a full house, with a long line of hugs and hellos from friends that I hadn't seen for five years. Stevie chose not to wear makeup for most of the trip, to remain incognito, so when I introduced her as my Californian musician girlfriend, nobody was the wiser.

We saw there was a small stage with instruments and microphones ready for playing. We got a round of food and spirits, plus Peruvian snow and sweet leaf. As the band began to play, I noticed that it included some

GET TUSKED

members of Chile's classic rock band, the Blops. After a couple of songs, out of politeness, they invited Stevie to join them at the electric piano. She was totally cool to the unsuspecting musicians and partygoers. They asked her what songs she knew. She asked them whether they knew "Dreams" by Fleetwood Mac. After the first few lines of her singing, a murmur started among everyone, as they began to realize this was no cover version, but the original Stevie Nicks in front of their own eyes!

The murmur turned to cheers and clapping, and everyone joined in the chorus. Friends and guests couldn't believe this was true, with many of them asking me, "What the fucking hell?!" I was so moved by what was going on that night, back in Chile with Tusk in the bag and the woman I loved doing her thing and capturing everyone's heart. Pure magic. Many of the people there spoke English, so Stevie had a wonderful night talking and being honored by all.

Stevie reflected on that moment in her diary:

> And Chile listened like a crystal jar while we played and sang my "Dreams" and enchanted them with "Blue Water," high above Santiago, as I was when I wrote it on the island of Maui a year ago.

Stevie connected with my mother, Maria Teresa, deeply, as they both shared a similar character: sensitive, romantic, and given to enjoy melancholic moments. They hung out and talked about memories and wisdom until dawn, resulting in Stevie writing her letters that she would leave under her door. Maria Teresa had a full set of pharmaceuticals available, including a medicine, Belladenal, that was good to treat Stevie's stomach cramps. Its main ingredient is the belladonna alkaloid, derived from the *plant.* "Belladonna" *became the nickname that Stevie gave to my mother, eventually becoming the name of Stevie's first solo album,* Bella Donna, *where she thanks my mother for the inspiration.*

During our stay, Stevie dropped letters under my mother's door with encouraging words to sooth her pains:

> *You are one of a kind. Never let anyone take love and goodness away from you—Never stop, never change.*

When we left, Stevie gave my mother a gold crescent moon pendant, a symbol of the Sisterhood of the Moon.

In a way, between the dinner invitations and the ski resorts and beach towns, Stevie and I hung out, as before, in a bubble. We did not witness the repression that was going on until one day, coming back from one of the parties before the end of the curfew, we were stopped by an armed military patrol. I had on the interior lights of our small Suzuki jeep and drove very slowly to show that we were not sneaking around, to prevent being shot at. Many of the streetlights had been extinguished by the military police so they could stay undercover and not be easy targets for the underground resistance.

The patrol pointed their M16s and Uzis at us and signaled us to stop.

We stopped.

They approached Stevie's window waving very fast, and as she rolled it down, they put a machine gun straight to her head.

Everything stopped.

We both freaked out, but somehow we managed to stay cool. I told Stevie not to worry, that I would give the proper explanations as to why we were out during curfew. Thankfully, the officer in charge was level-headed and listened to my story that I was driving a famous American artist to her hotel, and that we had no clear understanding of the curfew hours. My heart was pumping so fast I could hear it as I grabbed Stevie's hand and gave her all my empathy as to what had just occurred. She was in total shock and couldn't believe what had happened. This was something that only happened in the movies.

When we got home, we took some heavy-duty sleeping pills to recover from such a violent encounter. I thought about a friend of mine that was shot by mistake while passing a police barricade. The bullet hit his spine and he was left a paraplegic. We had been very fortunate and blessed to be allowed to continue, as anyone caught in the streets in those days was jailed or shot or both. I thought to myself for a long time how I could have faced Stevie's family and friends if the worst had happened. How could I have carried that deeply scarring guilt?

We changed our tickets and were on the next flight to Rio.

We booked a suite at the landmark Copacabana Palace Hotel that had a long history of distinguished guests, famous jet-setters, fabulous parties, and a luxury lifestyle. Its opulent art deco architecture, built in 1923, was featured in the 1933 film *Flying Down to Rio* that starred Fred Astaire and Ginger Rogers. No sooner had we arrived when Brazil's reputation for beauty and crime reared its head. We went for a stroll on a lovely beach and came back for lunch, only to discover Stevie's jewelry had disappeared and the hotel's management did nothing about it.

To make matters worse, the weather went from sunny to gray skies, which was very rare for Rio. We left the hotel and moved to a modern hotel on Ipanema Beach. There, we stayed mostly indoors with some rare outings to check out the music scene, which was quite muted due to Brazil's own cruel dictatorship, where all free expression was censored and repressed. After Stevie was bitten by a German shepherd at a dinner party, we concluded that the whole idea of an idyllic South American vacation was most assuredly cursed.

Speaking of curses, one funny thing did happen during our stay in Rio, though. Stevie had some crystal balls, lapis lazuli pyramids, animal figures, and incense she had acquired in Chile. When she would write, she would display them as if she were at an altar. We stayed up late, as was our habit, and got up late in the afternoon when the cleaning lady would come into our suite to do her job. On one occasion, Stevie was sitting down in front her shrine, lighting incense and singing while I was playing a Brazilian percussion instrument. The cleaning lady came in, looked at this scene with horror, genuflected while praying fervently, and ran out the door. Stevie and I looked each other and laughed. We found out later many of the poor Catholic favela dwellers held strong superstitions about black magic and voodoo. Our maid thought that we had it in for her.

By this time, management wanted Stevie to get back to LA. Tour rehearsals were starting up, and although that didn't appeal to her so much after a year of making Tusk with Lindsey, it presented a slightly less menacing environment. Even though no one was really speaking to one another, the band members had to stiffen their upper lip and prepare for a world tour that would last at least a year. That was the work ethic they had lived with for years, and Stevie and I knew they wouldn't change, even if the personal cost was threatening the band's very existence.

We flew back to Chile where a return flight would take her back to LA. I had to stay behind a few more days to handle some family affairs. Our good-bye was sad and very quiet. As her 747 took off, I sensed that some of the magic and love from our affair was maybe coming to an end. I felt uncertainty during the next few days prior to my return, somehow anticipating what the next encounter with Stevie would bring.

GET TUSKED

The tour rehearsals at Sunset Gower soundstage were in full swing by the time I got back, absorbing all of Stevie's time and energy. I noticed her hair was different, newly permed and piled in a Victorian topknot. The old tensions between her and Lindsey were back. He was stalking around in an Armani suit with an unusual new guitar, dictating to the band how to play his home-recorded songs live. When I was finally able to get Stevie alone, I realized that my intuition was right. Our closeness and warmth was gone. In spite of all the clear abuse from Lindsey, Stevie would fall back into their dysfunctional relationship, one that played out in front of their fans every night. We both knew she was leaving the next day to give herself to the world. So, with tears in our eyes, she told me how she had loved our whole time together and felt it necessary to stop our relationship due to her going on the road for such a long time. There was simply no way for us to continue under the circumstances, which was the truth.

Mayor Tom Bradley declared October 10, 1979, Fleetwood Mac Day in Los Angeles, where after a short ceremony and a few speeches, the band would receive their own star on the Hollywood Walk of Fame in front of Frederick's of Hollywood, which gave the band commemorative underwear. Fifteen USC Trojans marched through the store playing "Tusk," which was already moving up the charts and into the Top 10. Spirits were very high in the Fleetwood Mac camp, as if success were just a matter of course.

Mo Ostin, the respected and beloved head of Warner Bros. Records, had many kind words to say about Fleetwood Mac. Behind the scenes, Warner Bros. had been growing restless; for weeks it requested a chance to visit Studio D and have a listening session to get a feel for how *Tusk* was coming along and a sense for how to market it. The record company wanted to release one of the discs early and had an advertising agency from New York pitch its campaign to Mick. He turned both down. Platinum records, Warner Bros. explained, were a pretty common thing. These days, a band had to have multi-platinum records.

It's important to remember that in the not-so-old days of the music industry, every aspect was tightly controlled by the labels, with staff producers supervising every step of the process and reporting back up the chain. Staff producers chose the songs, the musicians, the studio, and how the music was both mixed and mastered. During the late '50s and early '60s, such artists as Frank Sinatra, Ray Charles, and Elvis Presley, who were big hit makers, were allowed some independence.

Even the Beatles had to battle for years to gain full autonomy under George Martin's production and EMI's strictures. By the late '60s, rock-and-roll bands that had reached superstar status had managed to convince labels that they, like the Beatles, could handle music production and recording with outside professionals very successfully. Still, such labels as Warner Bros., Columbia, RCA, and EMI had their own A&R people overseeing the artistic and financial management of most album productions. In the case of Fleetwood Mac, since it had gone from a cult British blues rock band to one of the biggest multi-platinum record-selling artists, it had achieved full independence. After *Rumours*, it was the darling of Warner Bros. Fleetwood Mac was self-managed and called all its own shots. That was its status when we started making of *Tusk*. Warner Bros. had placed all its hopes on *Tusk* to refill its coffers.

By the time the band finally agreed to have a listening session in Studio D to show Warner the progress on the album, there were loads of anxiety on both sides. The voice of resistance to this playback session came from Lindsey. He was against any suits, or silk jackets, as was often the case, being involved in anything that had to do with the creative affairs of the album. Regardless, after we spent a couple of days doing some rough mixes, the day had arrived. Lindsey sat expressionless, smoking joints and puffing the smoke in all of their faces. As was his sadistic habit, he made sure the playback volume was set on scald.

Lindsey would later remark with no small amount of satisfaction that the look on the Warner Bros.' record executives' faces was one where they saw their bonuses flying out the window. And he was right. To really rub it in, he ordered that "Tusk" be the first single off the album, and in quick fashion, the general public finally got to hear the sounds that were inside Lindsey's head and weigh them against the Knack's "My Sharona."

First, we had to master the digital album we had assembled in Salt Lake City. Just like for *Rumours*, I chose Ken Perry at Capitol Records Mastering to put the cherry on the top of our dubious work of art. I had known Ken for about five years, and I knew he cared as much for our album as we did. A mastering engineer is an experienced listener and it's his or her job to make sure each song has the same characteristics as the song before it and the one after, similar bass, treble, and volume. He or she listens and knows how to make your record sound the best it can be on most home stereo systems. I hoped that Ken could smooth out the rough edges between the girls' songs and Lindsey's. Another challenge would be to make sure the vinyl LP didn't skip due to the extreme left-right information in Lindsey's mixes. A record needle actually moves around inside the disc's grooves while playing, so too much movement and it could fly right out of the groove.

It took about one day per disc for Ken to learn all the moves he felt were necessary to make a great set of vinyl records. Last time, when we mastered *Rumours*, Richard and I hand carried each piece of warm vinyl down to a local pressing plant so the vinyl could be dipped in liquid silver and "frozen" before the soft, newly cut grooves could spring back and loose some of their sonics. But for *Tusk*, Warner had already made arrangements for a team of people to relieve Richard and me from that task. The mastering of *Tusk* was my last official duty for the band, which took us right up to the weekend before the artists started rehearsals.

Meanwhile, I couldn't get away from the band fast enough. This was the second time I'd finished a year-long project with Fleetwood Mac. And, as with any big event in one's life, after it passes, you are left with a void, a daily set of habits that needs restructuring, possibly like being released from prison after a long incarceration. After *Rumours*, it was catching up on mundane things like laundry, doctor appointments, catching up with old friends, or making minor repairs around the house. I got out of bed the day after *Tusk* ended and said, "What the fuck do I do now?" What was the next most important thing in my life to focus on? So, I decided to propose to Diane. To my eternal amazement and gratitude, she said yes.

We decided to take a break from LA and move up to my house in Lake Tahoe and experience a white winter with Scooter and Sky. I spent my first free weekend packing up my new red Jeep Cherokee Chief and anticipating a full winter of four-wheeling in Tahoe with Diane. We headed up north early on the morning of October 1, 1979, looking forward to the 400-plus-mile trip in my new jeep. I was feeling some anxiety about the album, but road-tripping with my bride to be pushed all those thoughts from my mind. We got to Tahoe three weeks before our wedding day and shortly before the album's release. In the back of the Jeep, next to the bags and tequila, we had a beautiful set of Waterford crystal for twelve that the band had bought us—of which only one Champagne flute survives—and a beautiful oak backgammon table from Stevie, which we still enjoy today.

On October 12, 1979, the double-album *Tusk* was unveiled to the public at the steep full retail price of $15.98, which is nearly $58 today. To complicate matters, one of Stevie's reference mix cassette tapes was stolen and sold to the RKO radio network, who announced it would play it in its entirety, and did just that in Boston, Los Angeles, New York, Memphis, Fort Lauderdale, San Francisco, and Chicago. Despite preliminary injunctions by Warner, these broadcasts allowed for massive home recording, and other stations boycotted the album, thinking the band sold an exclusive to RKO.

All the record-buying public really had to go on was the outlier single "Tusk" still being played on the radio. Listeners panicked. The band panicked. Warner Bros. panicked and rush released the largest ever shipment in history of 2 million copies of *Tusk* into the marketplace, with an accompanying advertising and media blitz. Regardless, sales languished as *Tusk* fought to compete with Led Zeppelin's *In Through the Out Door*, which had even more elaborate packaging, and the Eagles' *The Long Run*, a double album, which became a solo album that took eighteen months and five studios to finish.

Meanwhile, through all this, Fleetwood Mac was busy preparing for a back-breaking world tour, which meant it had to go through wardrobe fittings, stage design, and also arrange and rehearse over an hour and a half of music for live performance. The band chose around twenty-plus songs from all its albums, and only seven from *Tusk*, sometimes fewer, and usually just Lindsey's or Stevie's songs. The *Tusk* tour was essentially two world tours that started on October 26, 1979, in Pocatello, Idaho, and ended at the Hollywood Bowl on September 1, 1980. After spending nearly a year and a half in a small room together making a double album, now the poor souls had to travel the world for another year, playing what they had recorded.

The *Tusk* tour itself, became as infamous as the album for its extravagance and eyeliner, consisting of 111 concerts full of unfathomable amounts of alcohol, cocaine, and marijuana, consumed as a matter of habit, sustenance, and defense. Predictably, no matter how pampered or cocooned they were, the artists were done living out of a suitcase and couldn't stand the sight of one another, even fighting onstage. They brought back more baggage than they left with and I'd heard that they were close to breaking up. But it seemed the blood was too strong to let them. In the meantime, I was asked to continue recording a few shows during every leg of their tour so that a year later, I could sort through all the volumes of multitrack reels, going back to the *Rumours* tour, to find the best recordings and performances for *Live*, the band's first officially released live document.

If I go back to that foggy January morning of 1974 as the ship was leaving Valparaiso, full of anxiety for what the future was going to bring and the dream of being part of the music industry, none of what had just happened would have been in my wildest imagination. From my first days working with the band to the odyssey of Tusk, *it had all been a dream come true. Ken's search for precise hi-fi recording techniques and his full-hearted approach had been revelatory. It was a privilege to have him as a mentor and friend. The same went for Richard's spontaneous, intuitive, and fun approach to get the best creative juices from the artists in his care.*

Among music critics, there were immediately opposing visions of the album *from its release to this day. Some considered* Tusk *a grab bag of unfinished songs; whereas others were very positive, calling it "a peerless piece of pop art." In recent years, the work of Fleetwood Mac has been recognized by modern bands and artists as highly influential, and* Tusk, *especially, is singled out for praise. Commercially,* Tusk *is rightly considered a failure compared to* Rumours, *but we knew that going in—the sales expectations were, shall we say, unrealistic.*

This hasn't prevented many theories from surfacing over the years, including, but not limited to: the fact that the music sales in general were slumping due to stagflation; that the oil crisis had devastated the sale of vinyl; that double albums were too expensive; that a cassette copy of Tusk *was leaked to RKO Radio, which played the album in its entirety for greedy bootleggers, leading to a* Tusk *backlash by other radio stations; and that the lack of a strong single hobbled the album, despite two Top 10 hits. Obviously, the huge commercial and popular appeal of* Rumours *overshadowed* Tusk, *as it did every other album until* Thriller. *Michael Jackson took five years and well over a million dollars to make his follow-up,* Bad. *Fleetwood Mac's next biggest album,* Tango in the Night, *would take eighteen months.*

By 2018, Tusk *has sold 6.6 million albums, or 9.7 million when adding related releases, singles, and compilations. Beyond critical or commercial considerations,* Tusk *is a true and honest artistic expression of its musicians. Through their own creative expression, they shaped a collection of songs that reflected what was going on with them and their times, from deep heartache and pain to joy and love. The lustrous sounds and sharp edges of* Tusk *serve as a classic and key piece of rock and roll and pop music. The album represents not only an eclectic artistic moment of a band that in the past had risen from the roots of Delta blues to masters of some of the best rock pop*

TUSK IS HERE

songs in popular music, but also a cultural milestone that helped the birth of new styles of rock and new generations of singer-songwriters. The three main singles from Tusk*—"Sara," "Think About Me," and "Tusk"—speak to the uniqueness of each of the three songwriters. None of them could have written what the others had, and each song was made indescribably better by the collaboration of the others.*

Experiencing those thirteen months of inspiration and hardship made me who I am today, both professionally and as a human being. I was honored to be a part of the band's inner circle, helping to articulate its artistic vision. Stevie, Lindsey, Christine, John, and Mick, with all their light and darkness, their humor and rage, their vulnerability and their pride, made it a privilege. I'm just glad I made it out alive and somewhat sane.

Di and I decided our wedding day would be October 27, the day after the band left for the *Tusk* tour. By that point, I was ready to pack the band and ship it off myself. It seemed incredible to me that after all the work its musicians put in on the album, and with almost no time off, they would go straight into rehearsals and then follow that with nearly a year-long, around-the-world world tour. You had to hand it to them. Despite accusations of self-indulgence and waste, the band really did work hard for its money, and even harder at its craft.

I got a call from Mick while the band was on the road: "Ken, it's not looking good."

"Well, yeah, what happened to releasing the double albums separately for seven ninety-eight each? Warner released the whole thing at a ridiculous price! What happened to the plan, Mick?!" I asked, disappointed.

"Well, the label convinced me that everyone who bought *Rumours* would inevitably buy this and we'd make a killing on the release because more is more."

"That's not happening because Warner charged extra for it."

"We also didn't expect RKO to play the album before it was supposed to bloody come out. Now everyone's backbiting."

"Yeah, we heard it on the way up. Sorry, mate."

"Well, enough of that. I called on behalf of the band to wish you and Di well on your big day."

"Thanks, Mick, we appreciate it. Hang in there. So close, but yet so far."

"Cheers."

I hung up the phone and looked at Di, "We're screwed." I told her about our conversation, "Our royalties will definitely suffer because some bastard at Warner got greedy!"

She put her arms around me and said, "It's okay, honey. Come on, let's go to bed. I'll make you feel better." It was only noon, so naturally I agreed, smiling all the way to the bedroom.

Days before the wedding, I was busy running around buying Champagne and flowers for the big event. I had called Aspen Airways, which flew direct from LA to Lake Tahoe airport, and got all my friends who wanted to come a "charter" fare on a DC-3 prop plane. We had asked our friend, the local pub owner and part-time minister Joe Massini, to perform the ceremony on Saturday morning in the backyard of my home among the pine trees. While my house was being decorated, Diane and I booked the presidential suite at Harrah's Casino and partied with our closest friends until the wee hours of the morning.

"Good morning, Good Looking," I said, rolling over and stretching. "It looks like a beautiful day in paradise."

TUSK IS HERE

"Morning," she said, giving me a soft kiss. Her big almond eyes looked very sleepy. "What time is it?" she asked.

"Oh, crap!" I said. "Our wedding's in an hour!"

We leaped out of bed as if we we'd been electrocuted.

"I guess there's no time for a morning quickie?" I half-joked.

"Do you want to miss your own wedding?!" she asked.

"Well, *maybe*," I said, seriously considering the option.

"Dream on, Ken! Damn! We're going to be late for our own wedding!" she said, realizing there was no way we could be ready in less than an hour.

"Well, they can't start without us!" I comforted her. We were both moderately hung over as we hurried to vacate the massive hotel suite. "Boy, I like this suite! This is the way to go!" I said, pulling my pants on while taking a swig of warm, flat Champagne.

We pulled up in front of my house exactly one hour late, and it was clear that there was already a party in progress. Penny, Diane's maid of honor, ran out as soon as she saw us and gave us the customary and appropriate reprimand, "God, I've been worried sick! You guys are so late! What have you been doing? Couldn't you wait until after the wedding?! We're going to have to start the wedding late, but the limo is still picking you up at four to take you to the airport. And if you're late, you'll miss your connection in San Francisco to Europe!"

Diane jumped out of the car and ran downstairs to change into her bridal gown and put on some makeup while I fumbled with my bow tie.

Upstairs, all of our friends and family were already having the reception. It was Animal House. Hernan had brought most of his Chilean family and friends along with the Village crew. It was insane. They had been stuck at the airport in LA and already had big head start. My mom, dad, sister, and grandmother were there, as well as Diane's four beautiful sisters and brother, mom, and estranged father, and all were chatting in the backyard. Penny brought Diane upstairs and called the group to attention. Joe grabbed the wedding vows and stood at the top of the hill between two sugar pine trees. He ushered Di and me to face him and asked the group to gather around. Our vows ended with "for so long as we both shall love," and Di and I kissed long, and ever longer.

Afterward, it was time to cut the cake. My business manager, Brian Adams, raised his glass of Champagne and asked everyone to join him in a "warm and loving toast to Ken and Diane, and . . . to many *Tusk* sales!"

Acknowledgments

Hernan Rojas

First, I would like to thank my mentor, Ken Caillat, for sharing his friendship and professional sound and musical knowledge from our first encounter remixing the singles for Rumours *to the end of* Tusk, *and for trusting me enough to join him in the making of this book.*

I would also like to thank the devotion and craftsmanship of our editor, Dan Hoffheins, whose dedicated and passionate work has taken Ken's and my stories to higher grounds.

I would also like to thank my wife, Pascuala, for her love and relentless support during the intense writing sessions for this book.

I would like to thank, for their inspiration, and without whom I would have never taken the one-way-ticket trip to California: the Beatles, the Rolling Stones, Bob Dylan, Jimi Hendrix, Led Zeppelin, Pink Floyd, Joni Mitchell, Miles Davis, Violeta Parra, Los Blops, Los Jaivas, Víctor Jara, and Fleetwood Mac.

And finally I would like to thank Stevie Nicks for her friendship and trust during Tusk *that led to such wonderful songs, including the mesmerizing "Sara."*

(Special thanks from the authors to Lindsey Buckingham.)

In Memoriam

Robin Anderson

Gabrielle Arras

Terry Becker

David Bianco

Kenneth F. Caillat

John Courage

Danny Douma

David Elliott

Carla Frederick

Geordie Hormel

Michael Huber

Barbara Issak

Danny Kirwan

Dick LaPalm

Tom Petty

Greg Thomason

Bob Welch

Bob Weston

Judy Wong

Herbie Worthington

Selected Bibliography

Buckingham, Lindsey. "The Beach Boys." *Rolling Stone*, April 15, 2004.

Buckingham, Lindsey. "Fleetwood Mac's Lindsey Buckingham Turns Another Corner." Interview by Blair Jackson. *BAM*, January 30, 1981. https://www.fleetwoodmac-uk.com/articles/FMart72.htm.

Buckingham, Lindsey. Interview by Molly Meldrum. *Countdown*, ABC, October 21, 1979. https://www.youtube.com/watch?v=GSHPJiGe1DQ.

Crowe, Cameron, director. *Almost Famous*. Universal City, CA: DreamWorks Pictures, 2000.

Egan, Walter, songwriter/musician. Discussion with the authors. November 2009.

Flans, Robyn. "The Power of Fleetwood Mac." *Modern Drummer*, October–November, 1980. https://www.moderndrummer.com/article/october-november-1980-mick-fleetwood-power-fleetwood-mac/.

Fricke, David, senior editor *Rolling Stone*. Discussion with the authors. August 2017.

Jerome, Jim. "Fleetwood's *Tusk*." *People*, November 26, 1979. https://people.com/archive/cover-story-fleetwoods-tusk-vol-12-no-22/.

SELECTED BIBLIOGRAPHY

Lindsey, Ray, Fleetwood Mac guitar tech/roadie. Discussion with the authors. November 2009.

Lydon, John. "The Danceable Solution." Interview by Chris Brazier. *Melody Maker*, October 28, 1978. https://www.fodderstompf.com/ARCHIVES/INTERVIEWS/mm78.html.

McLane, Daisann. "Fleetwood Mac: They Dared to Be Different." *Rolling Stone*, February 7, 1980. https://www.rollingstone.com/music/music-news/fleetwood-mac-they-dared-to-be-different-243618/.

McVie, Christine. Interview by Nancy Collins. *Rock 'N Roll Women*, NBC, 1980. https://www.youtube.com/watch?v=QQ8oLODVE3U.

Nicks, Stevie. Interview by Molly Meldrum. *Countdown*, ABC, February 1980.
https://www.youtube.com/watch?v=Pm-U0oIKCHE.

Nicks, Stevie. Letter: Stevie Nicks to Hernan Rojas. Los Angeles, CA, October 1979.

Nicks, Stevie. Letter: Stevie Nicks to Maria Teresa Rojas. Santiago, Chile, October 1979.

Nicks, Stevie. Unpublished diary. September 1979–August 1980.

Salewicz, Chris. "Fleetwood Mac: Can't Go Home Again." *Trouser Press*, April 1, 1980. https://stevie-nicks.info/1980/04/fleetwood-mac-cant-go-home-again/.

Spain, Tom, dir. *Tusk Documentary*. Burbank, CA: Warner Bros. Pictures, 1980. DVD. https://www.youtube.com/watch?v=UIQrfFu5uTg.

Trucks, Rob. *Tusk*. New York: The Continuum International Publishing Group, 2011.

SELECTED BIBLIOGRAPHY

Unterberger, Richie. *Fleetwood Mac: The Complete Illustrated History.* Minneapolis, MN: Quarto Publishing Group, 2016.

Williamson, Nigel. "Fleetwood Mac: 'Everybody Was Pretty Weirded Out'—The Story of *Rumours*." *Uncut*, January 29, 2013. https://www.uncut.co.uk/features/fleetwood-mac- everybody-was-pretty-weirded-out-the-story-of-rumours-26395#zGfdrIQHz3LixQl6.99.

About the Authors

KEN CAILLAT is the producer and engineer for the Fleetwood Mac albums *Rumours, Tusk, Mirage, Live,* and *The Chain Box Set.* He has also had the pleasure of producing his daughter Colbie Caillat's albums *Coco, Breakthrough, All of You,* and *Christmas in the Sand.*

———

HERNAN ROJAS is a recording engineer, music producer, and on-air host of Sonar FM when not leading Great Place 2 Rock, a company dedicated to promoting change and transformation through music.

Index

ABBA, 21, 232
Adams, Brian, 207, 294, 350
"Angel," 261-266, 271-274, 315
Arras, Gabrielle, 136, 216

Bartner, Arthur C., 299-304
Beach Boys, 3, 18, 59, 74, 98, 110, 115, 195, 203, 255-258, 290, 317, 323
Beatles, 18-19, 56-57, 64, 92, 109-110, 127, 184, 250, 258, 317, 323, 341, 351
Beard, Peter, 192, 308
"Beautiful Child," 109-111
Becker, Terry, 76
Beckley, Gerry, 42
Bella Donna (Nicks), 242, 337

Bent, Lenise, 76, 78
Breakfast in America (Supertramp), 42, 78
"Brown Eyes," 12, 50, 80-85, 119, 162, 315, 317
Buckingham, Lindsey, 1, 3, 9-10, 12-15, 23-35, 37-38, 46, 49-55, 62-66, 69-70, 77, 79-84, 87-108, 116, 175-6, 179-80, 182-92, 1 95, 197, 199-206, 210-14, 217-19, 223, 228-33, 235-41, 243, 246-57, 262-63, 266, 273, 277, 279-301, 306, 308-9, 311, 315-16, 320, 323, 327, 330, 332, 339-42, 347, 351
Buckingham Nicks (Buckingham and Nicks), 143, 159, 161

INDEX

Caillat, Diane, 87-88, 101, 198, 207-208, 214, 218-220, 223-226, 251-255, 267-268, 270, 292-294, 307, 332, 343, 348-350

"Caroline No" (Wilson), 204, 257

Cey, Ron, 47, 101, 137, 292-294

"Chain, The," 66, 115, 154, 235

Clapton, Eric, 199, 203

Clash, 142, 182

Courage, John, 137, 315

Dashut, Richard, 1, 4-9, 13-14, 19-24, 27-30, 33-35, 47-49, 52-53, 62-65, 69, 72, 76, 83, 88, 94-97, 99-101, 108, 121-3, 126-8, 132, 135-6, 139, 146, 148-51, 155-6, 163, 165, 168-70, 173-80, 182, 185-6, 188, 192, 198-9, 201-2, 205-6, 210, 228, 230-1, 237-41, 243-4, 246, 249-54, 258, 263-5, 269, 271-4, 279, 281-5, 288, 293-4, 300-3, 305, 308, 311, 315-7, 320, 323, 325, 327, 343, 345

Dawes, Biff, 302, 304

"Dealer, The," 233, 235-6, 242

"Dreams," 57-58, 81-82, 109, 168, 191, 235, 266, 318, 336

Dodger Stadium, 191, 228, 297, 299, 304, 307, 332

"Don't Stop," 84, 115, 204

Eagles, 14, 48, 102, 153, 292, 344

Egan, Walter, 2, 61, 107, 152, 163, 286

"Farmer's Daughter" (Wilson), 255-58

Feldman, Rich, 196, 325, 327

Fleetwood Mac All-Stars, 47, 101, 295, 299

Fleetwood Mac, 4

Fleetwood, Mick, 3, 5-6, 8-13, 17, 21, 23, 25, 28-30, 33, 35, 46-48, 50-55, 62-66, 68-69, 72, 81-83, 89, 91, 93, 96-99, 102-04, 107-08, 113-14, 116, 120-21, 126, 132, 135-6, 139, 142-6, 148, 150-1, 154, 156, 160, 165-7, 169, 171, 174-5, 177-8, 182, 187,

INDEX

189-93, 199-202, 205, 209-11, 215-6, 218, 225, 228-32, 236-8, 240-1, 243-4, 246, 249-54, 257, 260-1, 263, 265-6, 271, 273, 280-3, 291, 293-4, 300-1, 306, 308-9, 315, 319-20, 323, 325, 327, 329, 332, 341, 347-8
Fleetwood, Sara, 10, 68, 131, 133, 136, 139, 293
Frederick, Carla, 76, 182, 219-20

Gaucho (Steely Dan), 26, 214
"Gold Dust Woman," 11, 153, 235
"Go Your Own Way," 29, 70, 188, 206, 248
Green, Peter, 20, 82, 85, 93, 113, 145, 199, 287

Hagadorn, Randall, 228, 271
Hamzy, Connie, 177, 179-80, 182
Harris, Carol Ann, 3, 9, 12-13, 29-30, 35, 46, 59, 106, 125-6, 128, 132, 135, 183, 247, 254, 263, 293
Harrison, George, 309

"Honey Hi," 80, 116, 118-19, 121, 162, 197
Hormel, Geordie, 2, 42, 120

"I Don't Want to Know," 202
"I Know I'm Not Wrong," 183, 189, 246-49, 288, 316
Issak, Barbara, 76

Jam, 182, 314

Katz, Gary, 214
Kirwan, Danny, 113, 287

"Ledge, The," 13-14, 28, 33-35, 37, 90, 144-5, 147, 155, 178, 184, 247, 316, 329
Lennon, John, 93, 170, 212, 249, 290, 334
Lindsey, Ray, 5-6, 8-9, 21, 31, 49, 59, 173, 185, 198, 215, 230, 237, 240, 250, 256, 265, 272, 327
Live, 345
Loggins, Kenny, 70, 311

"Magnet and Steel" (Egan), 2, 152, 286

INDEX

McCartney, Paul, 170, 285
McLoone, Annie, 137, 159, 163, 165, 169
McVie, Christine, 3, 5, 9-13, 23, 30-32, 34, 37, 48, 50, 55-7, 59, 63-64, 69-71, 80-84, 87, 89, 94-95, 97-98, 104, 108-9, 113-5, 118-21, 125-6, 132-3, 143, 154, 160, 171, 175-6, 184, 188, 199-202, 204-6, 216, 223, 233, 236-41, 246, 249-50, 256-58, 260, 262, 270, 293, 299, 301, 320, 323, 330, 347
McVie, John, 3, 9, 10, 12, 23, 27, 62, 67, 146, 148, 154, 156, 160, 167-9, 174, 179, 182, 187-91, 199-200, 202, 205, 209-11, 214, 228-32, 237-41, 246, 249-52, 259-61, 263-5, 271, 291, 293, 301, 306, 332, 347
Mirage, 80, 152, 154
Moncrieff, Tom, 132, 137, 159, 161-65, 167, 169

"Never Forget," 50-51, 55-56, 81, 114, 162, 175, 330

"Never Going Back Again," 230
"Never Make Me Cry," 84, 199-201
Nicks, Stevie, 3, 10-12, 23, 32, 47-48, 50, 55, 57-8, 61-3, 68-71, 77, 79, 81, 84, 96-98, 102-3, 105-6, 108-11, 114, 120-1, 126, 131, 133-4, 143, 146, 150, 153, 159-68, 171, 173-6, 189, 192, 199, 202, 204, 212-3, 223, 235-242, 247, 254-7, 262-6, 270-5, 277-281, 283-4, 287, 293, 295, 299, 301, 306, 311-4, 323, 333-40, 336, 347, 351
Not Shy (Egan), 163
"Not That Funny," 178-79, 183-5, 187, 211, 247-8

Odgers, Jayme, 308
Olsen, Keith, 4
"Over My Head," 120
"Over & Over," 12, 80, 114-5, 175, 317, 329

Penny, Ron, 6, 8-9, 21

"Rhiannon," 62, 131, 134

INDEX

Rumours, 1, 3-4, 6-7, 14, 19-21, 25, 27-30, 37, 40, 46, 66, 73, 76-77, 80, 98, 102, 107, 110, 139, 141-3, 149, 171, 190, 192, 195, 203-4, 213, 246, 260, 284-5, 288, 308, 319, 321, 324, 341-3, 345-7

"Save Me a Place," 90, 229-30, 233
"Sara," 50, 80, 159-74, 188, 199, 204, 212, 235-6, 263, 317, 326, 347, 351
"Say That You Love Me," 115, 154
Say You Will, 159
"Sentimental Lady" (Welch), 133, 183, 286
"Silver Springs," 171, 192, 319
"Sisters of the Moon," 11, 42, 62-64, 66, 68, 91, 162, 311
"Smile at You," 159, 213
Smile (Wilson), 204, 290
Soundstream Digital, 125, 195, 197, 325, 327-8
Spain, Tom, 228, 270, 281, 301
Spencer, Jeremy, 287

Starr, Gary, 20, 134, 251
Steely Dan, 20, 26, 79, 146, 214-5
Stewart, John, 107, 311-2
Stockham, Thomas, 324, 329
Stone, Sly, 234-5
"Storms," 10-11, 80, 96, 102-5, 162, 175, 327
Studio D, 2, 7, 11, 20, 22, 24, 26, 32, 59, 62, 67, 79, 80, 83-5, 87, 107-8, 110, 114, 119, 128, 133-4, 142, 156-7, 160, 162-5, 180, 182, 184, 187, 189-90, 199, 203-6, 209, 212, 215, 219, 230, 245-6, 251, 262, 271, 273-4, 277, 280, 312, 318, 325, 340-1
Supertramp, 42, 78-79, 291

Talking Heads, 142, 307
Tango in the Night, 309, 346
"That's All for Everyone," 90-94, 96, 102, 284, 316
"That's Alright," 154
"That's Enough for Me," 153-7, 165, 175, 247, 316
Then Play On, 287

INDEX

"Think About Me," 84, 202, 204-6, 236, 347

"Trouble," 94

"Tusk," 56, 142, 188, 191-3, 247, 297, 299, 300, 305-7, 309, 340, 342, 344, 347

Village Recorders, 2, 4, 7, 19-20, 22, 24-5, 42-43, 73-76, 78, 85, 87, 101, 109, 117-8, 120, 137, 155, 186, 199, 209, 230, 233-4, 243, 250-1, 265, 279, 288, 313-4, 316, 318, 324, 331, 349

"Walk a Thin Line," 284-8, 290-1, 309, 316

Wally Heider's Studio, 42, 47, 115, 292, 298, 305

"Warm Ways," 114

Warner Bros., 76, 82, 225, 245, 270, 316, 340-4, 347-8

"What Makes You Think You're the One," 210-3, 219, 326

Welch, Bob (musician), 107, 113, 133, 137, 183, 203, 286-7

Welch, Bob (pitcher), 47, 119, 297

"Whenever I Call You Friend" (Loggins), 70, 311

Wilson, Brian, 93, 107, 115, 118, 134, 151, 195, 203, 255, 258

Wilson, Dennis, 3, 11, 46, 58, 80, 83-84, 113-8, 121, 200-3, 256, 258, 293, 301, 332

Wolf, Frank, 76, 85, 195, 250, 331

Wong, Judy, 30, 47, 131, 225, 292, 301

"You Make Lovin' Fun," 115, 261, 272, 306

Zappa, Frank, 74